Hubert Keller's
Souvenirs
Stories & Recipes from My Life

with Penelope Wisner

Andrews McMeel
Publishing, LLC

Kansas City • Sydney • London

Hubert Keller's
Souvenirs

Stories & Recipes from My Life

with Penelope Wisner

Photographs by Eric Wolfinger

Other Books by Hubert Keller

Burger Bar: Build Your Own Ultimate Burgers

The Cuisine of Hubert Keller

Andrews McMeel Publishing, LLC
an Andrews McMeel Universal company
1130 Walnut Street, Kansas City, Missouri 64106

www.andrewsmcmeel.com

12 13 14 15 16 TEN 10 9 8 7 6 5 4 3 2 1

ISBN: 978-1-4494-1142-8

Library of Congress Control Number: 2012936737

www.hubertkeller.com

Design: Don Morris Design, New York
Photography: Eric Wolfinger
Photography by Henri Kugler: pages 288, 289, 293, 304, 305, 312, 313, 315

Pages ii and iii: Follow the little cut that starts below the hill on the left and travels below the bushes and around the corner on the right. My brother, Francis, and I walked that path after school to join our parents at their little vacation house in the mountains just beyond the hill. They closed the shop for a couple of days a week in the off-season and stayed there instead of taking a vacation.

In memory of Chef Paul Haeberlin,
L'Auberge de L'Ill, France

——————

And to my parents,
Yvonne and Henri Keller

"Memory is essential to what we are. We wouldn't be able to talk to each other without memory, and what we think of as the present really is the past. It is made out of the past....The past is always one moment that happened three minutes ago, and one moment is what happened thirty years ago—and they flow into each other in ways we can't predict....The idea that memory is somehow sentimental or nostalgic— nostalgia itself, the etymology of nostalgia is 'homecoming.' And home-coming is what we all believe in."

—The poet W. S. Merwin in a *Fresh Air* interview with host Terry Gross, aired when his book *The Shadow of Sirius* won the Pulitzer Prize in 2009.

A note about the recipes

♣ You will find weights included as well as volume measures for ingredients in some of my recipes. I've done this for several reasons. First, I think we often buy ingredients by the pound and it's helpful for a shopper to have some idea of what I mean, for instance, by a large onion. A second reason is that many of these recipes originate in professional kitchens where, if we measure at all, we most often weigh our ingredients. Another reason is the origin of some recipes. In Europe, even home cooks are in the habit of weighing ingredients. Especially in baking, precision is important; weights are more accurate than volume measurements and you will enjoy more consistent results if you weigh. Plus, it's faster and less messy. Often, you can place your mixing bowl on the scale and simply add the ingredients directly instead of stopping to measure first. I encourage you, if you don't have one already, to invest in a digital scale and to leave it out on your counter so you get in the habit of using it.

CHAPTER

1

Family Treasures

CHAPTER

2

Mentorship

By Three-Star Chefs

CHAPTER

3

Adaptation

When Creative Inspiration Saves the Day

CHAPTER

4

Modern French Cooking

Hits American Shores

CHAPTER

5

Pioneer

Seeking Adventure & Finding My Own Path

CHAPTER

6

*Love &
Partnership*

CHAPTER

7

*Holiday
Traditions*

"*For me the challenge is to put as much excitement into the professional side of cooking—the execution of a sauce, the combination of flavors, and the final presentation of a dish—as there is interest in the garden and its produce. Let the growers do what they do best, and then it is our turn to display our talent in the culinary arts, to put our skills and art to work on the ingredients.*"

—Hubert Keller, San Francisco, 2010

INTRODUCTION

WHEN I FIRST BEGAN collecting material for this book, I did not expect it to become a sort of memoir. But as I decided on one recipe and then the next, each reminded me of a story. And there are so many stories. They begin in my home village, Ribeauvillé, in Alsace, France, and in my father's pastry shop. We lived above the shop and my dad's mom lived on the floor above us. She cooked for my brother and me while our parents worked in the shop.

As I thought about what was most important to me, the recipes began to group themselves along certain lines. First, of course, came my family and its influence on me. And then my apprenticeship under the Haeberlin brothers, Paul and Jean-Pierre, at their Michelin three-star restaurant, L'Auberge de L'Ill. Their mentorship and friendship molded my career. I met Chantal, my wife and partner, during my apprenticeship and we have been together ever since.

Above: My home village of Ribeauvillé in the winter. You can see that many of the houses date from the early Middle Ages. *Right:* Whenever Chantal and I return home, we are treated to large family meals. Here is a *pâté froid*, the classic, coarse-textured terrine wrapped in brioche, like the ones my dad used to make for his shop. It's served with a celery root salad (page 12) and a shredded carrot salad (page 18).

Even when I was very young, I dreamed of traveling. After my apprenticeship and the army, I cooked on a cruise ship, sailing all over the Mediterranean, the North Sea, the Caribbean, and to the United States. Then Chantal and I traveled to the south of France, to South America, and then to San Francisco. We didn't speak Portuguese when we landed in Brazil, and we didn't speak English when we arrived in the United States. I still remember going to the corner store to buy beer. Its taste so surprised us. "What is this American beer?" we wondered. It turned out we had bought root beer.

In each new location I tried to stay true to my classic training and to also please our guests. That meant adapting recipes to local ingredients and tastes—using local fish in Brazil and not serving squab with the feet on in America. I was among the first of my generation trained in the new, lighter, modern French cuisine—called *cuisine légère* and *cuisine minceur*—to arrive in the United States. So I was kind of a pioneer at Fleur de Lys, our San Francisco fine French restaurant. While Chantal and my restaurant partner, Maurice Rouas, worked to remove the stuffiness that had been the style of French restaurants up until then, I brought a new emphasis on vegetables and created all-vegetarian tasting menus paired with wines, a radical approach in the mid-1980s.

The first time I ever thought about my "biography" was in the final show of the first season of *Top Chef Masters* when we were challenged to cook four dishes: the first was to re-create a food memory from our childhood that inspired us, a second was to cook a dish from our first restaurant job, and a third to present a dish from the first restaurant we had owned. For the fourth dish, we were to show what direction our cuisine was going to take. For each I stayed true to the original dish, re-creating them as I had done them way back then.

For the first I did a *Baeckeoffe* (page 30), a hearty, comforting casserole of meat and potatoes. Whenever I make it—and I often do for friends as well as occasionally to serve at Fleur de Lys—the aromas remind me of my home village and of my father's pastry shop. Pâtisserie Keller was a family affair: My father made the pastries, *viennoiseries* (baked goods from yeasted doughs such as brioche), and chocolates; my mother worked "the front of the house," dealing with our customers; and my brother and I often helped my father by filling doughnuts with jam (three good squeezes of the syringe), buttering the hundreds of *kugelhopf* molds we used daily, or adding flour to a batter as my dad folded it in. Both of my grandmas worked in the shop, too.

That family feeling followed me to my first real job as an apprentice at the Michelin three-star restaurant L'Auberge de L'Ill under Chef Paul Haeberlin. It was there that I was inducted into the three-star world, learning first great respect for our ingredients, and then the discipline, patience, and skills necessary to cook well and consistently. For the second dish of the *Top Chef Masters* challenge, I chose to make a classic dish from L'Auberge. It has always been called a salmon "soufflé" (page 90), but it is actually a thick layer of quenelles de brochet (mousseline of pike) domed over a salmon fillet. The mousseline puffs and browns as the dish bakes. The *brochets* arrived so fresh   they were a local fish—that they were often still alive. We then would have to kill them before we filleted them.

I worked four years at L'Auberge de L'Ill, three as an apprentice and one as a *commis*. It was an exceptional education. My years there provided a foundation and a model for how to run a kitchen. From our first day, apprentices were treated with respect. We might spend our day on the garde-manger station cleaning green beans, but we were never expected to wash pots or to scrub the floor, as was common in other kitchens. Calm reigned throughout the restaurant. It was only later, when I left to work in other kitchens, that I discovered a crazier world. But I had learned that the atmosphere at L'Auberge—on a different level, it was the same as in my father's shop—achieved as high a level of culinary excellence as anywhere else.

The restaurant was closed only one day. Everyone worked six days. We did Monday lunch, and then we were off Monday night and Tuesday. Otherwise it was around the clock. Our day started with our breakfast from 7:30 a.m. to 8 a.m. We worked preparing lunch throughout the morning, working until, if we were lucky, a two-hour break in the afternoon, and then back to work until we cleaned up after service, ending our day at 11 p.m. or later. We never felt that schedule was exceptional. I had grown up watching my father work that hard, and we watched our mentors work sometimes forty-eight hours straight (and we were straight, too, with no help from drugs that were not even around then). From their example we learned to do the same when we needed to.

When I trained, French cooking and food was very regional—*cuisine traditionnelle*, traditional dishes made with local ingredients. The food of Alsace, my home region, was based on butter and cream. We had foie gras because we made it locally. At home we cooked with peanut oil and Melfor vinegar, both produced by family-owned businesses in Alsace. We still do. One of our family recipes, the carrot salad (page 18), uses these simple ingredients.

Then, when I went to the south of France, I was exposed to so much I'd never seen before—a wild abundance and variety of fresh herbs and instead of the one, green zucchini I knew, there were six or more choices—yellow, pale green, striped, round, long, with and without flowers, or just the flowers. I found a colorful, happy cuisine.

Above: **Being French, I didn't really eat burgers until I started the research to open Burger Bar. Now a buffalo burger with sautéed spinach and caramelized onions on a ciabatta bun is my favorite.**

As saucier at Moulin de Mougins—Roger Vergé's then Michelin three-star restaurant in Provence—I experienced a new style of French cuisine, Vergé's cuisine of the sun, which excited me, spoke to me, and influenced my cooking even more than my native Alsatian cuisine. The cuisine focused on olive oil, herbs, and vegetables not because of health but because that was what was there.

I'd never before gone out to forage for wild foods, but we collected herbs and tiny green onions called *cebettes*. My first introduction to wild asparagus was at Le Chantecler, where I worked under chef Jacques Maximin, at Hôtel Le Negresco on the Riviera. One day, my wife Chantal and I went to pick wild asparagus from the fields. The ¼-inch-thick spears couldn't be seen. We had to lean over and sight along the tops of the waving grass and flowers to see the slim heads peeking up. The slow-roasted swordfish with carrot coulis (page 162) draws on my time with Maximin.

The way I was trained, I repeated dishes exactly the way I was taught. As chef of Roger Vergé's Brazilian restaurant, La Cuisine du Soleil, I was so happy that I could almost exactly reproduce the very popular St. Pierre (John Dory) with a red pepper coulis from Moulin de Mougins. But it was not well accepted by our guests. That experience opened my eyes. In a foreign country, everything—from the cooks' knowledge, to sourcing ingredients and equipment, to the tastes of the clientele—was different. I learned that to be successful I had to be flexible and adaptable, to keep my personality and my way of thinking but to shift my position to include new perspectives. Now it's fun to take traditional recipes and give them a twist, as we've done with the Tarte Flambée Alsacienne (page 116). Or to adapt ingredients and tastes from one country and use them in unexpected ways, as I've done with the chocolate quinoa pudding (page 134). I made that pudding recently—I hadn't in a long time—and it tasted so good.

I still remember the feeling in 1986 when, for the first time, I put my key in the door to Fleur de Lys. The feeling of ownership kicked in. And so for the third dish of the *Top Chef Masters* challenge, I cooked a signature lamb dish from Fleur de Lys: loin lamb chops stuffed with a whole garlic clove and wrapped in a lamb mousseline, then spinach, and finally caul fat (page 74). And that dish grew out of a dish we used to do at L'Auberge de L'Ill, a squab *côtelette* made from the breast and leg, wrapped in a forcemeat, and wrapped again in caul fat (page 67).

For Chantal and me the restaurant business is a passion and will always be a passion. There is always something new to work on. I like a challenge, to see if I can pull it off, even when it's an area in which I am not completely comfortable and have to learn as I go along. Every time I undertake something new, I get excited, and I also know I can lose it big-time. But I think I am most productive when I am put on the spot.

A decade ago the new challenge was Burger Bar. At the time, I didn't know much about burgers, but I learned fast and was the first to create the concept of the high-quality, build-it-yourself, premium burger restaurant. Now I have a favorite burger that we call the HK Burger (page 208). Next came the challenge of becoming a television chef and my cooking show, *Secrets of a Chef,* for public television. I've included several recipes from the show, including the duck terrine from season three, a variation on the terrines and pâtés we used to serve in France (page 92).

And a few years ago, we started Fleur by Hubert Keller in Las Vegas, a restaurant serving small plates with tastes from around the world. I think this is the future for restaurants. Guests love to be surprised by both the presentation and the taste of a dish. At Fleur, I've been able to play big-time. We were the first in Las Vegas to use nitrogen tableside to make frozen drinks and ice creams (see the nonnitrogen version of *Affogato,* page 234). And we created fantasy presentations for well-known foods such as oysters (page 215) and baby back ribs (page 220).

Above: The Ribeau-villois dress in medieval costume for Ribeauvillé's street fairs. The popular bacon vendor cooks skewered *lardons* on a burning, split log. *Below:* My brother, Francis, and his wife, Mireille, join Chantal and me at the window of our parents' apartment. All the houses have window boxes over-flowing with colorful geraniums.

As restaurateurs, Chantal and I are busy on holidays. But we always celebrate them, maybe beforehand or afterward. We especially love Christmas. Chantal starts decorating weeks in advance and the house is filled with a warm, festive feeling. It is our tradition to have a big Christmas dinner at our house with the same group of friends year after year. (When we first arrived in California, guests had to bring their own chairs.) We make the most of Christmas because we remember going with our families to the holiday street fairs in Alsace to shop, eat cones of roasted chestnuts, sip *Vin Chaud* (page 302), and lick the frosting from *Pain d'Épices* (page 298).

When you cook from this book, you can find dishes from all the parts and places of my life. Drawing on my experience as a teaching chef, I've written the recipes carefully. If you follow them and look at the step-by-step photographs of some of the techniques, I feel sure you can reproduce even the more sophisticated dishes.

It's an odd feeling to look back over your life. Through stories—not always easy ones—and recipes, I show how I was trained, how my thinking evolved, and how and why I built my business. There were moments when I wondered what I was doing. I am still excited about what I do. Sometimes it's crazy, and sometimes it's a little tight, but I'm still having the best time. And I've been able to do what I have because Chantal has always supported me, always been there, and shared equally in everything we have done. We never gave up our dreams.

CHAPTER

1

Family
Treasures

"On Sunday, everyone came in for special pastries and cakes for their family's lunch."

SUNDAY LUNCH IN RIBEAUVILLÉ

WHEN I WAS GROWING UP, my family lived on the first floor above my father's shop, Pâtisserie Keller, and his mother lived on the second floor. She was Grandma and cooked Alsace dishes influenced heavily by her experience of living through World War I and the food scarcity it caused. As my father's business flourished, he indulged in foods such as wonderful cuts of beef that were unavailable when he was growing up. And he no longer wanted to eat Grandma's budget-conscious traditional cooking. But my brother and I loved her cooking. Because my parents worked such long hours in the shop, Grandma was in charge of most meals for my brother and me.

A big Sunday lunch was a real tradition in Alsace. Every household would sit down to a big meal with all the family members—parents, children, grandchildren, aunts, uncles, and cousins. But for us,

Sunday was a little crazy at home. It was the only day we didn't eat together as a family. While Grandma kept us busy upstairs, Mom and Dad were busy downstairs. It was the busiest day of the week in the shop. Everyone came in for special pastries and cakes for their family's lunch.

In order to cook the midday meal and still have time for church, the women organized their menus around make-ahead and slow-cooked dishes. Early in the morning, Grandma would make marrow dumplings (page 16), dust them with flour, and then cover them with a towel. Then she would make a series of salads and hors d'oeuvres such as a carrot salad (page 18), celery root salad (page 12), and stuffed eggs (page 23). These would be ready to eat when everyone returned from church.

From left: My dad, Henri, and our family dog, Zezette. Me with a friend from childhood, Yves Baltenweck, on the first day of harvest in 2011. Pâtisserie Keller on the ground floor; my family lived on the floor above. A view of Ribeauvillé with the historic Église St. Grégoire in the foreground.

Pages 6 and 7: My brother, Francis, and me cooking together in his kitchen during a visit home to Alsace.

Clockwise, from left: A family Sunday lunch of roast venison loin, sautéed chanterelles and apples, nouilles Alsaciennes (noodles with toasted breadcrumbs). My mom, Yvonne, and me in the new Pâtisserie Keller, 1967. Meringues Glacées (page 50). Sunday lunch menu. Mom and Dad in front of the first Pâtisserie Keller.

For the main course, she frequently prepared a pot-au-feu (page 16), a large cut of beef cooked with carrots, turnips, leeks, and cabbage. It cooked slowly on the wood-fired stove during the long hours of worship. It's a one-pot dish served in two courses, first the broth and marrow-enriched dumplings and then the meat and vegetables moistened with a little more broth. The next day, the leftovers might be stuffed into tomatoes; turned into a salad of beef, onions, and cornichons moistened with broth and vinaigrette; or stuffed into a pasta roulade (page 42).

The menu worked well for whenever everyone could sit down together. Mom and Dad showed up when they took a break from the shop. Grandma would set my brother and me up, and then my father would come upstairs to eat while my mother looked after the shop. Then he would go down and Mom would come up. Even when served in this sort of hectic way, the flavors and textures didn't lose anything. Later my brother and I would both go down to the shop to choose something for dessert.

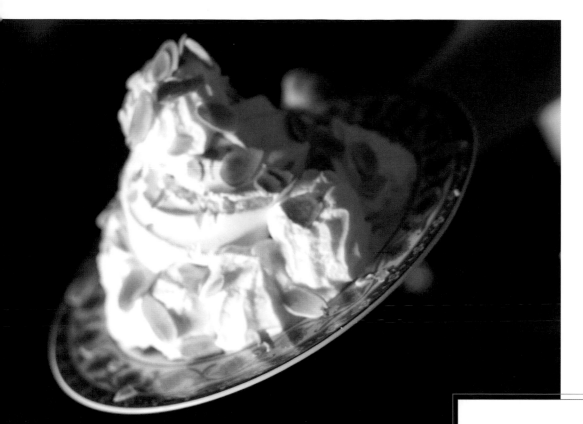

A SUNDAY LUNCH
IN RIBEAUVILLÉ MENU

♣ ♣ ♣

*Assorted Salads and
Hors D'Oeuvres*

Poached Leeks with Grandma's
Light Mayonnaise

Celery Root, Apple, and
Walnut Salad

Stuffed Eggs with
Smoked Salmon

Savory Carrot Salad

Pot-au-Feu

Soup with Marrow Dumplings

Sliced Beef and Vegetables

Mendiant

Henri's Bread Pudding

One of my favorites was my father's *mendiant*, a
three-inch-tall bread pudding baked in a pastry
shell. *Mendiant* means "beggar" in French and refers
to the dish's main ingredient—leftover bread. My
father saved leftover bits of brioche, soaked them
in milk and cream, and then beat in eggs, flavorings, and fresh
cherries. He poured the rich custard into a sweet pastry crust,
and when it was baked, he enrobed the whole in fondant. Dad still
makes *mendiant*, and I've included the home version (page 22)
that he taught me when I visited in 2010.

Celery Root, Apple, and Walnut Salad

WE USE CELERY ROOT OFTEN IN ALSACE, and this salad is one of Grandma's dishes that she prepared for us in the fall, when celery roots are harvested. This fresh, crisp, light-tasting salad is very much like an American slaw. Celery root by itself is underused, but it has a wonderful flavor and texture for salads, and you can braise it by itself. It's one of those earthy vegetables, like beets, that I think people are coming back to. When shopping for celery root, choose smaller ones—the big ones can be hollow and fibrous.

Serves 8

♣ Though Grandma would not have done this, you can substitute lime for the lemon juice if you like.

♣ To lighten the dressing a little, you can substitute Greek-style plain nonfat yogurt. Also, you can substitute other herbs for the chives, such as parsley, a little cilantro, basil, and nepitella (*calamintha nepeta*, a Tuscan favorite, in flavor a cross between mint and oregano).

Large handful (about 2 ounces) walnuts or pecans
3 tablespoons heavy cream
2 tablespoons mayonnaise
2 tablespoons Dijon mustard
Sea salt and freshly ground black pepper
1 lemon, halved, plus 2 tablespoons freshly squeezed lemon juice and more as needed
1 small celery root (about 1 pound)
1 tart green apple (about 8 ounces), peeled, halved, and cored
3 tablespoons finely minced fresh chives
Handful celery leaves or lovage, for garnish

Heat a small skillet over medium-low heat and add the nuts. Stir and toss until lightly toasted and fragrant, about 5 minutes. Pour onto a dish to cool, chop them coarsely, and set aside.

In a small bowl, whisk together the cream, mayonnaise, and mustard and season with salt and pepper. Set the mixture aside.

Because celery root oxidizes so quickly, some recipes will tell you to julienne and then blanch it to preserve its color. But I don't recommend that here as you will not get the right texture for your salad. Instead, fill a medium bowl halfway with water. Squeeze the juice from 1 lemon half into the water and drop in the peel. Working as quickly as you can, peel the celery root and rub the cut edges with the second lemon half to prevent discoloration. When finished, drop this lemon half into the bowl of water, too.

Cut the celery root into several pieces and drop them into the lemon water as you go. Shred the chunks with a coarse grater or with a food processor's grating disk. You should have about 4 packed cups.

Transfer the grated celery root to a large mixing bowl, toss with the 2 tablespoons of lemon juice, and season with salt and pepper. Coarsely shred the apple and toss it with the celery root. Add the reserved dressing, the walnuts, and half of the chives. Toss well until evenly combined. Taste and adjust the seasonings. Cover the mixture with plastic wrap and refrigerate for at least 1 hour and for up to a day or two.

When ready to serve, toss the salad with the remaining chives and taste for seasoning again. Add salt, pepper, and lemon juice if needed. Arrange the salad in a serving bowl and garnish with the celery leaves.

Grandma's Light Mayonnaise

Notes

♣ I recommend using a neutral-tasting oil for this mayonnaise, such as peanut oil or canola oil. If you are making an aioli or a rouille for a bouillabaisse (page 88), then olive oil is okay.

MY GRANDMA used to make this mayonnaise all the time. I don't know where the idea came from, but Chantal's mom used the same technique. It must have been a way of stretching ingredients. It's very useful for anyone who loves the silky richness of mayonnaise but cannot afford all the calories. Chantal and I often make this version. Because Grandma was religious, for Friday supper she made a dish of slowly cooked, melted leeks and served her mayonnaise on the side with the fish. Grandma's mayonnaise had a definite mustard flavor. And she always used peanut oil.

Makes about 1 cup

- 1 egg yolk
- 1 tablespoon coarse-grain Dijon mustard
   Pinch of sea salt and freshly ground black pepper
- 1 teaspoon white wine vinegar
- ¾ cup oil, such as canola or peanut
- 1 egg white

To make in a food processor: Place the yolk, mustard, salt, pepper, and vinegar in the bowl of a food processor and turn on the machine. Add the oil, drop by drop, until the mixture forms an emulsion. Add the remaining oil more quickly. Transfer the mayonnaise to a bowl.

In a separate bowl, whisk the egg white with an electric mixer until it holds firm peaks. With a whisk, gently fold the egg white into the mayonnaise until evenly blended and refrigerate until needed. Keeps for about 3 days.

To make by hand: In a medium bowl, whisk together the yolk, mustard, and salt and pepper. Add the oil drop by

drop while whisking vigorously until the mixture forms an emulsion, thickens, and turns a pale yellow. This can take up to 10 minutes. At that point, add the oil a little more quickly, whisking all the while. When the mayonnaise is very thick and glossy, it won't take more oil. (A food processor works so fast that you do not see this detail.) At that point, thin it with the vinegar. The mayonnaise will loosen and will then be able to absorb the remaining oil.

In a clean bowl with a clean whisk, beat the egg white until it holds firm peaks, about 5 minutes. Using the whisk, gently fold the egg white into the mayonnaise until evenly blended and then refrigerate until needed. Keeps for about 3 days.

From left to right: **Grandma Keller, my mom, and Grandma Young.** *Far right top:* **My mom and Francis in 2011. A page from a family album.**

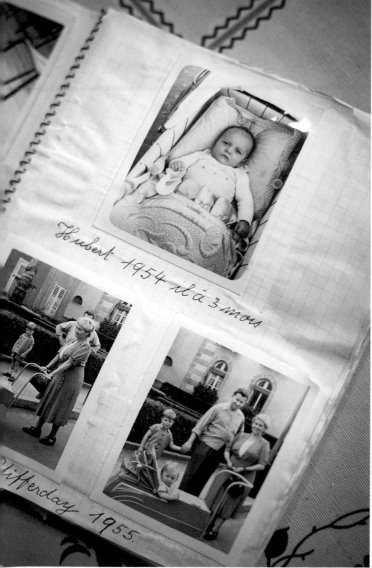

Hubert 1954 il a 3 mois

...fferday 1955.

The Road Not Taken

I had a little moment of doubt after I had been working at Moulin de Mougins for a time. I saw my friends progressing in their lives, with good jobs and money so they could enjoy themselves. I wondered where my career was headed after working so hard for so long. Right then, my father called with an idea.

A furniture store in Ribeauvillé, owned by a man he knew, was for sale. It had the largest storefront in town. My father suggested buying the store and turning it into a bakery/café/catering company. It would triple the size of his shop. I would make the food, and Chantal and I would run the business. We would work for ourselves.

When Chantal and I went back to Alsace, my father had already negotiated the price and the deal was locked in. My parents and Chantal and I went to the store owner's house to have a glass of wine and shake hands on the deal. But meanwhile, the owner had heard how excited we were by the opportunity and saw the potential of the idea. When we were already sitting down in his living room, he told us that, even though a price had been agreed on, he now wanted more. My father exploded, saying, "Okay. We are done here. There's no deal." We looked, but there was not another location we liked as well.

M. Jean-Pierre Haeberlin heard I was back home and thinking of settling down there. He got in touch with me and asked me to come over to talk with him. He said I should not settle in Ribeauvillé yet—my training was not over and I had more to learn. He suggested I go back to the south of France and work in another environment. That a new restaurant was opening with a new chef and that he knew the principals well. I knew that he and chef Paul Haeberlin must have discussed the idea. The restaurant was Le Chantecler at Hôtel Le Negresco in Nice to work under Jacques Maximin. And it was there that I discovered something that I did not expect. A fire was lit that has continued to burn to this day.

Pot-au-Feu with Marrow Dumplings

Notes

♣ Oxtail serves the same function here as a pig's foot does in the *Baeckeoffe* / Laundry Day Stew (page 30); they both add gelatin and lots of flavor.

♣ The saying goes that a good pot-au-feu "must have lots of eyes," meaning circles of fat floating on its surface. When you see the "eyes," you know the soup has been prepared with rich marrow bones and lots of meat. After working to achieve this richness, you usually do not want to defat the broth.

WHILE AT LE PRIEURÉ IN THE LOIRE VALLEY, I would make pot-au-feu and serve it in pretty copper casseroles. In formal service, the waiter presents the cocotte to the guest and then puts the cocotte on his waiter's trolley. In front of the guest, the waiter carves the meats, arranges them with the vegetables on a warm plate, moistens everything with some of the broth from the cocotte, and places the plate carefully in front of the diner. When Chantal was new in the dining room, the first time she served pot-au-feu she put the copper cocotte on the table directly in front of the diner and returned to the kitchen. She had not carved the meats and arranged them with the vegetables on a plate for the guest. We had a small argument until she went back out with a plate.

At a family-style Sunday meal, there is time between courses to prepare the next and serve everything hot. The meal opens with platters of crudités and cold salads. During the pause after these, you cook the dumplings in a pot of simmering broth to serve as a soup course. Finally, you arrange a large platter of the sliced meats and vegetables. Leftover meat can be used for the pasta roulade (page 42). Ask the butcher for center-cut (demi-canon) beef marrow bones cut into 2- to 3-inch lengths. You will need about 6 large marrow bones to make the dumplings.

Serves 8

Soup

1 pound beef short ribs
3 pounds beef chuck roast
1 pound oxtail (optional)
3 large yellow onions (8 to 10 ounces each), unpeeled, cut in half crosswise
5 whole cloves
6 cloves garlic, crushed
2 stalks celery, cut into 2-inch lengths, or 1 small celery root, peeled and halved
1 bay leaf
1 sprig fresh thyme
5 sprigs fresh flat-leaf parsley
1 sprig fresh rosemary
4 large leeks, white and green parts, left whole
½ large head green cabbage (about 3 pounds)
6 large carrots, peeled and cut into 2-inch lengths
6 medium turnips, peeled and quartered
   Sea salt and freshly ground black pepper
6 center-cut beef marrow bones, each 2 to 3 inches long, wrapped together in cheesecloth

Dumplings

1½ tablespoons semolina flour, plus more for dusting
    Marrow from the beef bones (about 5¼ ounces or 150 grams)

2 large eggs
1½ cups dried breadcrumbs
2 tablespoons unbleached all-purpose flour
1 large shallot, very finely chopped
1 clove garlic, very finely chopped
1 tablespoon finely chopped fresh flat-leaf parsley or a combination of chervil and parsley
   Freshly grated nutmeg
   Sea salt and freshly ground black pepper

Serving

Grandma's Light Mayonnaise (page 14)
Coarse sea salt
Freshly ground black pepper
Cornichons
Cream-style horseradish

To make the soup: Place the short ribs, chuck roast, and oxtail in a very large, heavy pot (12- to 16-quart size) and add cold water to cover (cold water helps clarify the broth). Bring it to a boil very slowly. Regulate the heat to maintain a gentle simmer. When the liquid first begins to simmer, the meat will throw off impurities. Skim these off for the first 15 minutes.

Meanwhile, heat a heavy-duty skillet such as a cast-iron pan over medium-high heat. Add the onions cut side down and let cook until nearly black, about 5 minutes. This process will add color and depth of flavor to your broth. Remove the onions from the pan, stick them with the whole cloves, and then put them, including the skin and charred bits, into the soup pot with the garlic cloves and celery.

Tie the bay leaf together with the thyme, parsley, and rosemary sprigs and add to the soup pot. Simmer very gently, partially covered, for 1½ hours.

While the meat cooks, trim the leeks. You want them to maintain their shape in the cooking pot, so trim away the root, leaving just a bit so the leek stays together. Then, without cutting through the root end, cut the leeks in half lengthwise. Thoroughly wash the leeks and then tie them, 2 by 2, into bundles, leaving one end of the string long enough to tie to the pot handle.

Cut the cabbage in half, core, and—if you want the quarters to stay in one piece for serving—tie each quarter with string or wrap in cheesecloth. Add the leeks, cabbage, carrots, and turnips to the soup. Season well with salt and pepper. Continue to simmer, partially covered, until the meats are tender, about 1½ hours. When a sharp knife pierces the meat without resistance, it is done. For a proper pot-au-feu, the meat must be very tender. Thirty minutes before the end of cooking, add the marrow bones and poach them for no more than 30 minutes.

To make the dumplings: Dust a baking sheet with semolina. Pull the marrow bones out of the soup, unwrap them, and push the marrow out into a large mixing bowl. Mash it into a paste with a broad wooden spoon or spatula. Mix in the eggs until evenly blended.

Add the breadcrumbs, flour, the 1½ tablespoons semolina, shallot, garlic, herbs, nutmeg, and salt and pepper to season. Mix together until the ingredients form a dough. Pinch off pieces and roll between your hands into ¾-inch balls. Place them on the baking sheet, cover with a towel, and set aside until ready to serve. The dumplings can be completed to this point several hours ahead of time. Refrigerate them if they will sit for more than 30 minutes or so. You will have 35 to 40 dumplings.

When ready to serve, bring the soup back to a very gentle simmer over low heat. Fish out the leeks, cut them into 1-inch lengths, and arrange them on a small platter. Set the platter on the table as part of the first-course salads with a bowl of Grandma's Light Mayonnaise (page 14) on the side.

Ladle about 8 cups of the broth into a separate saucepan with a wide circumference. Add the dumplings and poach them over very low heat (the soup should just steam, not even bubble), until cooked through, 5 to 7 minutes. As they cook, the dumplings tend to turn over on their own, but stir gently once to make sure they cook evenly.

When everyone has finished with the appetizer salads, serve the soup: Ladle some broth and several dumplings into warm soup plates and serve immediately.

For the main course: Fish out the meats, slice them, and arrange them in the center of a large platter. Arrange the vegetables around the meat. Ladle a little broth over all to keep everything moist. Set the platter in the center of the table. Have bowls of coarse sea salt, coarsely ground pepper, cornichons, and horseradish on the table so diners can season their meal to their liking.

♣ You can serve the vegetables sliced and drizzled with vinaigrette as a room-temperature salad. Or puree them with some of the broth, season with cinnamon, perhaps, lemon, and chopped fresh herbs for a soup to serve the next day, or freeze.

Carrot Salad with Alsatian Vinaigrette

WHEN I WAS RE-CREATING THE DISHES from my childhood, such as this simple salad, I remembered that back then olive oil was used only in the south of France. Instead we used Lesieur peanut oil, produced locally since the 1920s. Every Alsace kitchen also had a bottle of the local Melfor vinegar. Created from a Melfor family recipe, it blends a low-acid vinegar with a little local honey and an infusion of herbs. Lesieur and Melfor are still what everyone uses. Grandma made this carrot salad on Sunday just as every household did. It has a slightly nutty flavor because of the oil and a nice balance of tangy and sweet.

Serves 4 to 6

- 5 large carrots (about 1 pound), peeled
- 2 tablespoons red wine vinegar
- 2 teaspoons Dijon mustard
- ½ teaspoon wildflower honey or sugar
  Sea salt and freshly ground black pepper
- 2 tablespoons peanut oil
- 1 shallot, very finely chopped (optional)
- 2 cloves garlic, very finely chopped
- 1½ teaspoons finely chopped fresh chervil or flat-leaf parsley

Shred the carrots on a box grater or, more easily, in a food processor and put them in a serving bowl. You should have about 4 cups. In a small bowl, whisk together the vinegar, mustard, honey, and a good pinch each of salt and pepper. Whisk in the oil to form an emulsion and then stir in the shallot, garlic, and chervil.

Pour the dressing over the carrots, taste, and adjust the seasonings with salt, pepper, vinegar, or oil if needed. Set aside for at least 30 minutes and up to 4 hours, refrigerated, tossing occasionally to let the flavors develop. Serve cool or at room temperature.

Notes

♣ The honey and herbs of Melfor vinegar nicely complement the sweetness of carrots. Since Melfor is difficult to find in the States, I use red wine vinegar and add a little honey or sugar to the dressing.

Every time Chantal and I go home to visit, our families celebrate with big family meals. *From left:* **Chantal's brother Christian Martin, my brother, Francis, and me in our parents' dining room.**

Salade Vigneronne

I TALKED TO A FRIEND RECENTLY who had just returned to his home in Alsace after a trip. "The very first thing I did," he said, "was to get myself a *salade vigneronne*. I needed that salad." There are a few dishes you will find throughout Alsace, and this is one of them. The traditional salad combines lightly smoked *cervelas* sausage, a very popular local sausage (see Note) with cheese, celery, and radishes, all julienned and served very cold. Chantal loves it; my mother loves it. My father and I? Not so much. I think this version will appeal more to American palates even though it might cause a scandal back home.

Serves 4

1½ pounds small boiling potatoes, preferably a combination of red-skinned, purple, and yellow, unpeeled

　　Sea salt and freshly ground black pepper

2 shallots, very finely chopped

1½ tablespoons coarse-grain Dijon mustard

2 tablespoons Melfor vinegar (see page 19) or white wine vinegar plus ½ teaspoon honey or sugar

　　Juice of ½ lemon

⅓ cup extra-virgin olive oil

6 ounces mortadella or *cervelas* sausage, cut into ⅛-inch-thick slices

6 ounces Gruyère or Emmentaler cheese

2 stalks celery

¼ cup finely chopped fresh flat-leaf parsley or chervil

1 small bunch radishes, thinly sliced

2 hardboiled eggs, peeled and quartered lengthwise (optional)

　　About 2 ounces (a handful) walnut halves (optional)

　　Cornichons (optional)

1 ripe tomato, cut into wedges (optional)

Place the potatoes in a saucepan of cold water with a teaspoon of salt. Bring to a boil and cook until the potatoes are just tender, about 15 minutes, depending on their size. Don't overcook as we want to keep the skins on for their color. Drain the potatoes and slice them into rounds or, if they are more marble-sized, leave them whole

or simply cut them into halves or quarters. Pile the potatoes in a large bowl.

While the potatoes cook, in a small bowl whisk together the shallots, mustard, vinegar, and lemon juice. While whisking, add the olive oil until you have a well-blended dressing. Season with salt and pepper. Pour about half of the dressing over the potatoes while they are still warm.

Cut the sausage, cheese, and celery into matchsticks as similar in size (3/16 inch by 1 inch) as you can manage and add them to the potatoes with the parsley and radishes. Taste for seasoning and toss well, drizzling in the remaining dressing to your taste. Be careful when mixing the salad so as not to break up the potatoes. Make the salad an hour or so ahead of serving time and refrigerate to give the flavors a chance to develop.

Portion the salad onto plates and garnish each with quartered egg, walnuts, cornichons, and tomato wedges. Serve immediately.

Three castles command the hilltops above Ribeauvillé. It takes about 45 minutes to hike up to this one, Saint-Ulrich, a 12th-century "châteaufort." When we were young, our parents would send us up to practice "archaeology." It's always been a favorite place for Chantal and me.

21

Mendiant / Henri's Bread Pudding

MENDIANT IS FRENCH FOR BEGGAR. My dad showed me how to make this very typical dessert originally made from leftover kugel or brioche. Back when Dad had his shop, we tossed the leftover bits of brioche and kugel into a box that was stored above the stove. When it came time to make *mendiant*, we'd empty the box into milk and sugar. Now that he cooks at home, he uses a cracker very much like Melba toast. Whatever bread you use, don't worry about crusts—everything goes into the pudding. Because this is a dessert created by poor people being thrifty, it was not served with a sauce. However, softly whipped cream, ice cream, and crème anglaise would all be delicious additions.

Serves 10 to 12

- 2 tablespoons unsalted butter, plus more for buttering the baking dish
- 3 cups whole milk, or more as needed
- 6 tablespoons (2⅝ ounces or 75 grams) sugar
- 9 ounces brioche (page 126), kugelhopf (page 24), or Melba toast, broken into small pieces
- 1 tablespoon ground cinnamon
- 7 tablespoons (1¾ ounces or 50 grams) ground blanched almonds
- 4 large eggs
- 1½ pounds fresh cherries, pitted, or 24 ounces jarred sour cherries, such as morello or amarena, drained
- About ½ cup dried breadcrumbs
- Powdered sugar, for dusting
- Vanilla ice cream (optional)

Preheat the oven to 400°F. Generously butter the bottom and sides of a 2-quart baking dish such as a 9 by 13-inch oval gratin mold.

In a large saucepan, bring the milk and sugar to a boil over medium heat. Break the bread into a large mixing bowl. Pour the milk over the bread and stir so it is evenly moistened. Let sit for a few minutes, until the bread has softened and soaked up the milk. Whisk until the mixture is smooth and thick.

Whisk in the cinnamon and ground almonds. Continue to stir until the mixture has the consistency of a very soft, runny potato puree. Add more milk if necessary to get the right texture.

In a small bowl, whisk the eggs until blended and then whisk them into the milk mixture. Fold in the cherries. Pour the mixture into the prepared mold.

Sprinkle the breadcrumbs evenly over the top, dot the mixture with the remaining 2 tablespoons butter, set the mold on a baking sheet, and bake until the top is well browned and the pudding has set, about 45 minutes. It will barely jiggle in the center. Move the mold to a wire rack and let cool to room temperature.

Just before serving, dust the top all over with powdered sugar. Slice the *mendiant* into portions and arrange on dessert plates. Serve with the ice cream.

Notes

♣ You can pit the cherries, but leaving them in gives more flavor. We always left them in, even in the puddings we sold in my dad's shop. You can use the Spirited Sour Cherries (page 46). Drain them first and then use the syrup, sweetened to taste, as a sauce. Chantal liked the *mendiant* so much I had to ask her to leave some for the staff to taste later.

♣ Dad said the main thing to get right when making the dessert is the consistency. For *mendiant*, the bread and milk are stirred together until the texture looks like a milky mud or a very soft and runny potato puree.

Stuffed Eggs with Smoked Salmon

STUFFED EGGS WERE ALWAYS PART of a Sunday lunch appetizer buffet in Ribeauvillé. Everyone loved them, especially us hungry kids, who found it hard to wait for the big meal. Grandma did her eggs with just salt, pepper, mustard, and mayonnaise and a simple garnish of minced parsley, a single caper, and a last-minute dusting of paprika. Stuffed eggs are so homey that most of us would not think of them for entertaining. But adding smoked salmon takes them to another level. To go just a little further, add a tiny garnish of caviar or some truffle salt. Just as they worked for Grandma, stuffed eggs can work to make entertaining today easier.

Serves about 6

- 6 large eggs, at room temperature
  Sea salt and freshly ground black pepper
  About ¼ cup mayonnaise
- 4 to 5 ounces sliced smoked salmon
  About 1 tablespoon minced fresh chives
- 12 capers, drained
  Sweet paprika, for dusting

Place the eggs in a large saucepan and cover with cold water. Add a handful of salt, cover, and bring to a boil over high heat. Decrease the heat and simmer gently for 10 minutes. Remove from the heat and immediately plunge the eggs into cold water.

When cool enough to handle, crack the eggs and peel. Halve the eggs lengthwise and scoop the yolks into a food processor. Clean the whites well, rinsing them and letting them dry upside down on paper towels. Slice a thin strip off the bottom of the whites so they sit upright evenly. Use these bits for any patching that might be needed.

Pulse the egg yolks with the mayonnaise and salt and pepper to taste until the mixture is creamy. Coarsely chop about one-third of the salmon and then pulse it into the yolks just enough to blend but leave a little texture.

Make a decorative presentation by piping the yolk mixture into the whites. Use a round tip with a small pastry bag or cut the corner off a resealable plastic bag. Or spoon the yolks into the whites. Cut the remaining salmon into thin strips and curl them on top of each egg. Sprinkle with the minced chives and add a single caper in the middle. Just before serving, dust the tops with paprika using a small fine-mesh strainer.

Notes

♣ To peel hard-boiled eggs easily, put a handful of salt in the water. When I worked on the *Mermoz* cruise ship, we made hundreds of them every day for the passengers. When the cooked eggs cooled, we blew their shells off with a high-pressure hose.

♣ A fresh egg holds the yolk in the center. As they age, the yolks can move to the side. Once these older eggs are cooked and peeled, the whites might be very thin or even have a hole in the side. If this happens, you can patch them with the thin slices cut off the bottom of the whites to make the shells stand up straight. The green rim that sometimes forms around the hard-cooked yolk is caused by over-cooking.

♣ Grandma's Light Mayonnaise (page 14) is too thin for stuffed eggs. Use regular mayonnaise.

Chantal arranges garden flowers and I help prepare lunch in my parents' kitchen.

23

Pâtisserie Keller Kugelhopf

Notes

♣ The more you knead brioche, the better it is. I can still see my dad making brioche by hand. Once he had a dough formed, he would pick up the dough and sling it onto the table, then gather it—stretching it toward his body—and then bang it against the table again. And again, and again.

♣ When baked in the traditional swirling, fluted, high-sided mold, kugel develops a different texture from other cakes or brioche. It's denser and crisper because of all the surface area of the molds. Old molds were made of copper, which distributes heat very quickly, and earthenware.

THE WORD *kugel* means something round and *hopf* refers to the royal court. So a *kugelhopf* symbolizes a royal scepter. The village I come from, Ribeauvillé, is known as the capital of *kugelhopf* and celebrates with an annual festival. Traditionally, kugel was baked on weekends and eaten in the afternoon with a glass of wine or coffee. This recipe is a home version of the cake my dad baked in his shop. My grandmas liked it best several days old and even a little dry. The famous Paris pastry chef Gaston Lenôtre created a version that soaked the cake in a syrup and loaded it with fruit and nuts. But we in Alsace felt he had created a Parisian version of what is, at heart, a simple and handsome brioche.

One of my brother's and my jobs when we were young was to butter the kugel molds and lay in the almonds. The molds develop a particular smell from being baked and baked over the years. I brought two of those earthenware molds with me to America and keep them in a kitchen cabinet. Even today, when I open that cabinet, that smell from my childhood pours out.

When my father was an apprentice, almonds were expensive and unblanched. Apprentices had to soak them in hot water until the skins loosened and pinch each almond out of its skin. To prove they weren't eating any, the apprentices had to whistle the whole time.

Pâtisserie Keller Kugelhopf

My brother took over Pâtisserie Keller when my parents retired. He suggested the unorthodox rising procedure I've used here. The dough rises quickly in a very slow oven and results in a sweeter cake.

Makes 1 large cake, 11 or 12 inches in diameter (about 3½ pounds of dough)

½ cup whole milk, lukewarm (105° to 115°F)

2 envelopes (½ ounce) active dry yeast (about 2 tablespoons)

5 cups (25 ounces) plus ½ cup (2½ ounces) unbleached all-purpose flour, plus more as needed

½ cup (3½ ounces) sugar

1½ teaspoons sea salt

3 large eggs

1 cup whole milk, at room temperature

2 tablespoons (1 ounce) kirsch

12 tablespoons (1½ sticks or 6 ounces) plus 1 tablespoon unsalted butter, at room temperature

½ cup raisins

About 20 almonds

Powdered sugar, for dusting

Pour the ½ cup lukewarm milk into a small bowl. Add the yeast, whisk well, and then add ½ cup of the flour and whisk again until smooth. Cover with plastic wrap and leave in a warm place until the mixture begins to foam, at least 15 minutes.

In the bowl of a stand mixer fitted with the dough attachment, combine the remaining 5 cups flour, the sugar, and the salt. Add the eggs, the 1 cup room-temperature milk, and the kirsch to the bowl and knead on low speed until the dough comes together into a mass that clings to the dough hook, 5 to 8 minutes.

While the dough is kneading, cut 12 tablespoons of the butter into about 24 pieces. With the machine running on low, gradually add the butter, a few pieces at a time, until thoroughly incorporated. Continue kneading on low until the dough begins to clean the sides of the bowl, about 8 minutes. Scrape the dough off the dough hook and add the yeast mixture. Knead on low speed until the dough feels smooth and elastic, yet still fluffy and soft, about another 10 minutes. Finally, knead in the raisins until evenly distributed.

Dust a large bowl and countertop with a little flour. With a bowl scraper, scrape the dough onto the work surface, shape it into a ball, and place it in the prepared bowl. Cover the bowl with plastic wrap and leave in a warm place to rise until doubled in size, about 2 hours. When ready, the dough will not spring back when poked gently with a finger.

My dad, Henri, making croissants in his shop before he retired. We made Fleur de Lys aprons very soon after I joined the restaurant. He nearly wore his out but he still has it.

Melt the remaining 1 tablespoon butter over low heat or in a small dish in the microwave. Brush an 11- or 12-inch kugel mold or a 12-cup Bundt pan with the butter, making sure to cover all the surfaces. Place an almond at the bottom of each flute of the mold.

Punch the dough down and turn it out onto a lightly floured work surface. Shape it into a ball and use your thumb to make a hole through the center of the dough. Try to find the center of the dough so the ring of dough is even all around. Fit the dough into the mold, gently stretching the hole to accommodate the central funnel, and then use your knuckles to press the dough into the mold. Try not to disturb the almonds. The dough should fill about two-thirds of the mold.

Place an oven rack at the lowest position, put the mold in the oven, and close the door. Set the temperature to as low as possible and let the dough rise until it's just a ½ inch below the rim of the mold, perhaps in as little time as 30 minutes. (Kugel should develop a nice collar or edge as it bakes, so make sure to let the dough rise nearly to the top of the pan. As it bakes, it will form a dome over the central funnel.) Now crank the heat up to 400°F and bake until the cake browns and sounds hollow when tapped, about 45 minutes. If the cake browns too quickly—check after 30 minutes—cover it loosely with aluminum foil. Unmold the kugel onto a rack and let it cool. To serve, dust the cake generously with powdered sugar with a serrated knife. Serve the same day or toasted over the next day or two. Use leftovers for *Mendiant* (page 22), French toast, or bread pudding, or wrap well and freeze for up to 2 weeks.

Savory Kugelhopf Buns with Bacon, Onion, and Walnuts

WHEN FRENCH PEOPLE SAY "BREAD," we mean a dough made of flour, water, and yeast. When you add eggs and other ingredients—butter, for example—the dough becomes something else. But not bread. In the traditional way things used to be, the trades of baker and pâtissier were each legally protected: The baker could not put eggs and sugar in his bread dough and thus make cake, and the pâtissier could not leave them out of his dough and thus make bread. Since my father was a pâtissier, he could not by law sell bread.

My father's shop was open on Sunday because that is when he would sell the most pastry. Everyone would stop by on their way home from church to pick up a pastry or cake for dessert for the big family Sunday lunch, an event that included all the extended family. The baker, however, was not open on Sunday, so there was no fresh bread that day. As more tourists arrived in Alsace and Ribeauvillé, my father saw an opportunity to bake a "bread" so townsfolk and tourists alike could have a fresh loaf. He baked a savory kugel dough in a long loaf with a special identifying crosshatch on top, creating a *pain brioche* (brioche bread). I use this dough today to make the buns for our Kobe beef burger with Madeira sauce and black truffles. Use them for any burger, or toast them to serve with pâté, or for a holiday breakfast to serve with soft scrambled eggs.

Makes 10 (5-inch) burger buns or 20 dinner rolls (about 4 pounds of dough)

½ cup whole milk, lukewarm (105° to 115°F)

2 envelopes (½ ounce) active dry yeast (about 2 tablespoons)

5 cups (25 ounces) plus ½ cup (2½ ounces) unbleached all-purpose flour, plus more for dusting the work surfaces

2 thick slices nitrite-free bacon (about 2 ounces), cut crosswise into strips ⅓ inch wide

1 large yellow onion (8 to 10 ounces), finely chopped

1 tablespoon sea salt plus a large pinch

½ cup (3½ ounces) sugar

3 large eggs

1 cup and 2 tablespoons whole milk, at room temperature

12 tablespoons (1½ sticks or 6 ounces) unsalted butter, at room temperature and cut into about 24 pieces

5 ounces ham, cut into about ⅛-inch cubes (about 1 cup)

Large handful walnuts (about 1½ ounces), coarsely chopped

1 tablespoon finely chopped fresh thyme

2 tablespoons finely chopped fresh flat-leaf parsley

2 egg yolks whisked with 1 teaspoon water (optional)

Pour the ½ cup lukewarm milk into a small bowl. Add the yeast, whisk well, and then add the ½ cup flour and whisk again until smooth. Cover with plastic wrap and leave in a warm place until the mixture begins to foam, at least 15 minutes.

Place a medium skillet over medium heat. Add the bacon and stir and cook until crisp, about 4 minutes. Transfer the bacon to paper towels to drain and set aside.

Replace the same skillet over medium heat. In the bacon fat remaining in the pan, cook the onion, stirring and tossing, until very soft and translucent, about 8 minutes. Season with the pinch of salt, stir, and then drain the onion on paper towels. Set aside.

In the bowl of a stand mixer fitted with the dough attachment, combine the remaining 5 cups of flour, the sugar, and the remaining 1 tablespoon of salt. Add the eggs and the 1 cup and 2 tablespoons of room-temperature milk to the bowl and knead on low speed until the dough comes together into a mass that clings to the dough hook, 5 to 8 minutes.

With the machine on low, gradually add the butter, a few pieces at a time, until thoroughly incorporated. Continue kneading on low speed until the dough begins to clean the sides of the bowl, about 8 minutes. Scrape the dough off the dough hook and add the yeast mixture. Knead on low speed until the dough feels smooth and elastic, yet still fluffy and soft, about another 10 minutes. Finally, knead in the reserved bacon, onion, ham, walnuts, thyme, and parsley until evenly distributed.

Dust a large bowl and a countertop with a little flour. With a bowl scraper, scrape the dough onto the work surface, shape it into a ball, and place it in the prepared bowl. Cover the bowl with plastic wrap and leave in a warm place to rise until doubled in size, about 2 hours. When ready, the dough will not spring back when poked gently with a finger.

Line 2 baking sheets with parchment paper. Punch the dough down and turn it out onto a lightly floured work surface. Divide it into 6-ounce pieces. (For dinner rolls, divide the dough into 3-ounce pieces.) There should be enough for about 10 buns. Hold each piece of dough beneath your cupped palm. Rotate your hand in quick circles until the dough forms a nice, smooth ball. Let the dough stick very slightly to the counter to help pull it into a tight ball. Dust your hands and the counter very lightly with flour only if necessary. Arrange the balls on the prepared baking sheets, leaving plenty of space between the balls. Press them down lightly to form 4½- to 5-inch-diameter circles. Cover with a kitchen towel and let rest in a warm place until they begin to rise, about 30 minutes.

Preheat the oven to 400°F. Brush the tops of the buns with the beaten egg yolk or lightly dust the tops with flour. Score them with a razor blade in a diagonal checkerboard pattern. (If you wet the blade, it will slide more easily through the dough.) Bake until they are a handsome glossy medium brown, about 20 minutes. Rotate the pans front to back and top to bottom halfway through the baking time. Cool the buns on a rack. The buns are best eaten the same day they are baked, but they keep very well, wrapped in a paper or plastic bag, for a day or two at room temperature. The buns also freeze well; wrap in several layers of plastic wrap and freeze for up to several weeks.

Dinner Roll Variation

The rich dough makes a great canapé or savory dinner roll. Instead of kneading the onion, bacon, ham, and herbs into the dough, reserve them together in a bowl. Once the dough has risen, punch it down and roll it into a rectangle about ¼ inch thick. Sprinkle the dough evenly with the reserved ingredients. Starting from the long side of the rectangle, roll the dough into a log. Cut the log with a serrated knife into ¾-inch-thick slices. Arrange the slices, cut side up and about 1 inch apart, on parchment-lined baking sheets. Brush with egg yolk glaze and bake until golden brown, about 8 minutes.

Opposite: A collection of old, well-used *kugelhopf* molds. *Above:* Skewers of *lardons* (thick bacon) to be cooked over an open fire at one of Ribeauvillé's street festivals.

Baeckeoffe / Laundry Day Stew of Beef, Pork, and Lamb

THIS IS THE STEW THAT MADE SUCH AN IMPRESSION on the final episode of the first season of *Top Chef Masters*. Each of us had been asked to create a meal that would be an autobiography told through the dishes we would present to the judges. I immediately thought of *baeckeoffe* ("baker's oven"). The name refers back to the time when bakers used wood-fired ovens. After the bread was done, this dish would be baked long and slow in the falling temperatures of the cooling oven. Since everyone in town would see the baker every day for the family's daily loaf, each would often bring a casserole to be baked in the oven. It was traditional, particularly on Mondays, when the women went to the river to do their laundry. They would have marinated their meats and vegetables overnight, dropped their casseroles off in the morning on their way, and then picked them up—plus a loaf of bread—on their way home. Even though my father was not the bread baker and had a modern, gas-fired oven, people still took their casseroles to him. They liked to drop in because he always had some joke or story to tell. Before the village baker also invested in a modern oven and was still using wood, when my father turned over a fresh loaf of bread to give it the traditional blessing, he would sometimes see pieces of charcoal embedded in the crust. That would send my dad wild, muttering that "he [the baker] did not thoroughly clean his oven!"

I make this dish often, both at home and at the restaurant. But these days we tend to increase the vegetables and use less meat, and sometimes we use only vegetables and leave out the meat entirely. While there is never a mushroom in the classic recipe, you can add them or make a vegetarian version with mushrooms and a rich vegetable stock. I've also made this stew as the centerpiece for Christmas dinner, adding plenty of sliced black truffles. The classic dish uses a mix of meats including a pig's foot, which gives a rich, gelatinous texture to the stew. You may be able to special-order a pig's foot. Ask the butcher to slice it crosswise into three pieces. But even at the restaurant I sometimes have trouble ordering them, and your stew will still be delicious without one. You can also use just one or two kinds of meat instead of all three.

Serves 10

2 medium yellow onions, finely chopped

2 small leeks, white and pale green parts, finely chopped

1 large carrot, peeled and finely chopped

2 or 3 cloves garlic, very finely chopped

2 bay leaves

1 teaspoon whole juniper berries

1½ teaspoons finely chopped fresh thyme

3 tablespoons finely chopped fresh flat-leaf parsley

3 cups (one 750-milliliter bottle) dry white wine, such as an Alsatian pinot gris, plus more, if needed, for the pot

1 pound boneless beef chuck roast, cut into 1¼-inch chunks

1 pound boneless pork butt, trimmed and cut into 1¼-inch chunks

1 pound boneless lamb shoulder, trimmed and cut into 1¼-inch cubes

Sea salt and freshly ground black pepper

1 tablespoon extra-virgin olive oil

4 pounds Russet potatoes, peeled

In a large bowl or very large plastic bag with a secure seal, mix together the onions, leeks, carrot, garlic, bay leaves, juniper berries, thyme, parsley, wine, beef, pork, lamb, 1½ teaspoons salt, and 1 teaspoon pepper. Mix well, seal, and refrigerate for at least 12 hours

and up to 24 hours. Mix the meats and marinade occasionally; if they are in a bag, just turn it over once or twice.

When ready to cook, preheat the oven to 350°F. Smear the olive oil all over the bottom of a 6- or 8-quart Dutch oven.

Peel the potatoes if you like; using a mandoline, slice them thinly and season well with salt and pepper. Do not wash the potatoes after slicing. The potato starch thickens the broth. Cover the bottom of the pot with half of them. Strain the solids and meat from

the marinade, reserving both separately. Spread the meats and vegetables on top of the potatoes and then top with the remaining potatoes. Carefully pour the reserved marinade over the potatoes. If the liquid does not cover the top of the potatoes, add more wine or water until they are just covered.

Cover the pot and bring the stew to a gentle simmer on top of the stove. Place the pot in the oven and bake until the meats are very tender, about 3½ hours. Serve, directly from the casserole, in warm, generously sized soup plates.

Whenever we go home, we go to the Saturday farmers' market and shop at this stand. The vendor makes big sausages and mini ones for cocktails from so many kinds of meats, such as venison and wild boar. We always bring some home in our suitcases. *Pages 32 and 33:* A September view of Ribeauvillé. Parts of the town date back to the eighth century.

"A big Sunday lunch was a real tradition in Alsace. Every household would sit down to a big lunch with all the family members—parents, children, grandchildren, aunts, uncles, and cousins."

Above and right: The picking crew works up an appetite for the delicious, ample lunch provided by Yves Baltenweck *(shown at left with Chantal Herold)* and his wife, Lili. They prepared lunch in their blue-tiled harvest kitchen *(below).*

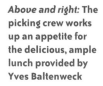

Harvesting with Family & Friends

Each September my friend Yves Baltenweck, the president of the Cave Cooperative de Ribeauvillé, gathers family, friends, and workers to pick his vineyard. With the first chardonnay grapes, he makes crémant d'Alsace, a lightly sparkling wine. Yves and I began the day tasting grapes and testing them for ripeness.

Traditionally, the vineyard owner provides a big lunch for all the pickers after harvest. Yves and his wife, Lili (standing in the photograph at right), served *coq au vin Riesling* and Lili's cheesecake (pictured at far left with her recipe in French).

Rabbit in Mustard Sauce

Notes

♣ For cooking
times, you have two
choices: short or
longer. At 30 to 40
minutes, the rabbit
meat will be firm
and moist; if you
prefer meltingly
tender meat that
falls off the bone,
cook for a longer
time, 1 hour or
so. Whatever you
do, do not boil the
rabbit or it will be
tough.

AS WE GREW UP, two weeks would not go by without rabbit for Saturday dinner, the day farmers brought them to market. Grandma would shop and bring home a single rabbit. My dad would ask why she had not come home with two to serve the four of us. And if she did buy two, he would still not be satisfied and would complain, "Did you have to buy the skinny ones?" When Chantal and I made this together on one of our Monday evenings at home, we invited a friend over and cooked two rabbits, thinking to have some left over. I served it at table from the cocotte I'd cooked in. Before we knew it, the cocotte was empty! Serve the rabbit with noodles or steamed potatoes and crusty bread for sopping up the sauce.

Serves 3 or 4

4   slices bacon (about 4 ounces), cut crosswise into narrow strips
4   ounces button mushrooms or baby portobellos, quartered (about 1½ cups)
    Sea salt and freshly ground black pepper
1   large rabbit (at least 2½ pounds), cut into serving pieces
½   cup Dijon mustard
2   tablespoons extra-virgin olive oil
1   medium yellow onion, chopped
1   large carrot, peeled and chopped
1   clove garlic, very finely chopped

1   cup dry white wine
1   bouquet garni (see page 65)
    About 2 cups low-salt chicken broth or water
¼   cup heavy cream
2   tablespoons finely chopped fresh flat-leaf parsley or chives

Place a heavy 4-quart casserole such as enameled cast iron or a large, heavy skillet over medium heat. Add the bacon and cook, stirring occasionally, until crisp, about 5 minutes. Transfer to a plate lined with paper towels to drain. Add the mushrooms to the casserole and cook them in the bacon fat without moving them until they have browned

From far left: The night sky above Ribeauvillé. Michele and Dany Haas host a simple supper on their deck surrounded by vines. They made us a really good dish of tripe.

on the first side, 1 to 2 minutes. Season with salt and pepper and then stir and cook until tender and browned all over, about 5 minutes. Transfer the mushrooms to a plate or bowl and wipe out the casserole with a paper towel if necessary.

Season the rabbit pieces well with salt and pepper. Using a pastry brush, lightly brush the pieces all over with about half of the mustard. Return the casserole to medium-low heat and add the olive oil. Working in batches, brown the rabbit, about 4 minutes per side. Make sure to regulate the heat so nothing scorches. As the pieces are done, transfer them to a plate.

Add the onion, carrot, and garlic to the casserole and cook, stirring occasionally, until the vegetables have softened, 5 to 10 minutes. Add the wine and stir and scrape all over the bottom of the pan until all the browned bits have loosened and dissolved in the liquid. Add the bouquet garni and the broth, bring to a very slow simmer, and return

the rabbit to the pan, putting the legs in first and the saddle pieces on top. Add just enough water, if needed, to barely cover the rabbit. Cover the pot, bring the liquids up to a bare simmer, and cook for about 30 minutes. Transfer the breast pieces to a plate and keep warm. Continue to simmer the legs and thighs until the meat is very tender, about another 20 minutes. Transfer the legs and thighs to the plate with the breast pieces.

Increase the heat under the casserole and boil the cooking liquids rapidly until they are slightly thickened and reduced by about one-third. You should have about 2 cups. Add the cream and continue to simmer for another minute or two. Whisk in half of the remaining mustard, taste the sauce, and add the remaining mustard to taste with salt and pepper. The sauce should have a nice mustard flavor. Return the rabbit to the pan with the reserved bacon, mushrooms, and the parsley. Heat very gently just until all is hot and then serve immediately.

37

Bretzels

Notes

♣ To develop more flavor in your bretzel, use half the amount of yeast (¾ teaspoon). Make the dough, shape it into a ball, place it in a bowl, cover it with plastic wrap, and refrigerate overnight. When ready to continue, remove the plastic wrap, cover with a kitchen towel, and leave it at room temperature for an hour or two before proceeding with the recipe.

♣ These bretzels are boiled in a baking soda solution before they are baked. The boiling helps develop their flavor; ensures even, deep browning; and gives the bretzels a nice shiny appearance. But it also softens the crust. If you prefer a crisp bretzel, omit the poaching step.

WHEN I VISIT MY PARENTS, my dad and I share a bretzel and beer before lunch and dinner every day. It's very traditional in Alsace to pair beer—mixed 3 parts beer to one part Amer Picon (a bitter orange liqueur) with bretzels. Bretzels are large, deeply browned, chewy breads in the shape of a pretzel. I buy them in a small shop, Coco LM, Biscuiterie de Ribeauvillé, on the Grand Rue (Main Street) in Ribeauvillé. The owner and baker, Sandrine Spielberg, always asks when I will need them and then bakes them especially for me so they are fresh and warm when I pick them up. They have a very short shelf life and are best consumed within an hour or so of baking. I am in her shop frequently. She also sells cookies and kugel, but her specialty is bretzels. You find bretzels in all the bistros, bars, and brasseries, where they hang on a tree stand on the bar. It's fun and not hard at all to make bretzels. They make great snacks for kids after school and for adults with cheese and, of course, beer. To refresh them, warm them on the bagel setting of your toaster or in a slow oven for a few minutes.

Makes 12 bretzels (about 2 ounces each; makes about 22½ ounces of dough)

1 cup lukewarm water (105° to 115°F)
1 tablespoon nondiastatic malt powder, barley malt syrup, or honey
2 teaspoons kosher salt
1½ teaspoons instant yeast
2½ cups (12½ ounces) unbleached bread flour, plus more for dusting the work surface if necessary
¼ cup baking soda
1 egg yolk
   About ¾ teaspoon cumin seeds for sprinkling (optional)
   About 1 teaspoon coarse salt, such as Maldon, or gray salt for sprinkling

In the bowl of a stand mixer, place the water, malt powder, salt, and yeast. Stir until dissolved. Add the flour and fit the machine with the dough hook. Knead the dough until it is very smooth and elastic, about 8 minutes. To test the dough, tug a small piece. It should stretch and not tear. If it tears, knead for another minute or so.

Remove the bowl from the machine, cover with plastic wrap, and let rise until nearly doubled in size, about 1 hour. This makes a fairly stiff, non-sticky dough. You probably won't need any flour at all on your work surface as you roll and shape your bretzels.

Turn the dough out onto a work surface and roll it into a log about 1 inch in diameter. Cut the log into 12 equal pieces. Cup your palms over each piece and roll them into tight balls. Cover with a kitchen towel and let rest for about 15 minutes.

To shape the bretzels, work sequentially, completing each step with all the dough and then returning to the first piece you worked with for the next step. This allows the dough to rest between manipulations and makes it easier to work. Line 2 baking sheets with parchment paper.

Preheat the oven to 450°F. Roll each ball into a log about 6 inches long. Then roll each of the logs into a long, thin rope about 2 feet long, tapering the ends to points, and immediately shape it and arrange it on the prepared baking sheet where you can neaten your bretzel shape. To make the classic twisted pretzel shape, leave the belly of the bretzel, the center of the rope, on the counter. Pick up the two ends and cross your hands, right over left. The end that was on the right is now on the left. Repeat for a second twist.

This was our welcome-home lunch in 2011 at Francis's house. It began with bretzels and beer mixed with Amer Picon, a favorite drink of my family and nearly all Alsatians, I think. The canapé is simple and good: buttered bread topped with cured ham and halved green olives. *Opposite:* Francis and I share a toast.

Keeping the belly of the bretzel on the work surface, lift up the ends and drape them over the bretzel, to the right and left of the belly, at 10 o'clock and 2 o'clock. You can leave the ends on top, where they will get very brown and crunchy, or flip the bretzel over, covering the ends with the sides of the bretzel. Either is correct. Make sure the ends are firmly secured to the body of the bretzel, or they might come apart when poached. Cover the shaped bretzels with kitchen towels and let them rest for about 15 minutes.

Meanwhile, fill a wide pot with about 2 to 3 inches of water and bring to a boil over high heat. Add the baking soda and lower the heat to maintain a gentle simmer. Poach the bretzels, 2 or 3 at a time, for about 30 seconds on each side, turning carefully with tongs or a large slotted spoon. Shake off excess water and return them to the baking sheets.

In a small bowl, whisk the egg yolk with a teaspoon of water and brush the bretzels with the egg glaze. Sprinkle with cumin seeds and coarse salt. Bake until very browned, about 10 minutes, rotating the baking pans top to bottom and front to back after 5 minutes. Serve them as soon as possible after baking.

Notes

♣ Have fun with your bretzel toppings. You can sprinkle them with seeds—cumin is one of my favorItes—singly or as a mixture, or sprinkle on minced onions or bacon. You can add color with exotic salts such as red, pink, black, or even smoked salt, or choose a simple coarse sea salt.

♣ As the bretzels rise before poaching, they may well split open here and there. Once baked, these splits create attractive color patterns. If you like, you can control this process by slitting the belly of the bretzels with a razor blade.

Fleischschneke / Pasta Roulade

Notes

♣ To make a vegetarian roulade, stuff the pasta with sautéed mushrooms, onions, winter squash, and herbs, adding some cheese or not, to your taste.

♣ To make the roulade ahead and freeze: Cut each roll in half crosswise; each half will serve 2 to 3. Dust them with flour, set them on a floured baking sheet, and freeze. Wrap each piece well in 2 layers of plastic wrap. To defrost, unwrap and let sit at room temperature for about an hour. Slice into portions and cook as directed. Since the slices may still be slightly frozen, simmer them for an extra 10 minutes.

HERE IS ANOTHER "MONDAY" DISH, to be made with Sunday leftovers. Ground meat is spread onto a sheet of uncooked noodle dough and rolled up just like a jelly roll cake. The spiral look gives the dish its name, *fleischschneke*, "spiral of meat."

In 2010, my mother-in-law invited Chantal and me to lunch up in the mountains at the popular Ferme-Auberge du Raedlé in the village of Sondernach. Chantal's mom and dad went there when they were young and then took their children. At lunch we discovered a classmate of Chantal's, Astrid Conreaux-Baumgart, in the kitchen. She had married Charles Baumgart, the grandson of the Auberge du Raedlé founder. Originally, auberges were popular rest stops for day hikers. You would go out for the day and stop at a farm and eat whatever was offered that day. When automobiles and Sunday drives became common, auberges got even more popular. Because of this popularity, *ferme-auberge* is now legally defined. It must not be a restaurant only but remain a farm—for example, it must have a certain number of farm animals.

Astrid makes *fleischschneke* on Wednesdays. Instead of the traditional presentation I've given here, she serves hers with a rich brown sauce with mushrooms. There are as many recipes for *fleischschneke* as there are cooks. This is mine, in tribute to our afternoon at Ferme-Auberge du Raedlé. Instead of making the pasta, you can purchase sheets at shops that sell fresh pasta. Sometimes the pasta dough for *fleischschneke* is made with fewer eggs and some water, but I think the dough has more flavor when made with all eggs.

Serves 8 as a main dish, about 2 slices each

Pasta Dough

17½ ounces (3½ cups) unbleached all-purpose flour, plus more for dusting the work surface

Large pinch of sea salt

6 large eggs

1 tablespoon champagne vinegar or white wine vinegar

Stuffing

1 pound cooked meat, such as leftovers from the pot-au-feu (page 16)

1 pound uncooked pork shoulder or ground pork

2 large eggs

About ¼ cup extra-virgin olive oil

1 large yellow onion (8 to 10 ounces), chopped

2 medium shallots, chopped

2 large cloves garlic, chopped

1 tablespoon finely chopped fresh flat-leaf parsley

1 tablespoon minced fresh chives or another tablespoon parsley, plus more for garnish

Pinch of freshly grated nutmeg

Sea salt and freshly ground black pepper

8 cups beef stock, such as the broth left over from pot-au-feu or low-salt beef broth

To make the pasta dough: Put the flour and salt into the work bowl of a food processor and pulse to combine. In a medium bowl, whisk together the eggs and vinegar until well combined. With the machine running, quickly add the egg mixture to the flour and process just until the dough begins to come together. Do not overwork. Transfer the dough to a floured work surface and knead lightly until smooth. You should have a soft, slightly sticky dough. Gather it into a ball, divide it in half, and flatten each into a disk. Wrap the disks well in plastic wrap and refrigerate for at least an hour.

While the dough rests, prepare the meat stuffing: Finely chop the beef and pork in a food processor and scrape into a large bowl. Beat the eggs together in a small bowl to break them up and then add them to the meat.

Heat 1 tablespoon of the oil in a medium skillet over medium heat. Sauté the onion and shallots until very soft and golden brown, about 10 minutes. Scrape them into the bowl with the meat. Add the garlic, parsley, chives, nutmeg, 1 teaspoon salt, and ½ teaspoon pepper. With your hands, knead the mixture together until evenly mixed. Pinch off a small nut of the meat mixture and cook it over medium heat in a small pan until cooked through. Taste for seasoning. Adjust the remaining meat stuffing with more salt and pepper as needed. The stuffing can be made, covered, and refrigerated a few hours. Let it sit at room temperature for 1 hour before proceeding with the recipe.

Flour your work surface and roll one disk of the dough into a very thin—no more than about 1/16 inch thick—rectangle about 13 by 20 inches. Using damp hands, spread half the filling evenly over the pasta, leaving a border of 2 inches all around. Trim any uneven edges. Starting from the longer edge, roll up the dough around the stuffing like a jelly roll, ending seam side down. With a very sharp knife, trim the ends neatly and cut the rolls into slices about 1¼ inches thick. Repeat with the second half of the dough and filling.

Bring the beef broth to a gentle simmer in a large saucepan. In a large nonstick skillet, heat another 2 tablespoons of the olive oil over medium heat. Lay the roulade slices flat in the pan and brown them well on both sides, about 5 minutes. You may need to do this in batches, adding more oil as needed.

If you are cooking just 4 portions, once they have browned, carefully ladle in enough hot broth to just submerge them in the skillet. Cover the skillet and simmer gently until the meat and pasta are cooked through, about 40 minutes. The pasta will swell as it cooks, which is why it is important to roll the pasta sheets as thin as possible. Check occasionally and add more broth as needed to keep the slices submerged.

If you plan to serve 8 people or do not have a skillet large enough to hold all the slices, preheat the oven to 375°F. When the roulade slices have browned on both sides, carefully transfer them to a roasting pan, fitting them together nicely in a single layer. Ladle the hot broth over them until submerged, cover with heavy-duty aluminum foil, and place in the oven to cook. Check after about 15 minutes to make sure that the broth is simmering gently. Add more broth and regulate the heat as needed to keep the slices submerged and simmering gently. Cook until done through, about 40 minutes.

To serve, arrange 1 or 2 slices in warm soup plates and ladle the broth over. Sprinkle each with a few chives and serve immediately.

♣ Once the pasta slices have been poached, they can be served with a sauce instead of in the broth. You would not see the roulade served in tomato sauce in Alsace. But a tomato sauce would be good with the roulade, as would a creamy mushroom sauce.

Francis with his wife, Mireille, and grandson Jules.

Henri's Breakfast Cake

MY DAD GAVE THIS RECIPE to Chantal a few years ago, and she makes it regularly. He bakes it at home in a tiny little oven. "It's so easy," says Chantal. "You just put everything in the food processor, and in two minutes it's done." I'll often have a piece when I get home from work on Saturday night, and we also have it toasted with coffee on Sunday morning. You can serve it any time of day with coffee or even with a glass of wine. It's particularly nice toasted or grilled and then served warm with marmalade or jam. Or serve it for dessert with berries and whipped cream.

Makes one 8½ by 4½ by 2¾-inch loaf

- 1¾ cups (7 ounces) powdered sugar
- 14 tablespoons (7 ounces) unsalted butter, at room temperature and cut into pieces, plus more for buttering the baking pan
- 1¾ cups (9 ounces) all-purpose unbleached flour, plus more for dusting the baking pan
- 5 large eggs, at room temperature
- 1 ounce (2 tablespoons) vanilla sugar or 2 teaspoons vanilla extract
- ½ ounce (3¼ teaspoons or 11 grams) baking powder
  Pinch of salt

Preheat the oven to 350°F. Butter and flour an 8½ by 4½ by 2¾-inch loaf pan.

Measure all the ingredients into the bowl of a food processor. Process just until the batter is smooth. Pour the batter into the prepared pan, smooth the top with a spatula, and bake for 20 minutes. With a razor blade, make a long cut down the middle of the loaf. Return the loaf to the oven and bake until a cake tester comes out clean, another 30 minutes. The cake will open and dome along the cut like a loaf of bread. If the cake browns too quickly, cover it loosely with aluminum foil.

When done, let the cake sit in the pan for about 5 minutes and then unmold it onto a rack and let cool. Cut thick slices to serve plain with coffee or toast slices until light gold and warm through. If well wrapped, the cake will keep for several days. Or freeze it.

Variation for Marble Cake

To make a marble cake, when the batter is made, pour half of it into a bowl. Add 3 tablespoons (14 grams, or ½ ounce) Dutch-process cocoa powder to the batter remaining in the food processor and pulse quickly until evenly combined.

Pour half of the vanilla batter into the baking pan, then add all the chocolate batter and smooth to the edges. Add the remaining white batter. If desired, run a knife in a zigzag pattern down the length of the mold to slightly mix the two batters to get more of a marble effect.

Notes

♣ This is a French version of the American pound cake. And you do need to use the food processor for the cake to come out properly. We use the German brand of baking powder, Dr. Oetker *levure chimique*, which is what everyone uses in Alsace. You can find it online; it comes in a 0.5-ounce / 11-gram packet. Use one per cake. Chantal always weighs her ingredients. You can flavor the cake with the zest of an orange or lemon.

Mom, Dad, and Francis in front of our shop.

Spirited Sour Cherries

WHEN SOUR CHERRIES (*griottes* in French) were in season, my father would preserve them in eau-de-vie for his Black Forest Cake génoise (page 318). The syrup moistened the génoise, and the cherries went into the filling. My brother and I would eat the cherries until we got a buzz. Before freezers, the only way to preserve the fruit crops would be to make jams, jellies, these fruits preserved in alcohol, and eau-de-vie. Alsace is famous for its eau-de-vie as well as for its cherries, plums, and pears. It was natural to do these cherries at home and pull out a jar for special occasions. We usually do not pit cherries even when baking or using them for preserves such as these, so be sure to tell your guests about the pits. If you do pit the cherries, the alcohol penetrates them more quickly. But they hold their shape better if not pitted. Serve the cherries on their own as a treat with after-dinner coffee or over ice cream or use some of the drained fruits in the *Mendiant* / Henri's Bread Pudding (page 22).

Makes 1 quart

  About 1½ pounds ripe but firm sour cherries
6 tablespoons sugar
  About 2 cups eau-de-vie, such as kirsch

Pack a clean, sterile quart-sized jar with a sterile lid with the cherries. Add the sugar and fill the jar with the eau-de-vie, leaving about ½ inch of headspace. Screw the lid on firmly and shake it well to dissolve the sugar. Store the jar in a cool, dark place for at least 4 weeks before use, shaking it occasionally. The flavor will continue to strengthen over several more months. Once you open the jar, store any remainders in the refrigerator.

46

The Pfiffe

Ribeauvillé's Pfifferdaj (Fiddlers') festival dates back to the Middle Ages and takes place on the first weekend of September. The Ribeauvillois dress in medieval costume (far left, bottom) and parade down the main street. Dozens of clubs work all year to build floats for the event. Members of my niece Carole's group (above) dance in orange and red, and members of my nephew Yvan's group in black and yellow ride their float (top left). The baker's float is at center left, and Chantal has a moment with one of the six giants who stride around on spring-loaded stilts doing their best to scare festivalgoers. The piper (left) hangs on the corner of what was Pâtisserie Keller. The fun lasts into the night (top) when the city throws an afterparty.

Grandma's Omelet Soufflé

WHEN OUR PARENTS WENT OUT TO A RESTAURANT on Sunday to have a night to themselves, they left my brother and me with Grandma. She could not keep us quiet by offering cookies or pastries because we had them all the time. But if she promised us an omelet soufflé, then we'd behave. The soufflé was the first thing I cooked for Chantal. Chantal had a little apartment with some kitchen equipment but not a nonstick pan. So we went out and bought one. It was our first purchase together. Make this at the last minute while your guests remain at the table and then serve it immediately.

Serves 4

- 2 pints strawberries, quartered if large
- 5 tablespoons plus 1 tablespoon sugar
- 1 tablespoon plus 1 tablespoon kirsch, Cointreau, or Grand Marnier (optional)
- 6 large eggs, at room temperature and separated
- 1 teaspoon freshly grated orange zest
- 1 tablespoon unsalted butter
  Powdered sugar, for dusting
- 8 fresh mint leaves

Preheat the oven to 375°F. In a large mixing bowl, toss the berries with 1 tablespoon of the sugar and 1 tablespoon of the kirsch. Set aside.

Once you start the omelet, don't get distracted. If you add the sugar to the yolks and walk away, you will burn them and they won't beat properly. In a large mixing bowl, beat the egg yolks, the remaining 5 tablespoons sugar, the remaining 1 tablespoon kirsch, and the orange zest with an electric mixer until very thick and pale yellow and the mixture forms a ribbon when the beaters are lifted above the surface. Set the mixture aside.

With clean beater blades, in a clean bowl, beat the whites until soft peaks form. Start the speed on low and gradually increase the speed to high. Try not to overbeat or the whites will be difficult to fold into the yolks.

With a large rubber spatula, stir about a quarter of the whites into the yolks to lighten the mixture. Fold in another quarter, and then the remaining whites just until incorporated.

Heat the butter in a very large (at least 14 inches), ovenproof nonstick skillet over medium heat. When melted, swirl the pan to coat it and then scrape in the omelet mixture. Even the surface with the spatula and let cook until it has browned around the edges and the center has puffed slightly, about 3 minutes. Put the pan in the oven and cook for another 3 minutes. To cook on top of the stove, cover the pan with a lid, and cook over low heat.

Once the top has begun to set, with a slotted spoon, scatter half the berries just off center on top of the soufflé. Return the pan to the oven (or re-cover and leave on low heat) for another 2 minutes to warm the berries.

To serve, give the pan a good shake to loosen the omelet so it slides easily. Hold a serving dish in one hand and grasp the skillet handle in the other. Slide the omelet onto the dish, upending the skillet so the omelet folds in half, enclosing the berries. Spoon the remaining berries and their juices around the soufflé, dust generously with powdered sugar, and then scatter the mint over and around the dessert. Serve immediately.

Notes

♣ In the summer, Grandma made the soufflé with strawberries. But you can use other berries or even sliced peaches. In winter, we had it plain and it still motivated us to be good.

♣ You can easily cut the recipe in half to serve 2; use a 12-inch skillet. When cooking for 4, if you do not have a skillet larger than 12 inches, you might want to use 2 skillets so the omelets cook through. When slightly smaller, they are also easier to handle.

Francis's daughter Carole and her son Jules.

Meringues Glacées and Meringues Chantilly

WHEN I WAS GROWING UP, you could not buy ice cream at a store. So my brother and I were so excited when my dad bought the first ice-cream machine in the village. He turned the machine on in the late spring, and then, when the summer season was over, he turned it off until the next year. No one would even think of buying ice cream out of season. On Sunday—and only on Sunday; no one would serve meringues glacées on a Wednesday—while the family waited at the table after the main course, one of the kids would be sent to Dad's shop with a big serving bowl. Dad would fill it with two meringue shells per person and, in ice-cream season, a scoop went into each shell. He piped whipped cream generously over all and sprinkled the white pile with toasted almonds. And then the child rushed home before the ice cream melted. The rest of the year, the meringues were topped with just whipped cream and toasted almonds.

Dad baked his meringues very slowly overnight. They were slightly browned and, when broken open, revealed drops of caramelized sugar. Chantal still talks about my dad's meringues. If I had kids, I would want them to have the same taste memories I do. I think that is why my brother still makes all the same desserts for my nieces and nephews and the grandkids.

Serves 4 to 6; makes about 8 (5 by 2-inch) meringue shells

Meringues

- 4 large egg whites, at room temperature
- 2 teaspoons vanilla extract
- Pinch of salt
- ½ cup (3½ ounces) superfine sugar
- ½ cup (2 ounces) powdered sugar

Crème Chantilly

- ½ cup heavy cream
- 1½ teaspoons superfine sugar

Serving

- 1 or 2 pints premium-quality ice cream, such as vanilla, strawberry, or raspberry, or Maple Syrup and Fromage Blanc Ice Cream (page 124)
- Toasted sliced almonds

Preheat the oven to 225°F. Line a baking sheet with parchment paper.

To make the meringues: In the bowl of a stand mixer fitted with the whisk attachment, place the egg whites, vanilla, and salt. Begin to whisk the whites at medium speed until frothy. Slowly add about half the superfine sugar and continue to whisk for another minute. Increase the speed to high and slowly pour in the remaining superfine sugar. Whisk until the meringue holds stiff peaks—when the whisk is lifted the peaks stay upright.

Remove the bowl from the machine and sift the powdered sugar over the meringue. Using a large rubber spatula, fold in the powdered sugar until smooth.

You can shape the meringues with a pastry bag or, more simply, with a spoon. To shape with a pastry bag, scoop the meringue into a pastry bag fitted with a medium star tip. Pipe out ovals, about 5 by 2 inches. Begin in the center and pipe concentric ovals until you have the correct size and then build up the sides, piping one or two layers on top of each other to form a little nest. Leave 1 to 2 inches between meringues. To shape with a spoon, spoon some of the meringue onto the baking sheet and then use the back of the spoon to smooth it into shape and make a depression in the center.

Bake until the meringues are a pale beige color and are crisp and dry, about 1½ hours. Pull the parchment paper off the baking sheet onto a rack to cool for a few minutes and then carefully pry the meringues off the paper. Let

cool completely. The meringues can be made ahead and stored in an airtight tin for several days.

When ready to serve, make the whipped cream and leave the ice cream out to soften slightly. In a medium bowl, whip the cream with the sugar until it forms soft peaks.

To serve, place 2 meringue shells on each dessert plate. Place a scoop of ice cream in each and then top with a spoonful of whipped cream. Sprinkle with toasted almonds and serve immediately.

♣ You can mix Dutch-process cocoa powder into the meringues (use 4 tablespoons for 4 egg whites) or dust the tops of the vanilla meringues with cocoa powder. Instead of vanilla extract, you could use almond extract, a nice combination with berries. Lavender sugar, about 1½ teaspoons, would be another fun addition. And you can serve the meringues with seasonal fruit such as fresh berries or sliced peaches. Or you could pull out a jar of your Spirited Sour Cherries (page 46) and spoon the cherries and some of their syrup over the shells and ice cream.

Mentorship

By Three-Star Chefs

A THREE-STAR PRODUCT

I COME FROM A FAMILY BUSINESS where the grandmas, parents, and kids were all involved. My parents worked together in the pastry shop all day every day—my father doing the baking and my mom as the gracious presence interacting with the customers. The environment was always calm.

The Pâtisserie Keller became so popular because my father insisted on quality. He could have made the mille-feuille, a classic puff pastry dessert sold only on Sundays, on Saturday. But then it would not have been fresh and crisp. So he worked every day; he made the mille-feuille on Sunday. Showing profits was less important than the quality of his pastries. Of course, when you are a kid, you don't understand what you are absorbing. But that is what you see, that is what you learn, and that is what has stayed with me.

"At L'Auberge de L'Ill, from the kitchen to the front of the house, the choice is for quality without shortcuts."

When, at sixteen, I apprenticed at L'Auberge de L'Ill, I found the same quiet intensity in the kitchen, the same dedication to quality. L'Auberge de L'Ill was, and is still, a Michelin three-star restaurant. From the kitchen to the front of the house, the choice was for quality without short-cuts. On a different scale that's what my dad did in his shop.

The original L'Auberge, a tiny little restaurant specializing in *carpe frite*, sat next to the bridge across the river in Illhaeusern, very close to the German border. As the Germans retreated over the river L'Ill during World War II, they blew up the bridge and the little L'Auberge exploded as well. Eventually, the Haeberlins got a little funding from the government to help rebuild. Chef Paul Haeberlin with his talent, and Jean-Pierre Haeberlin, with his

From left: L'Auberge de L'Ill today. Jean-Pierre Haeberlin (owner, mentor, and brother of chef Paul Haeberlin), Chantal, and me at dinner in 2011. The famous *mousseline de grenouilles*.

Pages 52 and 53: Marc Haeberlin, my friend from school days and now the chef/owner of L'Auberge de L'Ill, and me before dinner at his restaurant.

Above: Marc keeps the signature dessert, Pêche Haeberlin, on the menu in tribute to his father. *Above, right:* Jean-Pierre Haeberlin and me on the outdoor dining patio of L'Auberge de L'Ill. Marc's daughter Laetitia, who worked with us at Fleur de Lys, stands just behind me.

artist's vision, together with their mother and aunt Henriette rebuilt that little L'Auberge and turned it into the internationally recognized L'Auberge de L'Ill. They earned their first Michelin star in 1952, the second in 1957, and finally the third in 1967, a few years before I arrived there.

Mme. Haeberlin, "Grandma," and Henriette were around for the entire time I was there. We slept in the house above where Chef lived. (We always addressed chef Paul Haeberlin as Chef and Jean-Pierre Haeberlin as M. Jean-Pierre.) When we came down in the morning, Grandma would have prepared the café au lait, baguette, *beurre*, and her homemade confiture. When Grandma passed away, Chef did the breakfast. The chef was always the first one in the kitchen. Always. Before the apprentices and everybody else came down. And he was always the last to leave.

Henriette's day began in the laundry about 4 a.m. and her windows directly overlooked the restaurant parking lot. As

56

L'Auberge de l'Ill

"Chef Paul Haeberlin was always the first one in the kitchen in the morning, and he was always the last to leave at night."

apprentices we were not authorized to go out after service on Saturday night. Chef locked the door to keep us in. So we had to find a way to sneak out and then in past Henriette. The kitchen floor had a trap door with a garbage can placed underneath. When we swept the floor, a foot pedal opened the chute and we brushed everything into the can. It was emptied from the outside. So when we snuck in, we removed the garbage can and climbed into the kitchen and pulled the trash can in behind us. When Henriette caught us, she would go see the chef. She'd say, "They went out again last night; I saw them coming in at four."

One of M. Jean-Pierre's watercolors of L'Auberge de L'Ill is reproduced in the restaurant's cookbook.

In order to maintain discipline in the kitchen, Chef needed one person to put us straight when we got loose. Monsieur Daniel was that one, the chef of L'Auberge de L'Ill directly under Paul Haeberlin. He was extremely well respected by everyone in the kitchen. M. Daniel lived in Ribeauvillé, seven kilometers from Illhaeusern. Every morning he drove to the restaurant, arriving at eight o'clock. His feeling was, "If I have to drive from Ribeauvillé to L'Auberge de L'Ill, and I walk in the kitchen and you apprentices are still eating breakfast? That's wrong. You should already be at work." Often, as we were just dipping the last bite of our baguette into our coffee, we'd hear the sound of his Citroën 2CV approaching. Then we'd scramble to put our blue aprons on.

Above: The Great Chefs of France, including Paul Bocuse, gave a cooking class at the Greystone campus of the CIA (Culinary Institute of America) in Napa, California, and several of us French chefs in America came to help out. *Above, right:* Me, Roger Vergé, and Paul Bocuse when M. Vergé was presented with a lifetime achievement award at the Ritz-Carlton Laguna.

One of the dishes we served at L'Auberge de L'Ill was *truite au bleu*, a classic preparation that can only be done if the restaurant keeps their trout alive until just before they are cooked. Occasionally, the trout pond needed cleaning. If you were the apprentice who had earned M. Daniel's disfavor that day, instead of your afternoon break you went out to the pond, caught all the fish, put them in a big plastic tub with some of the water, scrubbed the pond with a long-handled brush, refilled the tank, and returned the fish. By then it was time to return to the kitchen and start cooking again.

Every lunch and dinner, at the end of service, the routine was the same: M. Daniel, a big, tall man made even larger by his toque, would stand, his arms crossed, watching us with his apron on while we polished our Molteni stoves, which are big cooking islands manned by a team of chefs on opposite sides. M. Daniel would walk around each one to assess our work. So we competed with each other, trying to outdo the team on the opposite side of the stove. We rubbed a regular design of even, overlapping circles with our oiled stainless-steel pads onto the stoves until they shone and even the screws sparkled like gems. We could not stop until M. Daniel removed his apron. So everybody was on it. When he felt the stoves were clean, he undid his apron. That meant we could take ours off and relax.

I still use the techniques I learned at L'Auberge de L'Ill every day. Some are so simple—the bouquet garni (page 65) used to flavor stocks, the braising method for vegetables (page 73) that brings out their sweet flavors, the wrapping of meats in caul fat before cooking to preserve their moisture (page 74). Some reach back to folk ways, such as cooking with hay (page 71). And some, such as the complex wrapping of lamb chops in multiple layers (page 74), I've adapted and updated to create a new dish and presentation.

My apprenticeship at L'Auberge de L'Ill gave me a foot in the door to the world of three-stars. Once you were in that circuit, as long as you were serious and did well, you didn't have to worry about a job. The Haeberlin brothers guided my early career, sending me to positions with many of the greatest chefs of the time, including Gaston Lenôtre in Paris, Roger Vergé in Provence and later in Brazil (the Orange Tartlets with Lavender Meringue, page 94, capture the essence of his *cuisine du soleil*), and Jacques Maximin on the Côte d'Azur. I've included a Bouillabaisse (page 88) that reminds me of my year there. Through M. Vergé, I worked with Paul Bocuse at his restaurant near Lyon. Those great chefs, who revolutionized the cuisine of their day, knew they were training us to be a three-star product.

Frisée Salad with the Perfect Poached Egg and Panisse Croutons

Notes

♣ You can reheat *panisse* in a low oven. And they can be baked instead of fried. Preheat the oven to 375°F. Butter or oil a large baking sheet. Lay out the croutons and then brush or spray the tops with butter or oil. Bake until browned and crispy, about 20 minutes. Turn over about three-fourths of the way through. While still warm, sprinkle with salt and dust with Spanish hot paprika if you like.

♣ If you use a pan deeper than ½ inch, the *panisse* dough may not release easily. In that case, score the dough in the pan and use an offset spatula to lift up the dough triangles.

THERE WAS A POACHED EGG DISH we made at L'Auberge de L'Ill only when the whole restaurant was sold out for a party. The poached eggs needed to be perfectly shaped. They were glazed in a lobster *chaud froid* (a lobster sauce thickened with gelatin) that gave the egg an orange, shiny coating. Then we put the coated egg in an oyster shell and topped it with a truffle slice and an oyster we'd lightly poached in white wine and shallots. But poached eggs can also be comfort food. Use my simple technique and you can turn out a nicely shaped poached egg every time. This frisée salad with bacon and a poached egg is classic French bistro fare. When you cut into the yolk, it runs into the salad, creating a satiny, savory sauce. *Panisse*, made from chickpea flour, is a specialty of southern France. The frisée salad is almost always served as an appetizer, but I think it would make a very good dish for brunch or lunch.

Serves 4

Panisse Croutons

    Pinch of sea salt
1   tablespoon extra-virgin olive oil
¾   cup (2¾ ounces) chickpea flour
    About 3 cups vegetable oil or sunflower oil for deep-frying

Vinaigrette

1   tablespoon sherry vinegar or red wine vinegar
½   teaspoon Dijon mustard
    Sea salt and freshly ground black pepper
3   tablespoons extra-virgin olive oil
2   teaspoons very finely chopped shallots
1   clove garlic, very finely chopped

Salad

3   (¼-inch-thick) slices bacon (3 ounces), cut crosswise into ¼-inch strips
4   large eggs
    Extra-virgin olive oil
    Sea salt and freshly ground black pepper
4   or 5 radicchio leaves
2   cups loosely packed frisée lettuce
1   cup loosely packed baby spinach or arugula
    About 2 whole chive blossoms or a few nasturtium flowers

    Handful mixed nasturtium leaves and celery leaves (optional)
    Fleur de sel (optional)

To make the panisse croutons: Bring 2 cups of water to a boil in a medium saucepan and then lower the heat to maintain a simmer. Whisk in the salt and the olive oil and then slowly sprinkle in the chickpea flour, whisking all the while.

Cook the mixture, stirring frequently and scraping all over the bottom of the pot with a wooden spoon or silicone spatula, until very thick, about 7 minutes. Immediately scrape the mixture into a food processor and process until smooth. Scrape down the work bowl several times and process again. Any lumps can cause the croutons to burst when cooked.

Working very quickly to prevent a skin from forming, pour the batter into an ungreased 8-inch square baking dish. (You can also simply pour the batter onto a small baking sheet and let the batter spread naturally. If you rap the pan smartly to remove air bubbles, you will not need to work them out with a dowel as described below.) Make sure the pan is flat so the batter forms

an even layer. Use an offset spatula to smooth the top. Rap the pan smartly against the counter to release any bubbles. Lay a sheet of plastic wrap directly on the surface of the batter and gently roll a wooden dowel over the surface to work out any bubbles. Lift up the corners of the plastic wrap to release air bubbles and resmooth the wrap. Rap the pan again against the counter to work any bubbles up to the surface, and then smooth again. Refrigerate for at least 2 hours and preferably overnight.

To prepare the vinaigrette: Whisk together the vinegar, mustard, and a pinch each of salt and pepper in a large mixing bowl until the salt has dissolved. Whisk in the olive oil, shallots, and garlic until the dressing has emulsified. Cover and set aside for up to 1 hour. Don't let it stand for longer or the garlic flavor may become too strong.

To make the salad: Line a plate with paper towels. Place the bacon in a nonstick skillet over medium heat and cook, while stirring, until crisp. Remove with a slotted spoon and drain on the paper towels. Reserve.

Prepare the eggs for cooking. Spread an 8- or 10-inch-long sheet of plastic wrap on a counter. Spray or smear it with oil and season the center with salt and pepper. Line a round coffee cup with the prepared plastic wrap. Crack an egg into the lined cup without breaking the yolk. Carefully gather the ends of the plastic wrap together until the egg is completely enclosed in the wrap without any air bubbles. Twist the ends together and then tie the wrap into a knot or with string to make an airtight pouch. Repeat with the remaining eggs. Fill a large pan with 3 inches of water and bring to a boil over high heat. Lower the heat to a rolling simmer.

Preheat the oven to low. Line a baking sheet with paper towels. Heat the oil in a deep fryer or deep saucepan to 360°F. To unmold the chickpea dough, run a knife around the edges and invert it onto a counter. Trim the edges, if needed, and cut the batter into 1/4- to 1/2-inch wide strips. Cut the strips on a diagonal at 1-inch intervals to create diamond shapes. Working in batches, fry the *panisse* croutons until crisp and golden brown, 3 to 4 minutes. Transfer them with a large skimmer to the prepared baking sheet to drain. Sprinkle liberally with salt and keep warm in the oven.

Cut the radicchio into 1/4-inch-wide strips and place them in a large bowl with the frisée, spinach, and bacon. Add half the vinaigrette and toss well. Add more vinaigrette and toss again until the salad is dressed to your palate. Taste and adjust the seasoning with salt and pepper. Break up the chive blossoms into individual flowers and reserve in a small bowl.

Lower the eggs into the simmering water and cook for about 5 minutes. If they've been wrapped without bubbles, they will sink under the water. Try to keep them submerged. Meanwhile, divide the salad among 4 plates, arranging the portions to accommodate the poached eggs, and add some *panisse* croutons to each. When the eggs are done, carefully pick them up by the ends of the plastic wrap and gently place on a work surface. One by one, release the eggs by cutting with scissors just below the tie. Unwrap the eggs and place them on top of the salads. Sprinkle with the chive flowers and nasturtium leaves, season with freshly ground pepper and fleur de sel, and serve immediately.

Chicken Demi-Deuil

♣ The flavor of the dish depends on very good broth, so make your own or buy prepared broth and reduce it by about half before you use it.

♣ Use a good-quality olive oil for the vinaigrette that is well balanced and not pungent or powerfully flavored.

♣ Once you have bouquet garni on hand, it's so easy to improve the flavor of packaged broth by simmering the broth with a bouquet garni for a few minutes.

THIS VERY SPECIAL DISH IS FROM MY APPRENTICESHIP at L'Auberge de L'Ill. *Demi-deuil* refers to the tradition of wearing black when grieving for a loved one. Here, black truffle slices are slid under the bird's skin before cooking, giving it a black and white appearance, or half (*demi*) in black (*deuil*). The dish is really a pot-au-feu, but with chicken instead of beef. In France, we would make this with one of our best-quality chickens. For an elegant dinner party, try the recipe with Cornish game hens or squab, Chantal's favorite bird, serving one per person. Then you will not have to do any carving at table. (See the variation for details.) Poached chicken is not much in fashion, but this would make a great holiday dinner.

The original recipe included an early sort of *sous-vide* cooking called *en vessie*. The chicken was poached first until it was almost but not quite cooked through. Then we'd cook a little ragout of vegetables; add cooked, diced sweetbreads; bind it with a cream sauce; and stuff the chicken with it. We had a supply of previously cleaned and dried pig bladders. We soaked a bladder until it became supple, rubbed with it cognac, and turned it inside out. Then we blew it up to make a balloon. We put the chicken in the balloon and tied it tightly. The balloon was set afloat in a pot of simmering broth to complete the cooking. The waiter presented the chicken-filled balloon to the diner at table and then returned it to the kitchen where it was carved and then presented again to the diner.

Serves 4

5 large carrots, peeled	¼ cup balsamic vinegar, or more as needed
1 large onion (8 to 10 ounces), halved	
4 whole cloves	3 tablespoons toasted hazelnut oil
3 to 4 quarts low-salt chicken broth or water	1 small tomato, peeled, seeded, and chopped (optional)
1 clove garlic	2 tablespoons finely chopped fresh herbs (such as chervil, basil, and flat-leaf parsley)
1 bouquet garni (page 65), including 1 sprig rosemary	
2 stalks celery, cut into about 1-inch lengths	
1 large fresh black truffle (about ½ ounce)	
1 pasture-raised chicken (about 3½ pounds), at room temperature	
Sea salt and freshly ground black pepper	
1 small bunch basil (optional)	
2 medium leeks, white and pale green parts, halved and tied into a bundle with string	
½ pound pearl onions, blanched and peeled	
½ pound brussels sprouts	
2 medium zucchini, about 1 inch in diameter	
2 medium turnips, peeled	
8 ounces fresh haricots verts (optional)	
½ cup extra-virgin olive oil	

Cut 3 of the carrots into 1-inch lengths and cut the remaining 2 into ½-inch-thick diagonal slices. Set aside separately. Stick the onion halves with the cloves and place them in a large stockpot with the broth, garlic, bouquet garni, the 3 carrots, and the celery. Bring to a boil over high heat and simmer, uncovered, for 30 to 40 minutes. Strain the broth into another large stockpot and discard the vegetables.

While the broth simmers, cut about 10 very thin slices from the truffle. Finely dice the remaining truffle and set aside. Slide 5 slices under the chicken skin on each side of the breast. Salt and pepper the chicken inside and out and then stuff the cavity with the bunch of basil. Tie up the legs.

When the broth is ready, submerge the chicken in it, bring to a boil, and simmer, uncovered, very gently with the remaining 2 sliced carrots, the leeks, and the pearl onions until the chicken juices run clear, about 45 minutes.

While the chicken cooks, prepare the remaining vegetables. Halve the brussels sprouts or quarter them if large. Cut the zucchini lengthwise into quarters and then cut these into ½-inch lengths. Cut the turnips into a size that matches the zucchini. Trim the haricots verts into 1-inch lengths.

Fish out the chicken and place it on a warm platter. Cover it with plastic wrap or a damp kitchen towel so it does not dry out. Keep warm. Dip out 2½ cups cooking broth into a clean saucepan, bring it to a boil over medium-high heat, and cook until reduced to about 1 cup, about 15 minutes. Remove from the heat and let cool.

Meanwhile, add the brussels sprouts, zucchini, and turnips to the pot with the remaining broth and continue to simmer slowly, uncovered, until the vegetables are nearly tender, another 10 to 15 minutes. Add the haricots verts and simmer until just tender, about 2 minutes. The broth should barely simmer.

To make the dressing: In a medium bowl, whisk together the remaining diced truffle, the reduced cooking broth, olive oil, vinegar, hazelnut oil, tomato, and fresh herbs. Taste and adjust the balance by seasoning with salt, pepper, and perhaps more vinegar.

To serve, strain the vegetables out of the broth, reserving both separately. Cut the string holding the leeks together and then arrange all the vegetables around the chicken on the platter. Moisten everything with some of the broth. Carve the chicken at the table and pass the dressing separately.

Cornish Game Hen or Squab Variation

Buy one bird per person, each weighing about 1½ to 1¾ pounds.

Insert 2 or 3 truffle slices under the skin on each side of the breast, 4 to 6 per bird. Poach the birds until their juices run clear, about 30 minutes for both the Cornish game hens and the squab. Cut the strings tying the feet together and discard the herbs inside. Arrange one bird per person on warm dinner plates, arrange some of the vegetables around the bird, and moisten all with some of the broth. Pass the dressing at table.

Bouquet Garni

Makes 1

A bouquet garni combines the traditional aromatics of French cooking in a single bundle that you can pluck out of the dish once its job is done. The basics are leek, bay leaf, parsley, celery, and thyme. But you can construct your own depending on the flavors you want in your final dish. For example, you could make a Provençale bouquet garni with orange or lemon zest and more herbs such as oregano, rosemary, or basil.

1   (3- to 4-inch) single layer of the white part of a fat leek
1   bay leaf
1   (3-inch) piece celery
4   to 5 sprigs fresh flat-leaf parsley
2   sprigs fresh thyme

Hold the leek layer in one hand and fit the bay leaf, celery, parsley, and thyme inside it. Fold the leek over your bundle and tie it up securely with string. You can assemble several of these and keep them, wrapped in a plastic bag, in the refrigerator for several days or in the freezer for about a month.

♣ Change the vegetables you use to flavor the broth and for serving according to the season. When leeks are plentiful, use them. Chantal and I love parsnips and add one or two when available.

♣ You will have lots of flavorful broth and vegetables left over. We enjoy it as a light lunch with salad. Also, you can use any leftover dressing for a salad.

Marinated Squab en Crépinettes with Juniper and Red Wine Sauce

THIS IS A DISH WE USED TO MAKE at L'Auberge de L'Ill with squab and partridge. It is based on a classic dish, *côtelette Pojarski*, from the Russian court. *Côtelette* means *chop*, but *côtelette Pojarski* was made with chopped veal shaped to resemble a chop. When I first served this at Fleur de Lys, I served the birds as we did in France—with the feet still attached. In the morning I would call the only shop in San Francisco licensed to butcher live birds. They were killed, cleaned, and delivered (feet on) in the afternoon. I thought the presentation would show our customers how fresh the squab were, how unprocessed and natural. But it was a disaster. No one wanted to see feet on their dinner.

Serves 4

Squab and Marinade

- 5 squab
- 2 cloves garlic, peeled and lightly crushed
- 2 bay leaves
- ½ bunch fresh thyme
- 1 tablespoon juniper berries, lightly crushed
- 1 tablespoon cracked black pepper
- 2 tablespoons cognac
  About 3 cups dry red wine

Sauce

  All the trimmings and bones from the squab
- 1 tablespoon extra-virgin olive oil
- 1 small yellow onion or 2 shallots, very finely chopped
- 1 large carrot, peeled and diced
- 2 stalks celery, diced
- 2 cloves garlic, peeled and lightly crushed
  Sea salt and freshly ground black pepper
- 1 tablespoon tomato paste
- 1 bouquet garni (page 65)
- 6 cups low-salt chicken broth, boiled until reduced to 3 cups

Filling

- 3 ounces pork back fat or 1½ ounces rendered pork fat
- 3 ounces boneless loin of veal or chicken breast
- 1½ ounces chicken livers

  Reserved 3 ounces boneless squab meat, uncooked
- 2 large egg yolks
  Sea salt and freshly ground black pepper

Assembly and Serving

- 1 tablespoon extra-virgin olive oil
- 8 ounces wild mushrooms (such as black chanterelles, chanterelles, shiitakes, and morels), sliced ¼ inch thick
- 1 tablespoon finely chopped shallots
  Sea salt and freshly ground black pepper
- 8 to 10 ounces caul fat (see Note, page 74)
- 2 tablespoons unsalted butter

To prepare the squab: One squab will be used for a filling. Set it aside while you prepare the remaining 4 birds. Remove the breasts from 4 of the squab so that you have 8 boneless, skinless half breasts. Trim them of any fat. Remove the whole legs from the backbones and bone just the thighs. Transfer the breasts and legs to a large, nonreactive container and add the garlic, bay leaves, thyme, juniper berries, cracked pepper, cognac, and enough red wine just to cover the birds. Cover and refrigerate overnight. For the fifth squab, bone the breasts and weigh out 3 ounces of the meat. Reserve it, covered, and refrigerated, to use for the filling. Reserve the trimmings and bones from all the squab in a bowl, cover, and refrigerate until needed for the stock.

Notes

♣ The sauce is a reduction of the marinade and broth. The more you reduce red wine, the more acidic and strong the flavors. Swirling a little butter into the sauce at the end really smooths out the flavors.

To make the juniper and red wine sauce:
Drain the squab, reserving it and the marinade separately. Transfer the marinated squab to a bowl, cover, and refrigerate until needed. Set the marinade aside for a moment.

Break the squab carcasses into small pieces. Heat the olive oil in a large heavy sauté pan over medium heat. Add the carcasses and bones and trimmings and sear them, stirring so they brown all over, about 10 minutes. Add the onion, carrot, celery, and garlic, season lightly with salt and pepper, and cook until the vegetables have browned lightly, about 10 minutes. Add the reserved marinade with the tomato paste and bouquet garni. Bring to a boil and cook until reduced by two-thirds, about 15 minutes. Add the chicken broth, bring to a boil, lower the heat to a very gentle simmer, and cook— frequently skimming off any foam or scum that rises to the top—until the sauce has reduced to a bit more than ½ cup, about 50 minutes. The more you skim, the clearer your sauce will be. Strain the sauce through a sieve into a small bowl. Discard the solids. Skim any fat off the top of the sauce.

While the sauce reduces, make the filling:
With a meat grinder or food processor, finely mince the pork fat, veal, chicken livers, and reserved 3 ounces squab

meat. Transfer the mixture to a bowl and mix in the egg yolks and a good pinch each of salt and pepper with a wooden spoon until well combined. Scoop out a small spoonful of the filling and cook in a small skillet over medium heat until cooked through. Taste for seasoning and adjust the remaining filling as needed.

To assemble the squab chops: Preheat the oven to 375°F. Heat the olive oil in a large skillet over medium-high heat. Add the mushrooms, making sure not to crowd the pan, and cook for 1 minute without disturbing them, until they have browned. Then stir and cook for another 2 minutes. Add the shallots and season with salt and pepper. Continue to cook until the mushrooms are thoroughly tender, 2 to 3 minutes. Set aside to cool and then chop finely.

Remove the squab breasts from the refrigerator and season with salt and pepper. Lay out the caul fat into eight 8-inch squares. To make sure you have enough filling to finish the job, separate it into 8 equal portions. Each squab breast will need 2 layers of filling, so plan accordingly. Place a little filling in the center of each piece of caul fat, spreading it to the size of a squab breast. Lay the squab breasts (with what was the skin side down) on the filling. Position a squab leg so that the thigh slightly overlaps the breast and the drumstick protrudes much like the rib bone of a chop. Cover each breast with a thin layer of the mush-

Left to right: **Me, Marc Haeberlin, and Jean-Pierre Haeberlin in the sparkling kitchen of L'Auberge de L'Ill.**

rooms and then cover with another layer of filling. Fold the caul fat over the filling, making sure that everything is completely enclosed but leaving the drumsticks exposed so that the wrapped packages look like chops.

Heat 1 tablespoon of the butter in a large ovenproof sauté pan over medium heat. Season the squab "chops" with salt and pepper. Place them in the pan, seam side up, and cook until brown on both sides, about 3 minutes. Set the pan in the oven and roast for 10 minutes.

Transfer the sauce to a small saucepan and reheat over low heat until hot. Little by little, whisk in the remaining tablespoon of butter so that it emulsifies into the sauce. Taste and season with salt and pepper.

When the squab chops are done, transfer them to a cutting board and let rest for 2 to 3 minutes. Cut the breasts into ½-inch-thick slices but keep them together to retain the chop shape. The breasts should still be pink in the center. Arrange 2 chops each on 4 warm dinner plates. Moisten the chops with the sauce and serve immediately.

Rack of Lamb Cooked in Hay

THERE'S NO MISTAKING WHEN IT IS HAYING TIME; you can tell by the good smell in the air. When you cook this dish and crack open the lid at the table, the hay releases a beautiful, rustic aroma. Cooking with hay is one of those old techniques we used to do in Alsace that I've noticed popping up on menus recently. This is a very fun dish to cook—at least once you've sourced your hay (see Notes). Ask the butcher for 2 racks of lamb chops. Suckling pig loin chops are about the same size as lamb racks, and pork cooked this way would be equally delicious. In the old days when we poached a whole fresh ham, we put lots of hay in the water, and it would infuse the ham with its sweet, herbal flavor.

Serves 4

Red Wine–Shallot Sauce (page 211, optional)

2 lamb racks (1 to 1½ pounds trimmed weight each) or baby pork racks

Sea salt and freshly ground black pepper

2 tablespoons extra-virgin olive oil

Several large handfuls freshly dried hay

3 bay leaves

1 large bunch fresh thyme, preferably lemon or lavender thyme

4 cloves garlic, peeled or unpeeled and lightly crushed

Make the sauce first and have it ready before you cook the meat. Add the butter just before serving.

If the butcher did not french the rib bones of the lamb rack for you, with a small, sharp knife, scrape the ends of the rib bones clean of meat. (This is not absolutely necessary but makes for a nicer presentation.)

Preheat the oven to 500°F. Let the racks come to room temperature and season them all over with salt and pepper. Heat 1 tablespoon of the olive oil in a large skillet. When hot, sear the racks on all sides and both ends until they turn a rich, golden brown, about 6 minutes total. Set aside.

Brush the bottom of a cast-iron Dutch oven—with a lid and large enough to hold the racks in a single layer—with the remaining 1 tablespoon olive oil. Spread the hay in a layer over the bottom of the pot. Add the bay leaves, thyme sprigs, and garlic. Arrange the racks over the herbs, fat side up.

Place the pot over medium-high heat for 2 minutes to get it hot, cover, transfer it to the oven, and cook for 15 minutes for medium meat. For rare to medium-rare, just cut back on the time in the oven by a few minutes. Remove from the oven, and with the lid still on, let it rest for 5 minutes. Transfer the racks to a cutting board and let them rest for another 5 minutes before carving into chops. Reheat the sauce gently over low heat. Add any pan juices to your warm sauce and swirl in the butter. Arrange the chops on warm dinner plates and spoon some of the sauce around each. Serve immediately. Pass the remaining sauce at the table.

Notes

♣ Don't confuse hay with straw. Freshly harvested hay is slightly green, includes the seed heads and often legumes, and is used for animal fodder. Straw is the stubble left in the field and is used for animal bedding and mulch. You can find hay even in cities. Perhaps there's a riding stable or one of the local schools has started a school farm, a growing trend in San Francisco. When testing this recipe, a couple of generous sheep and goats shared their feed hay with us. Look for fresh, clean, organic hay.

♣ If you have an herb garden and not a hay field, harvest handfuls of the overgrown stems, collecting an abundance of whatever you have, and line the pot with them. This would be a terrific way to cook a loin of pork as well.

A Traditional Apprenticeship
THE REAL MEANING OF A BLUE APRON

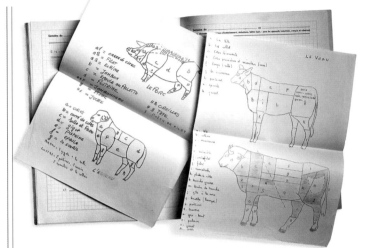

The classic apprenticeship program I entered does not exist now. We studied and worked in the restaurant kitchen wearing our apprentice uniforms: a white chef's jacket worn under a blue apron with a bib that covered our chests, checked chef's pants, and a short toque. After three years, in order to receive our CAP (*certificat d'aptitude professionnelle*), we took both a written and a practical exam to test our proficiency. (See pages from my 1973 exam books above.) It was given just once a year, and the best chefs in the region were our judges. Without that credential, it would be very difficult to progress as a chef and impossible to get a bank loan to open a business.

If we passed, we earned the right to wear the kitchen uniform of a *commis*: a taller toque, a white jacket, and a white apron that tied around the waist. The apron, without a bib, showed that we knew how to work cleanly, and we were motivated to work for it. The hierarchy of the kitchen staff was very like the army. There was the chef, and under him a chef de cuisine, and then the sous chef. The "officers" were the *chefs de parties*. A *partie* is a section or station including sauces, fish, meat. Each *chef de partie* had two, three, or

even four *commis*. Under the *commis* were the apprentices. It was very structured, and we worked our way up from apprentice to *commis* and then to *chef de partie*.

Our careers were mapped out by our mentors and their relationships with other three-star chefs. They talked to each other and traded young chefs. But becoming a better cook was what drove us. And to be recognized as a real professional we needed to move from kitchen to kitchen. As we moved up the hierarchy there were fewer of us. We wanted to do our best and succeed so that our performance reflected well on our mentors, and we knew if we failed there were many in line to take our places.

An informal mentoring practice does still exist. When my friend Marc Haeberlin, Paul Haeberlin's son and now the chef of L'Auberge de L'Ill, wanted to give his daughter Laetitia restaurant experience outside France, he called me. She came to us at Fleur de Lys for a year and a half. Chantal and I were proud and happy to act as her American parents and mentors.

Winter Vegetable Ragout

I COOK THIS DISH AT HOME FOR CHANTAL. I learned this braising technique at L'Auberge de L'Ill. It brings out the sweetness of the vegetables. You might think that if you blanched the vegetables and then sautéed them in butter you would get a similar result. But the difference is night and day. Braising gives a more intense flavor. You can use this cooking technique with many vegetables, including brussels sprouts, parsnips, carrots, celery root, whole heads of endive, turnips, pearl onions, and radishes. Serve the ragout with roasted meat, fish, or fowl, as an omelet filling, or—with some curls of Parmesan on top—as a first course on its own.

Notes

♣ This is a comparatively large amount of shallots, but don't worry; I mean it to be that way.

Serves 4

16 to 20 fresh or dried morel mushrooms (about 1 ounce dried)

3 medium rutabagas (about 1¼ pounds), peeled

2 tablespoons extra-virgin olive oil

4 medium shallots, very thinly sliced

2 cloves garlic, very finely chopped

1 teaspoon brown sugar
  Sea salt and freshly ground black pepper

1 teaspoon finely chopped fresh thyme
  About 1½ cups low-salt chicken or beef broth or water

1 tablespoon unsalted butter (optional)

2 tablespoons finely sliced chives

If using dried morels, put them in a medium bowl and add just enough hot water to cover them. Set aside until they soften. Drain the mushrooms, reserving the soaking water, and cut off and discard the stems. Cut the caps open and rinse them well in two changes of water. Filter the soaking liquid through a coffee filter, put in a small saucepan, and boil until reduced to about 2 tablespoons. If the mushroom halves are very large, cut them in half again. Set aside. If using fresh morels, remove and discard the stems or save for stock. Cut the caps open and wash well in two changes of water. Set aside.

Cut the rutabagas into no less than ¼-inch-thick slices and cut these into ¼-inch-wide strips about 2 inches long. Heat 1 tablespoon of the oil in a medium saucepan over medium heat. Add the shallots and cook until soft, about 3 minutes. Add the rutabaga, garlic, brown sugar, 1 teaspoon salt, ½ teaspoon pepper, the thyme, and the broth to a depth of about ⅓ inch. Cover the pan and bring to a simmer. Cook, partially covered, very slowly until tender, 20 to 25 minutes. The rutabagas should retain their shape.

While the rutabagas cook, sauté the morels in a skillet with the remaining 1 tablespoon olive oil over medium-high heat until tender, 2 to 5 minutes. Season with salt and pepper. If you have reserved mushroom-soaking liquid, add it just as the mushrooms are tender and cook and toss until the pan is dry.

When the rutabagas are tender, add the morels, butter, and chives. Toss gently and taste for seasoning. Serve immediately.

Fleur de Lys's Signature Roasted Lamb Chops with Merlot-Vanilla Sauce

Notes

♣ Butchers often carry or will special-order caul fat for you. It freezes beautifully, so even if you have to order some pounds of it on the Internet (Amazon.com is one source I found) it will not go to waste. In fact, a pound would make a much-appreciated gift to any friend who loves to cook. But you can use it yourself to wrap lean meats like venison, rabbit, chicken breasts, and buffalo to keep them moist as they cook.

THIS IS A DISH I MADE on the first season of *Top Chef Masters*. Until then, I had promised myself I would never compete because of my experience as an apprentice. After winning our professional credential and graduating from apprentice to *commis*, it was customary to enter *Le Meilleur Apprentis de France* competition. The first part was a regional competition in Colmar. There I earned the title Meilleur Apprentis d'Ouest. For the national competition in Paris, we would prepare three dishes from Auguste Escoffier's compendium of classic French haute cuisine, *Le Guide Culinaire*. My performance would reflect back on L'Auberge de L'Ill and its chef de cuisine M. Daniel, who had prepared me for the competition by drilling me until I was perfect. In Paris, the last dish to cook was a soufflé, something I had done countless times. But we had just a single oven and drew straws for when we would be able to bake our soufflés. I drew last, and by then, with the continuous opening and closing of the oven to check other dishes, the temperature rose and fell and my soufflé never fully developed. I decided that if competitions depended more on luck than on skill, then they were not for me.

Toward the end of my time at Sutter 500 in San Francisco, I started working on this lamb dish. The original idea came from L'Auberge de L'Ill, where we did a similar dish with squab (page 67). The version I present here is the one I created for Fleur de Lys, just after I partnered with Maurice Rouas. We had so little help in the kitchen that Chantal would come in and help with the chops. She must have stuffed and wrapped thousands—well, many hundreds—of them. It is still unusual, I think, to pair lamb with vanilla. But lamb is often paired with merlot wines. And merlot's flavor is often described as having a vanilla component, probably from the oak barrels in which it ages. This is definitely a restaurant dish and somewhat technical to assemble, but I believe if you follow the steps carefully you will achieve success. I prefer to use Colorado lamb for this dish. It is wonderful meat and has longer rib bones, which look more elegant in this presentation. Let's get cooking!

Serves 4

1 lamb loin rack, well trimmed
8 small whole cloves garlic
1 tablespoon plus 1½ teaspoons extra-virgin olive oil
   Sea salt and freshly ground black pepper
24 large spinach leaves or white chard leaves
6 to 8 ounces caul fat (see Notes)

Mousseline

2 tablespoons extra-virgin olive oil
1 tablespoon finely chopped zucchini
1 tablespoon finely chopped yellow squash
1 tablespoon peeled and finely chopped carrots
1 tablespoon finely chopped celery
1 tablespoon finely chopped yellow onion
1 tablespoon peeled and finely chopped red bell pepper
1 tablespoon finely chopped garlic
1 teaspoon finely chopped fresh thyme
   Sea salt and freshly ground black pepper
3 ounces boneless lean lamb (from the shoulder, leg, or loin)
3 ounces pork back fat or 1½ ounces rendered pork fat
3 ounces boneless veal loin

1½ ounces chicken livers

2 large egg yolks

1 tablespoon finely chopped fresh cilantro

Sauce

½ teaspoon extra-virgin olive oil

2 tablespoons finely chopped shallots

1 clove garlic, very finely chopped

1 cup merlot

1½ cups low-salt chicken or beef broth

2 tablespoons ruby port

⅓ plump, moist vanilla bean, split lengthwise

1½ teaspoons cornstarch

Sea salt and freshly ground black pepper

To prepare the lamb chops: If the end pieces of the rack are ragged, trim them and reserve for the mousseline. If the rib bones are not well cleaned, scrape them clean with the back of a knife. Separate the rack into four 2-rib chops. Remove one of the rib bones from each chop: cut it out by cutting around the knuckle with a small, sharp knife.

Bring a little pot of water to a boil, drop in the garlic cloves, and simmer for 1 minute. Drain off the water and repeat twice more. Heat 1½ teaspoons of the oil in a small nonstick skillet over medium heat. Add the garlic and cook and stir until lightly colored. Season with salt and pepper, scrape into a small bowl, and let cool.

HOW TO WRAP THE LAMB CHOPS

Cut a small incision into the center of each chop. Push a cooked garlic clove all the way into the meat so that it is enclosed.

Lay a circle of caul fat on a work surface and arrange a circle of blanched spinach leaves in the middle with the rib sides up.

Bring a saucepan of water to a boil over high heat and add salt. Prepare an ice-water bath. Invert a small mixing bowl or colander on a dinner plate. Very quickly blanch the spinach leaves in 2 to 3 batches, just in and out until limp and bright green, about 5 seconds or less. Immediately plunge them into ice water. Fish the leaves out of the water one by one and lay them carefully over the bowl to drain. If you cook the spinach more than an hour ahead of time (it can be done up to 24 hours ahead), wrap the bowl with the leaves on it in plastic wrap and refrigerate. You can cook the garlic up to 2 hours in advance as well.

To prepare the lamb and vegetable mousseline: Heat 2 tablespoons of the oil in a medium skillet over medium heat.

Add the zucchini, squash, carrots, celery, onion, and bell pepper. Sauté the vegetables until soft, about 5 minutes, adding the chopped garlic, thyme, and salt and pepper to taste after 2 minutes. Scrape the vegetables into a medium bowl and let cool. Refrigerate until cold.

In a food processor, pulse the lamb, pork fat, veal, and chicken livers until finely ground. Add the yolks and pulse in with the cilantro and a good pinch each of salt and pepper. Pulse in the cooked vegetables just until mixed. You do not want a smooth puree but want to retain some texture. In a small skillet over medium heat, cook a small nugget of the mousseline and taste for seasoning. Adjust the remaining mixture with salt and pepper as needed.

Drain blanched and cooled spinach leaves on an inverted bowl. You can do them ahead; wrap and refrigerate.

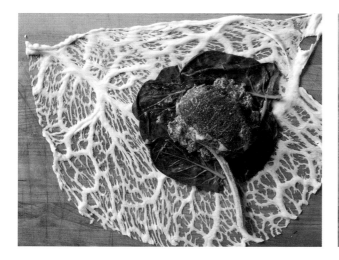

Press a small round of mousseline on top of the spinach and then center a chop on top.

Press more mousseline on top of the chop and wrap it in the spinach. Add more leaves if needed to cover all the meat. And leave the rib bone exposed.

Notes

♣ Since caul fat sticks to itself, it self-seals. Use it to keep a stuffing inside a chicken breast; at L'Auberge de L'Ill we called preparations with that shape *alouettes sans têtes* (little birds without heads). Make sure to cook caul-wrapped foods over moderate heat. If the pan is too hot, the caul fat will melt away.

To make the sauce: Heat ½ teaspoon of the olive oil in a small saucepan over medium heat. Add the shallots and cook until soft, about 3 minutes. Add the chopped garlic and cook for 1 minute. Add the wine and simmer until the pan is almost dry. Add the broth and stir and scrape all over the sides and bottom of the pan to loosen any browned bits. Add the port and the vanilla bean and simmer very gently for 8 to 10 minutes. Place the cornstarch in a small jar with twice as much water, shake well, and dribble into the gently boiling sauce while whisking and watching for signs of thickening. Season with salt and pepper. Set aside until needed.

To assemble the lamb chops: Holding a small, sharp knife parallel to the work

surface, make a small incision into the center of each chop. Insert the cooked garlic cloves so they are enclosed by the meat. Season the meat on both sides with salt and pepper.

Spread the caul fat out on a work surface. The easiest way to work with it is to wrap one chop at a time, cutting the caul fat around each chop and leaving enough margin to enclose the chop. Then smooth out more of the fat and wrap the next chop. Arrange 3 or more spinach leaves (rib sides up) to form a circle on the fat, points to the center and shoulders to the outside.

Divide the mousseline into 4 equal portions. Wet your hands, pick up half of one portion of the mousseline, and press it into a flat pancake about

Trim the caul fat so there is just enough to wrap the chop nicely.

Lift up the edge of the caul fat and begin wrapping the chop. Again, leave the bone exposed.

⅜ inch thick. Place it in the center of the spinach leaves and lay a chop on top of the mousseline. Again with wet hands, pat the remaining half of one portion of mousseline into a disk and lay it on top of the meat. Press this disk down around the chop and press the edges together with the lower disk so the chop is completely enclosed by the mousseline with just the rib sticking out. Carefully pry up the spinach leaves and wrap them all around the chops, completely encasing them except for the bone. Now cut the caul fat around the chop, lift up the edges, and overlap them over the chop. Line a baking sheet with plastic wrap and place the chop on it, seam side down. Repeat with the remaining 3 chops. You can make the chops in the morning and cook them in the evening. Wrap well with plastic wrap and refrigerate.

To cook the lamb chops: Preheat the oven to 375°F. Rewarm the sauce gently over low heat. Heat the remaining 1 tablespoon of oil in a large ovenproof nonstick skillet over medium heat. The pans should be hot but not smoking. Add the chops, seam side up, and sear them delicately, just until lightly colored, about 1 minute. Flip them over and place them in the oven to roast for 10 minutes. Transfer the lamb chops to a cutting board and let rest for 3 to 4 minutes. Carefully peel off the caul fat and cut each chop into thick slices to display the green wrapping, pink meat, and garlic clove.

Spoon some sauce on warm dinner plates and arrange a chop on each. Moisten with more sauce and serve immediately.

I was so proud to win the Ivy Award in 1991 given by *Restaurants and Institutions* magazine. The photo shows how we served the lamb chops "back in the day."

Try to maintain a smooth wrap without pleats or puckers.

The completed, wrapped chop ready to cook. Notice the seam side of the caul fat is underneath. The chops should be cooked seam side up.

Tomahawk Steak with Béarnaise Sauce

Notes

♣ You can substitute tarragon vinegar for the white wine vinegar and the fresh tarragon, but avoid dried tarragon.

♣ Even when I grill a steak, I put the cast-iron skillet right on the grate to heat and cook the steak in the pan. That way I keep the fat and juices and can baste the steak as it cooks. Basting keeps the meat moist and helps it cook evenly.

ONE OF THE SIGNATURE DISHES of L'Auberge de L'Ill was a rib eye for two with béarnaise sauce. I remember M. Daniel, the chef de cuisine, grilled the steak and garnished the plate with artichoke hearts filled with béarnaise and topped with a nice slice of truffle. Ten years ago in France you would probably not see a dish like this in three-star restaurants because it was too simple in execution. But today with the focus on highest-quality ingredients, steaks are making a comeback. The Tomahawk is a very thick, bone-in rib eye steak but with the whole rib bone left on so that it looks like a hatchet. It's very impressive when it shows up on the table. At home I like to cook the steak in a cast-iron skillet on the grill.

Serves 2

1 (40-ounce) tomahawk-cut steak about 3 inches thick
  Sea salt and freshly ground black pepper
1 small head garlic, separated into cloves and peeled
2 tablespoons extra-virgin olive oil, plus more for tossing
1 sprig fresh rosemary plus 2 to 3 sprigs for presentation
1 small bunch fresh thyme
6 tablespoons plus 2 tablespoons unsalted butter
1 medium shallot, finely chopped
1 tablespoon plus 1 teaspoon finely chopped fresh tarragon
2 tablespoons white wine vinegar
  Freshly ground white pepper
2 large egg yolks
1 teaspoon finely chopped fresh flat-leaf parsley

Preheat the oven to 400°F or build a fire in a grill. Season the steak generously with salt and black pepper. Scrape the rib bones clean of any meat and wrap them in foil to protect them from the heat while cooking. Season the garlic with salt and pepper and toss with olive oil.

Place a very large cast-iron skillet over high heat and add the 2 tablespoons olive oil. Add the steak and garlic, and sear the steak until browned on the first side, about 5 minutes. Turn the meat and sear the second side, lowering the heat to medium-high, until well browned, about another 5 minutes. Scatter the rosemary and thyme sprigs around the meat.

Place the skillet in the oven and roast 15 to 20 minutes (for medium-rare meat, about 125°F), basting the steak and garlic every 4 to 5 minutes with the fat in the pan. This will also give you a chance to check the internal temperature of the meat with an instant-read thermometer. Begin checking at 10 minutes; you do not want to overcook the steak.

Transfer the skillet from the oven to the stove top, or uncover the grill, put the 2 tablespoons butter on top of the chop, and continue basting for 3 to 4 minutes. Transfer the steak to a cutting board, tent with aluminum foil, and let rest for at least 5 minutes in a warm place.

While the steak cooks, prepare the béarnaise sauce: Melt the remaining 6 tablespoons butter in a small saucepan over low heat. Skim off the white foam that forms on top. Set the skimmed butter aside and keep warm.

Combine the shallot, 1 tablespoon of the tarragon, the vinegar, and a pinch of white pepper in a small saucepan and place over medium heat. Bring to a boil and cook until the pan is nearly dry. Remove the pan from the heat, let cool until lukewarm, and whisk in the egg yolks and a tablespoon of water. Return to low heat and whisk vigorously and continuously until the mixture thickens and emulsifies. Move the pan off and on the heat so the eggs

80

do not overcook. When the eggs turn lemon-yellow and you can see the bottom of the pan when you pass over it with the whisk, whisk in the melted butter little by little, making sure each addition is fully incorporated into the emulsion before adding more. Again move the pan off and on the heat. Leave the white, milky butter solids behind in the pan. Whisk in the parsley and the remaining 1 teaspoon tarragon. Season to taste with salt and white pepper and keep warm. Makes about ½ cup béarnaise.

With a chef's knife, remove the giant bone and cut the meat on the bias into ¼-inch-thick slices. Arrange the steak on a warm serving platter and display the bone and the roasted garlic next to it. You can decorate the plate with one or two nice sprigs of rosemary. Serve the béarnaise sauce on the side.

♣ I wrote out the béarnaise recipe exactly as I learned it from M. Daniel. He never added salt when cooking the shallots down with the vinegar, so I don't either.

Pommes Paillasson

♣ Cutting the potatoes on a mandoline gives a spikier, more *paillasson* look to your cake. But the coarse blade of a food processor is also fast and easy. You can also make this dish with a combination of parsnip and potato.

♣ If you want to add some black or white truffle, chop it and toss with the potatoes. You could also sprinkle the finished cake with truffle salt or truffle oil. Adding herbs is a colorful and nice addition. Thyme is always appropriate, and Chantal and I both love minced rosemary in these potatoes. You could top the cake with smoked salt and a dollop of crème fraîche, too.

♣ I make this dish with butter or a combination of butter and oil, but you can use all olive oil.

WHEN CHANTAL AND I FIRST STARTED DATING, we did not have the money to go out. A steak and these potatoes was a favorite meal. We cooked the potatoes in our first joint purchase, a nonstick pan. At L'Auberge de L'Ill we served the potatoes, larded with truffles, with a New York strip steak. It's a shredded potato pancake, very crisp on the outside and soft inside. The name, *paillasson*, refers to its spiky, flat look; a *paillasse* is a straw mattress or doormat. Serve the potatoes with a dish with sauce so they can soak it up and as a side dish to fried eggs.

Serves 4

3 large Russet potatoes (about 1½ pounds), peeled
   Sea salt and freshly ground black pepper
   About 4 tablespoons (½ stick or 2 ounces) unsalted butter, melted
2 tablespoons extra-virgin olive oil

Cut the potatoes into a fine julienne with a mandoline or with the coarse shredding blade of a food processor. Once they are grated, do not rinse the potatoes; you need their starch to hold the potatoes together. Transfer them to a baking sheet, season well with salt and pepper, and let sit for a few minutes. Place the sheet on a tilt; the salt will begin to wilt the potatoes and they will begin releasing water.

Heat 1 tablespoon of the butter and 1 tablespoon of the oil in a 9- or 10-inch nonstick skillet over medium heat. Squeeze the potatoes very hard between your hands to remove as much water as possible and then add them to the pan. With the back of a large spoon, neaten the edges and lightly press the potatoes to make a flat cake.

Cook for a few minutes and then rub all around the edge of the pan with a tablespoon-sized nut of butter so that it melts and runs under the potatoes. Cook over medium heat until crispy and brown, about 10 minutes. Slide the cake carefully out onto a plate, cover it with a second plate, add another piece of butter to the pan, and then invert the plates and slide the cake back into the pan to cook the second side.

Cook, adding butter or oil as needed around the edges and tilting the pan, until the cake is crispy underneath and the potatoes have cooked through, another 7 to 10 minutes. Regulate the heat so the cake browns and caramelizes but does not burn. Slide it onto a cutting board, blot any excess oil with paper towels, cut into 8 wedges with a sharp knife, and transfer to a large round serving platter. Sprinkle with salt and serve immediately.

Feuilleté of Crayfish, Scallops, Summer Vegetables, and Basil in Hollandaise Sauce

THIS IS A DISH I LEARNED FROM JACQUES MAXIMIN at Le Chantecler, and I put it on my menu at Le Prieuré as well. Until Maximin, *feuilletés* were filled with a creamy, rich béchamel-based sauce. Using an airy, almost foamy hollandaise gave the dish a much lighter, fresher feel and flavor. At L'Auberge de L'Ill we kept the crayfish alive in long wooden boxes sunk in the river and attached to the bank with a chain. When a guest ordered them, one of the apprentices had to run down and around, haul out the box, scoop out a large portion of the crayfish, and then return to the kitchen to cook them. The customer could watch the action through the large windows of the dining room.

Serves 6 as an appetizer or fish course

Sea salt and freshly ground black pepper

1 bouquet garni (page 65)

1 medium yellow onion, peeled and quartered

12 baby carrots, about 2 inches long, peeled

12 small red pearl onions, peeled

12 young green beans, preferably haricots verts, topped, tailed, and cut into 2-inch lengths

½ cup shelled fresh young peas or frozen petit pois

2 tablespoons champagne vinegar or white wine vinegar

24 live crayfish, or unpeeled medium shrimp, or the meat from 1 lobster

1 sheet puff pastry (11 by 15 inches)

Unbleached all-purpose flour, for dusting

6 large egg yolks, divided

¼ cup heavy cream

12 fresh large basil leaves or the leaves from 1 sprig fresh tarragon

12 tablespoons (1½ sticks or 6 ounces) unsalted butter, melted

Juice of 1 lemon

12 ounces fresh wild mushrooms, such as chanterelles

3 teaspoons extra-virgin olive oil, divided

8 large sea scallops, cut in half horizontally

20 almonds, preferably fresh new crop almonds, skinned; if dried, halve or split the blanched nuts lengthwise

1 large tomato, peeled, seeded, and diced

Bring a large pot of water to a boil over high heat and add 1 tablespoon of salt. Add the bouquet garni and the quartered onion. Let simmer, uncovered, for 5 minutes. Meanwhile, prepare a large ice-water bath. Return the water to a rolling boil and add the baby carrots. After 2 minutes, add the pearl onions and cook for 3 minutes. Add the green beans and cook until almost tender, about 2 minutes. Add the peas and keep boiling until tender, about 30 seconds. Scoop out the vegetables with a large skimmer and immediately immerse them in the ice water. When cooled, drain well, discard the bouquet garni and yellow onion, and set aside.

Preheat the oven to 400°F and return the pot of water to a boil. Add the vinegar and the crayfish and poach at a simmer just until they turn red and are cooked through, about 3 minutes. Transfer them immediately to the ice-water bath. If the crayfish have roe attached to their underbellies, transfer it to a separate, small container and refrigerate. Use the roe as a garnish. Drain the crayfish well and shell them by separating the tails from the bodies with a careful twist. Then pinch the tails gently until they crack. Pinch off the legs and gently peel off the shells, keeping the tails in a single piece. Place them in a bowl, cover, and refrigerate

Notes

♣ Make the hollandaise as close to serving time as possible. You want the sauce to be very light, even frothy for the best effect. Have everything you need hot and ready to assemble quickly in order to maintain the airy quality. Six is probably the most you can serve without sacrificing quality.

85

Notes

♣ Fresh almonds, newly harvested and in the shell, have a delicate and sweet flavor that's very different from dried almonds. The fresh ones are used a lot in the south of France in meat, poultry, and vegetable stews. All you do is crack them, remove the shells, and peel off the skins by hand. You don't need to blanch them.

until needed. Save the shells and heads separately for another use, such as a seafood stock.

Arrange the pastry on a lightly floured surface. Whisk 2 of the egg yolks together with 1 teaspoon of water in a small bowl and brush the pastry with the egg wash. Make a decorative pattern in the egg wash, using the tines of a fork or the back of a knife blade to create crisscrossing diagonals without cutting into the pastry. Using a sharp knife, cut the pastry into 6 squares. First cut the sheet into thirds crosswise. You will have three 10 by 5-inch strips. Cut these in half crosswise to make six 5-inch squares. Line a baking sheet with parchment paper and transfer the pastry to the baking sheet. Sprinkle the baking sheet with water to create some steam in the oven. Bake the pastry until crisp and golden brown, about 15 minutes. Let the pastry cool on a rack. Carefully cut the top off the rectangles; these will be the lids. Using a fork, hollow out the interior of the baked pastry. Set the pastry cases aside and keep warm.

In a small bowl, whisk the cream until stiff and set aside. Stack the basil leaves one on top of the other, roll up together, and cut into thin shreds. Set aside.

To make the sauce: Place the remaining 4 egg yolks and 1 tablespoon of water in a stainless-steel mixing bowl that fits over a pan of water without touching the surface. Bring the water to a simmer and place the bowl over it. Whisk the yolks vigorously and continuously until they double in volume and thicken. Be careful not to let the eggs get too hot, or they will scramble. While continuing to whisk, slowly drizzle in the melted butter bit

by bit and whisking after each addition to form an emulsion. Remove from the heat and whisk in the lemon juice, also bit by bit. Taste for balance after you've added about half the juice. You want a sauce with a moderately strong lemon flavor. Season with salt and pepper. Cover the sauce and keep warm until needed. If the sauce gets too thick, whisk in a few drops of water.

Brush the mushrooms to remove any dirt. If they are very dirty, rinse them quickly and halve them if large. Do not allow them to get waterlogged. Heat a nonstick sauté pan over medium-high heat. Add 1½ teaspoons of the olive oil and the mushrooms. Cook, stirring and tossing, until tender, 3 to 4 minutes, and until the pan is dry. Season with salt and pepper. Transfer the mushrooms to a bowl and keep warm.

Replace the pan over high heat and add the remaining 1½ teaspoons olive oil. Season the scallops with salt and pepper and sear them quickly, about 1 minute, on each side. Lower the heat to medium, add the mushrooms, crayfish, vegetables, and almonds, and delicately stir and toss the ingredients together until hot. Remove from the heat, and, with a large spatula, fold in the hollandaise and then the whipped cream, half the basil, and the tomato. Taste again for seasoning and adjust as needed with salt and pepper.

Arrange the puff pastry cases on warm dinner plates. Spoon the crayfish mixture into the pastry shells and spoon any extra around on the plates. Divide the remaining basil among the *feuilletés*. Top each shell with its lid and serve immediately.

CHEF PAUL HAEBERLIN'S
Eightieth Birthday Party

Me, Marc Haeberlin, and his father (and my mentor) chef Paul Haeberlin.

Chef Haeberlin accepted only one new apprentice per year. An apprenticeship lasted three years. But when I started, the three-star chef Jean Troisgros sent his son to L'Auberge de L'Ill for his apprenticeship, so we were two apprentices together and became really close friends. During the time I was there, I also overlapped with Jean-Georges Vongerichten (now in New York) and Jean Joho (in Chicago), who was hired at L'Auberge de L'Ill as a *commis*.

As Chef's eightieth birthday approached, his son Marc asked him, "What do we do to celebrate your birthday?" Chef said, "I don't want a party, and remember I do not like surprises." So his family said, "Okay, we'll just keep it in the family. Meanwhile, there's a company in Paris—we didn't want to tell you before—that wants to buy out (reserve) the whole restaurant for a special event on your birthday." M. Jean-Pierre had set it up so well that letters arrived from the company in Paris confirming the details. Chef believed the story and started work on the party.

But the night before the party, worried that the surprise might cause Chef a heart attack, the family sat him down and said, "Chef, tomorrow the party is actually your party." But he didn't know who was coming. We flew in from all over the world—chefs and restaurateurs, many of whom got their start at L'Auberge de L'Ill. Friends and patrons of the restaurant from the worlds of politics, society, and art all came. And of course Paul Bocuse, one of Chef's closest friends, arrived. I remember Chef standing at the door as we all called, "Surprise! Surprise!"

Jean Joho came from Chicago, I came from San Francisco, and Jean-Georges Vongerichten from New York. The party was the only time over so many years that Chef and the three of us were together. Chef died at age eighty-four in 2008.

Bouillabaisse

WHEN I WORKED WITH Jacques Maximin, chef of Le Chantecler at Hôtel Le Negresco, we sometimes went to dinner together on our night off. One time he and his wife took Chantal and me to the famous Côte d'Azur restaurant Le Bacon in Cap d'Antibes. If you wanted real bouillabaisse, this is where you went. They started their broth correctly with many pounds of small fish called *poisson de roche*, and then whole, large fish were poached in the soup. It came to the table in a big copper pot. And, right at tableside, waiters dipped out the fish and filleted them for us. Scalloped potatoes cooked with saffron were just delicious with that great soup poured over them. Le Bacon is sixty years old now and still serving great bouillabaisse.

Serves 4

Two "lefties" in the kitchen: Jacques Maximim and me in the kitchen of Le Chantecler on the Côte d'Azur. The copper pot with the aluminum foil next to me was my improvised steamer. Steaming fish was a brand-new technique in French cuisine back then.

1 baguette, thinly sliced on the diagonal

3 tablespoons extra-virgin olive oil, plus more for brushing

4 cloves garlic, very finely chopped, plus 1 whole clove garlic (optional)

1 medium yellow onion, halved and thinly sliced

1 bulb fennel, quartered and thinly sliced

1 small celery root, peeled, quartered, and thinly sliced

1 (14½-ounce) can diced tomatoes with juices

10 small fingerling potatoes, thinly sliced

6 cups fish broth or clam juice

1 cup dry white wine

1 bay leaf

2 sprigs fresh thyme

2 sprigs fresh cilantro

3 sprigs fresh tarragon

1 teaspoon saffron threads

5 ounces halibut fillet, skin on, cut into 4 equal pieces, or monkfish

5 ounces red snapper fillet, skin on, cut into 4 equal pieces

5 ounces salmon fillet, skin on, cut into 4 equal pieces

Sea salt and freshly ground black pepper

8 large prawns, head and shell on, deveined

8 large sea scallops

1 quart clams, in the shell, well scrubbed

1 quart mussels, in the shell, well scrubbed

1 teaspoon freshly grated orange zest

Rouille (page 89)

Aioli with miso (page 89)

1 cup freshly grated Parmesan

Harissa (page 276)

Preheat the oven to 375°F. Brush the baguette slices on both sides with olive oil and arrange on a baking sheet. Toast in the oven until brown, about 15 minutes. Rub the whole garlic clove over the toasted bread. Set aside.

Heat the 3 tablespoons olive oil in a large Dutch oven over medium heat. Add the onion and sauté, stirring, until the onion has softened, about 10 minutes. Add the finely chopped garlic and cook for another minute.

Add the fennel, celery root, diced tomatoes, fingerling potatoes, fish broth, and wine; stir to combine and bring to a boil. Add the bay leaf, thyme, cilantro, tarragon, and saffron and stir well to mix the herbs throughout. Turn the heat to low, cover, and simmer until the vegetables are almost tender, 10 to 15 minutes.

Season the halibut, snapper, and salmon lightly with salt and pepper. Gently push the halibut into the stew so that the pieces are almost completely submerged in the liquid. Cover the pan and let simmer for 2 minutes. Repeat with the snapper, and then the salmon, prawns, scallops, and clams, simmering for 2 minutes after each addition.

Finally, add the mussels and sprinkle the orange zest evenly over the stew. Re-cover the pan and simmer until the clams and mussels have all opened and all the seafood has cooked through, 2 to 3 minutes. Discard the herb sprigs. Taste and adjust seasoning with salt and pepper.

Serve in warm, deep soup plates with the croutons to the side. Pass the rouille, aioli, Parmesan, and harissa at the table.

Rouille

Makes about 1½ cups

Rouille is the classic condiment for the famous soup from the south of France, bouillabaisse. It is basically a spicy, garlicky mayonnaise. I've given it a little twist by adding fresh orange zest. It would also make a nice spread for a roasted chicken or salmon sandwich, or use it as a sauce for grilled vegetables (page 277) and grilled potatoes (page 281).

- 2 large egg yolks
- 1 tablespoon Dijon mustard
- 2 cloves garlic, very finely chopped
- ½ teaspoon ground saffron
  Pinch of sea salt and freshly ground white pepper
- 1 cup extra-virgin olive oil
  Pinch of cayenne
  Finely grated zest of ½ orange

Place the egg yolks, mustard, garlic, saffron, and salt and pepper in a food processor and process until fully incorporated and smooth. With the machine running, very slowly drizzle in the olive oil until the mayonnaise is thick

and creamy. Pulse in the cayenne and orange zest, and check the seasoning. Adjust with salt and pepper.

Aioli with Miso

Makes about ⅓ cup

I love mayonnaise, but it took my going to the south of France to cook with Roger Vergé to learn about the garlicky mayonnaise-based sauce called *aioli*. Here in San Francisco, we have a habit of adding Asian ingredients to classic dishes. Adding miso to aioli gives it just a little twist, a little greater savory taste. Serve it with the bouillabaisse but also with poached fish; steamed, roasted, or grilled vegetables (page 277); and hardboiled eggs. It makes a great condiment for burgers as well and a great dip for fries of all kinds.

- 5 tablespoons mayonnaise
- 1 tablespoon coarse-grain Dijon mustard
- 1½ teaspoons freshly squeezed lemon juice, plus more if needed
- 1 teaspoon finely chopped garlic
- ½ teaspoon white or yellow miso (optional)
  Pinch of cayenne
  Sea salt and freshly ground white pepper

In a small bowl or small food processor, mix together the mayonnaise, mustard, lemon juice, garlic, miso, cayenne, and a pinch of pepper. Miso can be salty, so mix well until thoroughly blended and then taste for seasoning. Adjust with salt, pepper, and more lemon juice if needed. Refrigerate in a covered container for up to 3 days, remembering that the garlic flavor will strengthen over time.

Classic Salmon "Soufflé" Paul Haeberlin

THIS IS ONE OF THE BEST-KNOWN DISHES from L'Auberge de L'Ill, a salmon fillet covered with one of the most delicate mousses that you will ever taste. It does not puff up like a soufflé, but like a soufflé it does get nicely browned on top. As a tribute to Paul Haeberlin when he passed away, Jean Joho, Jean-Georges Vongerichten, and I all put this dish on our menus for a month. We had met when we worked at L'Auberge de L'Ill. So this signature dish was on menus in New York, Chicago, Las Vegas, and San Francisco. It was so popular at Fleur de Lys that it remains on the menu today. For this version, I've stayed with Chef's original with its clean, straightforward, and delicious flavor.

Serves 4

Tomatoes

1 pint cherry tomatoes
   Sea salt and freshly ground
   black pepper
   Extra-virgin olive oil

Mousseline

4 ounces sea bass fillet
1 large egg white, chilled
   Sea salt and freshly ground
   white pepper
½ cup heavy cream, chilled

Fish

4 skinless, boneless salmon fillets (about
   5 ounces each), pin bones removed
   Sea salt and freshly ground
   white pepper
   Extra-virgin olive oil for
   oiling baking dish
1 tablespoon finely minced shallots
1 tablespoon dry vermouth
1 cup fish broth or clam juice

Vermouth and Tarragon Sauce

3 tablespoons dry vermouth
1 tablespoon finely minced shallots
½ cup heavy cream
1 tablespoon finely minced fresh
   tarragon
   About ¼ cup oven-dried
   cherry tomatoes
   Sea salt and freshly ground
   white pepper
   Freshly squeezed lemon juice

To prepare the tomatoes: Preheat the oven to 200°F. Toss the tomatoes in a bowl with salt and pepper to taste and a good drizzle of the olive oil. Spread the tomatoes on a sheet pan and bake until they've lost about half their volume. You don't want them to get too dry; check them after about an hour. Scrape the tomatoes into a clean container, cover, and refrigerate until needed. Use the tomatoes for an extra fillip of flavor in salads and omelets and just about anywhere else.

To prepare the mousseline: To ensure a smooth, thick mousse, make sure all the ingredients are well chilled, including the mixing bowl. Place the sea bass in a food processor and process until finely ground. Put the work bowl with the fish in the freezer until very cold. Stir the mixture occasionally. You want it chilled, not frozen. Replace the work bowl on the processor and pulse in the egg white until incorporated. Add a good pinch each of salt and pepper and pulse several times again. With the machine running, very slowly add the cream through the feed tube. Scrape the mixture into a chilled mixing bowl, cover well with plastic wrap, and refrigerate for at least 15 minutes and for as long as a day.

To cook the fish: Preheat the oven to 400°F. Season the salmon fillets on both sides with salt and pepper. Generously brush olive oil all over the bottom of a casserole large enough to hold the fillets in a single layer. Sprinkle

the pan with the shallots. Spread or pipe the mousseline over each fillet, mounding it generously. Place the fillets in the casserole and add the vermouth and broth. You should have at least ½ inch of liquid in the casserole; if not, add enough water to make up the difference. Bake until the mousseline is golden brown, 15 to 20 minutes. Drain the cooking liquids from the fish into a warm measuring cup and keep the fillets warm.

To prepare the sauce: Place the vermouth and shallots in a small saucepan and bring to a boil. Cook until the pan is almost dry. Add the reserved cooking liquid to the saucepan, bring to a boil over high heat, and cook until reduced to about ¾ cup. Add the cream and simmer slowly for a few minutes, until the cream has thickened slightly. Stir in the tarragon and the oven-dried tomatoes. Taste and adjust the seasoning with salt and pepper and a squeeze of lemon juice. Arrange the fillets on warm dinner plates and spoon the sauce equally around them. Serve immediately.

Duck Terrine with Pistachios and Green Olives

WHEN I LAUNCHED Roger Vergé's Cuisine du Soleil restaurant in Brazil, it was still a time when diners expected a cold terrine and a soup when they ate out. Often the reputation of a restaurant hinged on the quality of its pâtés, terrines, and soups. This duck terrine comes from my time at M. Vergé's Moulin de Mougins. I also made it for the third season of my public television cooking show, *Secrets of a Chef*. It's a rough-textured mix of diced duck confit bound in a matrix of duck, pork, and chicken liver forcemeat. You could save yourself time by purchasing the confit, but it is not difficult to make and it is a good technique to know. Serve the terrine with toasted baguette or country bread, small cornichons or pickled vegetables, Dijon mustard, and a frisée salad.

Serves 12 to 15

- 4 bay leaves, torn into small pieces, divided
- 1 tablespoon plus 1 teaspoon coarsely chopped fresh thyme
- ¼ cup (2¼ ounces) coarse sea salt
- 7 to 8 large duck legs, both drumsticks and thighs (about 12 ounces each)
- 4 cups (2 pounds) duck fat or rendered pork fat
- 4 cloves garlic, crushed
- 1 teaspoon cracked black pepper
- 1½ teaspoons extra-virgin olive oil
- 4 medium shallots, coarsely chopped (about ½ cup)
- 1½ cups pitted green olives (1 can, drained weight 6 ounces)
- 1 pound boneless pork shoulder, coarsely chopped
- 1 pound pork back fat, coarsely chopped
- ½ pound chicken livers
- 1½ tablespoons cognac
  Sea salt and freshly ground black pepper
- ¾ cup (3 ounces) whole pistachios

Notes

♣ For the terrine you need a pound of confit and a pound of raw duck leg meat. If you buy large duck legs such as those from Muscovy ducks, you will need only about 4 legs for the confit and perhaps 3 for the raw duck meat. Extra confit is never a problem. If you are going to make the confit, double the recipe. For 8 legs, double the seasonings, but you will need only about 6 cups of fat. The confit keeps for up to 2 weeks, refrigerated in the cooking fat. When you want some, just pull out a leg and reheat it in a skillet over low heat until the skin is crispy and the meat is hot through. You can also bone out the confit and toss it with pasta.

In a small bowl, combine 2 of the bay leaves, 1 tablespoon of the thyme, and the coarse salt. Rub the salt mixture generously all over 4 of the duck legs. Put the seasoned legs in a bowl, cover or seal in a heavy-duty plastic bag, and refrigerate for 24 hours, but no more.

Rinse the duck legs under cold running water to remove the salt. Pat them dry with paper towels and put them in a large deep saucepan with the duck fat, the remaining 2 bay leaves, the remaining 1 teaspoon thyme, the garlic, and the cracked pepper. Put the pan over low heat and cook, covered, until the duck is very tender, 2½ to 3 hours. Once the fat has melted off the duck legs, they will be submerged in the fat. Keep the temperature of the fat between 190° and 200°F. If it gets hotter, the duck will dry out.

Once the legs are very tender, remove them from the fat and set them on a rack to drain and cool. Remove the skin and bones and spread the meat on a sheet pan. You should have about 1 pound of duck meat. (If you have extra, wrap well and refrigerate or freeze for another use.) Cover and refrigerate. Once the meat is cold, it will be easier to cut into a nice dice to fold into the rest of the terrine ingredients.

Preheat the oven to 325°F. Heat the olive oil in a small skillet over medium-high heat, add the shallots, and cook until soft and translucent, about 3 minutes. Scrape them into a medium bowl, cover, and refrigerate. Bring a small pot of water to a boil, add the olives, and quickly blanch them, about 1 minute. Drain and cool. Cut the olives in half lengthwise and add them to the bowl with the shallots.

Skin and debone the remaining 3 or 4 duck legs. You should have about 1 pound of meat. Chop the meat coarsely and place it in the work bowl of a food processor with the pork shoulder, pork fat, chicken livers, and cognac. Season well with salt and pepper and process until smooth. Scrape the mixture into a large bowl.

Cut the duck confit into ⅓-inch dice. Add to the bowl with the shallots, olives, and pistachios. Mix with a wooden spoon until evenly blended. Set a small skillet over medium heat and add a small nut of the mixture. Cook until done through and taste for seasoning. Adjust the rest of the duck terrine mixture with salt and pepper.

Line a 2½-quart terrine with plastic wrap, making sure to leave several inches of overhang all around. Heat a teakettle full of water to a boil. Press the meat mixture into the terrine and smooth the top. Fold the extra wrap over the terrine to enclose it and tightly cover the terrine with aluminum foil. Set the terrine in a larger pan, such as a roasting pan, and put it in the oven. Carefully pour the boiling water around the terrine. Bake until the terrine registers 160°F on an instant-read thermometer, about 90 minutes. You can also test for doneness by inserting a metal skewer into the center of the terrine. When the juices run clear, the terrine is done.

Remove the terrine from the oven and set the mold on a rack. Weigh down the terrine by laying a couple of cans or a wine bottle on top of it. Let it cool and refrigerate for at least 12 hours before serving. You can keep the terrine for up to 5 days well covered and refrigerated. To serve, cut the terrine into ¼-inch-thick slices.

Le Tour de France

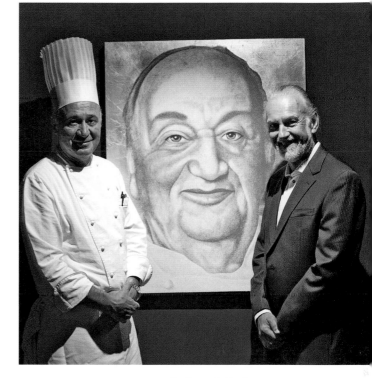

Marc Haeberlin and I flank a portrait of his father, chef Paul Haeberlin.

In those days, it was common practice for talented apprentices to be sent by their mentors from one restaurant to another to gather experience. It was typical to spend just a year in each place before moving on. We called this *le tour de France*.

This practice gave me trouble when I applied for a U.S. visa. The American authorities questioned my stability—"You stay only a year in any job!"—and my skills—"You only have experience in three-star restaurants. That's not very many stars." Steven Stiller, Roger Vergé's lawyer, had to prepare a thick dossier explaining the three-star system to the authorities to prove that I did have skills very rare at that time in America.

Orange Tartlets with Lavender Meringue

WHEN I MOVED TO THE SOUTH OF FRANCE, I found so many foods and flavor combinations new to me. This recipe from Roger Vergé and his Moulin de Mougins restaurant combines the bright, sunny flavors of citrus with lavender that grew on the hillsides and really did scent the air. It is a good example of why I consider the cuisine of the south of France a happy cuisine.

Serves 6

Pâte Sucrée

- 2 cups (10 ounces) unbleached all-purpose flour
- ¾ cup (5¼ ounces) sugar
- ¼ teaspoon sea salt
- 12 tablespoons (1½ sticks or 6 ounces) unsalted butter, at room temperature and cut into pieces, plus more for buttering molds
- 4 large egg yolks

Citrus Filling

- 1 Meyer lemon
- 1 thin-skinned orange (such as Valencia)
- ½ cup (3½ ounces) sugar
  Pinch of sea salt
- 3 large eggs
- 4 tablespoons (½ stick or 2 ounces) unsalted butter, at room temperature

Lavender Meringue

- 3 large egg whites
- ¼ teaspoon sea salt
- 1 cup (4 ounces) powdered sugar plus 2 teaspoons for dusting
- 1 teaspoon ground dried lavender flowers plus ½ teaspoon dried whole lavender flowers

To make the dough: Combine the flour, sugar, and salt in a food processor with a couple of pulses. Scatter the butter pieces over the flour and process until the mixture has the texture of coarse sand. Add the yolks and process until the dough almost—but not quite—forms a ball. Do not overwork the dough. Scrape the dough onto a lightly floured work surface and knead briefly until smooth. Shape it into a disk, wrap well in plastic wrap, and refrigerate for at least 2 hours and for up to a day.

Meanwhile, prepare the citrus filling: Leaving the skin on, quarter the lemon and the orange and remove any seeds. Place the fruit in a food processor. Add the sugar and salt and process until the citrus is evenly ground with the sugar. Add the eggs and the butter and process until you have a fairly smooth puree. Transfer to a mixing bowl and refrigerate for at least an hour and up to a day.

Preheat the oven to 375°F. Using a brush, butter six 4-inch tartlet molds. On a lightly floured work surface, roll out the dough until it is about ⅛ inch thick. Cut out six 6-inch circles by cutting around a small plate with a sharp knife. Carefully fit the pastry into the molds and prick them with a fork. Trim off extra pastry and chill the lined molds for at least 30 minutes and up to 2 hours.

Meanwhile, cut six 7-inch squares of aluminum foil. Line the tart shells with the foil, shiny side down. Fill the molds with dry beans or pastry weights. Bake the tart shells for about 10 minutes, or until they have firmed up. Remove them from the oven, remove the foil and beans, and bake until the tart shells turn a light golden color, another 5 to 10 minutes. Divide the filling equally among the tart shells and bake until the custard has puffed slightly and lightly browned, about 20 minutes. Leave the oven on and cool the tartlets on a rack for 10 minutes.

Notes

♣ Grinding whole citrus with sugar releases the aromatic oils in the skins. But if the skins are too thick, you might get too much bitterness— a little is good, though, and offsets the sweetness of the meringue. Use a Meyer lemon and a thin-skinned orange such as Valencia to capture the flavor of Provence.

♣ Because it is really cookie dough, you always roll *pâte sucrée* a little thicker than *pâte brisée*. When *pâte sucrée* is thicker, it tastes better. Make sure the dough is well chilled. If it gets sticky while you work with it, return it to the refrigerator to firm up. You can turn extra dough into cookies (roll it out, dust it with sugar, cut into shapes, and bake) or freeze for up to a month.

While the tarts bake, prepare the meringue: Whip the egg whites and salt in a mixing bowl with an electric mixer on medium-low speed until frothy. Increase the speed to medium and add the sugar by spoonfuls, whipping until stiff peaks form. Beat in the 1 teaspoon ground lavender. Transfer the meringue to a pastry bag fitted with a large star tip. Pipe the meringue attractively in a rosette pattern on top of the tarts. Sprinkle the remaining ½ teaspoon lavender flowers over the tartlets and bake until the meringue turns golden brown, 10 to 15 minutes. Remove from the oven and dust lightly with the remaining powdered sugar. Using the tip of a sharp knife, carefully pry the tarts out of their molds. They should lift out easily. Serve warm.

Adaptation

When Creative Inspiration Saves the Day

"Everything is positive; everything is good."

LEARNING FROM ROGER VERGÉ

When I did my apprenticeship, it was to learn to cook. My training did not include any business school for running a restaurant. So far I had worked to understand the techniques and the recipes and to see how restaurants operated. Then in 1977 I joined Roger Vergé at his three-star Moulin de Mougins as saucier, a *chef de partie*. And I saw that there was another step.

M. Vergé had traveled a lot after his training at the Paris three-star La Tour d'Argent and at the Plaza Athénée. The school of life had taught him to be flexible and resourceful. He learned to adapt, to make things happen, to make high-quality food even out of lower-cost goods if necessary. For example, he had developed a technique for cooking mushrooms so that their essence tasted like truffle. I imagine that one day for a special dinner the truffles had

From left: In the
kitchen at Sutter 500.
A thank-you note
from Roger Vergé
after I'd prepped the
food in San Fran-
cisco and shipped it
to Las Vegas for an
event for the French
singer Silvie Vartan.
After Chantal and
I learned our way
around São Paulo a
bit, I bought a car,
a Ford Galaxie 500.
I think it was a '74
or '75.

Pages 96 and 97:
Roger Vergé and me
at Sutter 500 in San
Francisco.

not arrived, and M. Vergé had to change his menu and be creative.
Many years later, I found myself in a similar situation cooking
pasta in a dorm room (on an episode of *Top Chef Masters* season
one), and my training helped me find an unconventional way to
cool the pasta for my mac and cheese (page 118).

M. Vergé moved to the south of France to be the chef of Le Club
in the little town of Cavalière and earned two Michelin stars in
1967. From there, he decided to open his own place. But he didn't
have any money. He would have to take over something that
was nothing. In 1969 he found Moulin de Mougins, which had
housed four or five bankrupt restaurants. It was located right on
a curve of a tiny road, and you couldn't see the driveway. But his
many friends and the visibility of having earned two stars brought

Above: Roger Vergé and me consulting during one of his visits to his San Francisco restaurant Sutter 500.

people up the road to enjoy his "cuisine of the sun." He called it a "joyful cuisine," naturally healthy, combining local ingredients in surprising ways that could be very simple. The honey-caramel sauce with lavender (page 131) reminds me of him.

A few years later, working for M. Vergé in Brazil, I learned to adapt his cuisine by using local ingredients and making basics I needed—mustard, almond paste—that did not exist there. It's a thread that runs through all my cooking, from the quinoa chocolate pudding (page 134) to the combination of maple syrup and fromage blanc in an ice cream (page 124).

Roger Vergé's vision for his restaurant was different from what I was used to. He built it as a business, with a sharp eye on the bottom line. He did not build a state-of-the-art kitchen the way the

LE FEUILLETÉ DE POIRE WILLIAM, SAUCE CARAMEL ET
    LA COROLLE DE GLACE VANILLE

A Feuilleté en forme de losange glacé au
    sucre et fourré d'une crème Diplomate,
    plus sun de vie et dés de poire.
B Glace vanille en corolle avec pointe de gousse de vanille
C Sauce caramel D Demie poire pochée en éventail

LE FEUILLETÉ DE FRAISES AVEC SON SABAYON AU VIN
    DE CHAMPAGNE

A Feuilleté rond et glacé, fourré d'une
    confiture de fraises allégée d'une chantilly
    non sucrée. - Bouquet de menthe
B Fraises coupées en quartiers et nappées de sabayon froid

LE MILLE-FEUILLE A LA COMPOTE DE FRAISES T.G.

    Écraser des fraises à la fourchette, en
    les mélangeant avec de la crème double
    et du sucre. Cuire une bande de feuilletage
    sucrée sur le dessus, puis la détailler en 2 ou 3 rectangles
    Monter ce mille-feuille tout en nappant le fond de
    l'assiette d'un coulis de fraises. A l'aide d'un cornet
    de crème double, tracer un cercle sur le coulis de
    fraises et avec la pointe d'un couteau d'office réaliser
    le décor "Mille feuille".

Haeberlins had at L'Auberge de L'Ill. He invested in the guests' environment—in the front of the house, the dining room, and in the quality of the hospitality. Yet, as M. Vergé knew we could, we cranked out some great food, as well executed as any from a showplace kitchen.

M. Vergé combined his personal charm, marketing smarts, and cooking talent to achieve his vision and did really, really well, earning his third star at Moulin de Mougins by 1974. He also redefined what you might find on the menu of a three-star restaurant. I think he was the first one in France to put a pig's foot on his menu. Usually at three-stars it is only the best cuts—the rack of lamb, the heart of the filet mignon—that are served. But M. Vergé stuffed his pig's foot with foie gras and truffles and it was the best pig's foot ever. My red-wine-braised beef cheeks (page 112) uses the same principle, creating an elegant presentation from rustic ingredients. M. Vergé set a different tone, gave his menu and his restaurant a different twist. Probably the greatest lesson I adopted—and use every day—was his attitude "This is what I have; this is what I want to do. How can we make it happen?"

Above center: **Entertaining the press in São Paulo: Maksoud Plaza general manager Roberto Maksoud, the food critic of the local paper, and Roger Vergé are flanked by me and Peter Fuchs, the executive chef of the Maksoud Plaza project.** *Above:* **A page from one of my notebooks. Ever since I was an apprentice, I've drawn dishes to remember the presentation and details. On this page, I was comparing recipes and platings from several chefs.**

Anchoïade and Crudité Platter

WE MADE *anchoïade* on the cruise ship *Mermoz*. And we made it, too, at Moulin de Mougins and at Le Chantecler. Those days were before food processors, so we had to melt the anchovies over low heat and then build up the sauce from there. It's much quicker to make now. You can serve the crudités as an appetizer or make a meal of the dish by adding hardboiled eggs, cooked large white beans, and olives. This is a great dish for those times when you never know how many people will show up; you can just add more vegetables as I did here for a lunch for eight, adding cherry tomatoes, quartered avocado, broccoli and cauliflower florets, and more of everything else.

Serves 4 or more

1 lemon

2 small artichokes

2 beets, preferably a striped Chioggia beet and a golden beet

4 thin scallions

4 leek thinnings, about ⅛ inch in diameter (optional)

1 bunch radishes, well scrubbed, with an inch or so of their greens attached

2 to 4 baby carrots, well scrubbed, with an inch of their greens attached

1 celery heart, cut lengthwise into thin slices

1 fennel bulb, cut lengthwise into thin slices

1 small head endive

   Juice of 1 medium orange

1 teaspoon freshly squeezed lemon juice

2 small cans good-quality oil-packed anchovies (1.7 ounces net weight each), drained

2 to 3 cloves garlic, peeled

1 shallot, peeled and halved

1 teaspoon finely chopped fresh thyme

1 teaspoon finely chopped fresh marjoram (optional)

   Small handful fresh basil leaves

   Freshly ground black pepper

2 tablespoons sherry vinegar

1 cup extra-virgin olive oil

   Unsalted butter, at room temperature for serving

   Coarse sea salt or fleur de sel for serving

1 baguette, thinly sliced and toasted or grilled

To prepare the vegetables: Have ready a small bowl of water; squeeze half of the lemon into it and drop in the peel. Trim the artichokes, rubbing the cut surfaces with the second lemon half as you go, until you have only the palest green, tender parts left. Halve them and remove any fuzzy choke. Slice them very thinly and set aside in the lemon water.

Prepare several bowls of ice water. Peel the beets, very thinly slice them on a mandoline, and transfer, keeping the colors separate, into small bowls of ice water. Trim the root ends and the dark green parts from the scallions and leeks and set them aside in ice water. Place the radishes and carrots together in ice water and the celery and fennel together in ice water. Separate the endive into leaves, wrap well in plastic, and refrigerate.

To make the sauce: In a very small pan, bring the orange juice to a boil and cook until syrupy. Add the lemon juice and set aside. In a food processor, process the anchovies, garlic, and shallot until very finely chopped. Scrape down the sides of the work bowl as needed. Add the thyme, marjoram,

basil, and several good grinds of black pepper with the vinegar and reduced orange juice mixture. Process until evenly blended. With the machine running, slowly drizzle in the olive oil. Taste and adjust the seasoning, adding pepper and vinegar or lemon juice as needed. The anchovies should provide plenty of salt. Pour and scrape the *anchoïade* into a lidded container and refrigerate until needed.

When ready to serve, pour the sauce into a bowl and let it come to room temperature. Arrange the chilled vegetables on a large platter with the sauce. Have small pots of unsalted butter and coarse sea salt on the table. Serve the *anchoïade* and crudités with a basket of toasted or grilled baguette.

Beet Salad with Cumin Ice Cream

THIS VERY COLORFUL SALAD has been on the menu at Fleur de Lys for a while now. It's a great way to begin a meal because cumin seeds are said to aid digestion. Plus, cumin and beets together taste really good. I've played with the classic combination, having some fun with it. But the key to adapting classic combinations is to not compromise the flavors. Instead of sprinkling the beets with cumin, the seeds infuse the base for an ice cream served alongside the beet salad.

Serves 6

Ice Cream

1   tablespoon and 1 teaspoon cumin seeds

2   cups whole milk

½   cup heavy cream

¼   cup (3 ounces by weight) honey

4   egg yolks

Beet Salad

2   pounds baby beets, preferably a mix of colors such as deep red and yellow

Sea salt and freshly ground black pepper

1   tablespoon sherry vinegar

2   tablespoons extra-virgin olive oil, plus more for drizzling

3   pearl onions, peeled and thinly sliced

2   cups vegetable oil for deep-frying (optional)

1   large raw beet, peeled and cut into a very fine, threadlike julienne or thinly sliced (optional)

Fleur de sel (optional)

Cumin seeds (optional)

Handful of sprouts or celery leaves (optional)

To make the ice cream: Toast the cumin seeds in a small dry pan over medium heat until fragrant, stirring frequently, 1 to 2 minutes. Add the toasted seeds to a large saucepan with the milk, heavy cream, and honey and bring to a simmer over medium heat. Let simmer very slowly for 10 minutes to allow the cumin to infuse the milk. Turn off the heat and let sit another 5 minutes.

In a large mixing bowl, whisk the egg yolks until smooth. While whisking vigorously, very slowly pour the

hot milk through a fine sieve into the yolks. Return the yolk mixture to the saucepan and place over medium-low heat. Cook, while whisking all over the bottom and sides of the pan, until thick enough to coat the back of a spoon, about 5 minutes. Do not let the mixture boil.

While the custard cooks, prepare an ice-water bath. Pour the cumin custard through a fine-mesh strainer into a large mixing bowl and put the bowl in the ice water to stop the cooking and cool the custard. Stir occasionally until the mixture is quite cold. Refrigerate the custard for several hours or put it in the freezer until very chilled. Freeze in an ice-cream machine according to the manufacturer's instructions. The ice cream can be completed a day ahead of time. Makes about 1 quart.

To make the salad: Preheat the oven to 400°F. Place the baby beets in separate baking dishes by color, season with salt and pepper, and drizzle with olive oil. Cover tightly and bake the beets until tender, about 45 minutes, depending on their size. Let cool and slip off their skins.

In a small bowl, whisk together the vinegar with the 2 tablespoons olive oil. Season with salt and pepper. Cut the baby beets in half and put them in separate mixing bowls. Divide the onions among the bowls. Drizzle the dressing over and toss until well combined.

In a deep, heavy saucepan, heat the vegetable oil to 375°F. Cover a plate with paper towels. Deep-fry the raw beets in batches until crisp, 2 to 3 minutes, drain on the paper towels, and season with salt and pepper.

To serve, arrange some beets of each color in chilled, shallow bowls and add a neat scoop of cumin ice cream. Add a tuft of fried beet or beet chip to the top of the ice cream and a light sprinkling of fleur de sel, cumin seeds, and sprouts. Serve immediately.

Notes

♣ If you use baby beets, just cut them in half. You can use bigger beets, too, in which case cut them into ³/₈-inch cubes.

♣ To speed plating, make sure your plates are chilled. You can also shape quenelles of ice cream just before the meal, cover them well, and keep in the freezer until ready to serve.

Brazil & the Moulin de Mougins Menu

Our Cuisine du Soleil restaurant menus in São Paulo were written entirely in French, no matter what the local language was. This one shows my notes as I began to change the menu and incorporate Brazilian ingredients.

In the beginning at La Cuisine du Soleil in Brazil, we tried to reproduce the menu of Moulin de Mougins as closely as possible. We had two problems. One was the ingredients themselves. When I ordered lobsters, I would get huge thirty-year-old guys alongside little babies that should not even have been harvested. Lamb racks were often as tough as a shoe. A case of "small" zucchini contained big, seedy vegetables as well as tiny ones.

The second issue was our guests' response to the food. Some of the dishes we did were highlights of the Moulin de Mougins. I knew my Brazilian versions were as close as I could get to M. Vergé's dishes. And then the guests would reject them. I had a choice: I

could get frustrated and think: *These Brazilians don't know what good food is!* Or I could open up, expand, and begin to understand what was going on.

I decided I would cater to their taste by offering some of the foods Brazilians were familiar with and considered upscale. Instead of the local lobster, I started serving these big prawns from the north of Brazil. Spinach was hard to find, but there was kale. I made the mousseline of sole with *namorado*, a great Brazilian fish. And the Brazilian diners began to connect to the cuisine. After a while, when M. Vergé would visit he would suggest this or that dish. And I would be able to tell him whether it was going to work or not. For the first time, he began to ask me what I thought and he would listen. I felt I had graduated to a new level as a chef.

Brazil is where I learned to make mustard. The import tax made Dijon mustard too expensive. But mustard seeds were all over. I had made flavored mustards but not mustard itself. I had to research how to do it. I remember that when I made my first batch, I was kind of disappointed. It did not have a strong mustard flavor and was a little bitter. But I didn't want to throw it out; I put it in the refrigerator and forgot about it. Then a week later, I ran across it and tasted it again. It had changed completely. None of my sources had said anything about aging the mustard. The flavor got more intense and hotter over time. The mustard now had the flavor I was looking for.

One of the advantages of M. Henry Maksoud (the owner / developer of Maksoud Plaza and La Cuisine du Soleil, see page 125) being so wealthy is that he would occasionally buy us a special piece of equipment. One was a state-of-the-art ice-cream machine. We were the only ones in town to have such a modern one. My idea was to introduce flavors Brazilians would think special. There was a tiny berry that grew only in the Amazon. M. Maksoud sent his plane up to the North to bring us a regular supply of the berries and the prawns. News stories about the special ingredients helped create great buzz and the place was hopping.

Baked Potato Shells Stuffed with Warm Potato Salad, Soft Scrambled Eggs, Oysters, Smoked Salmon, and Caviar

I WAS INTRODUCED TO POTATO SKINS through Burger Bar. The general manager, the chef, and I were talking about bar snacks when they brought up potato skins. This is my interpretation, and it might be the fanciest version of stuffed potato skins you and your friends have ever had. As you dig past the smoked salmon and bright-tasting potato salad you reach the creamy surprise of scrambled eggs.

Serves 4

- 4 ounces sliced smoked salmon
- ½ cup extra-virgin olive oil, plus more for oiling the potatoes
- 4 large Russet potatoes
  Sea salt and freshly ground black pepper
- 2 tablespoons red wine vinegar
- 4 large eggs
- 1 tablespoon plus 1½ teaspoons unsalted butter
- 1 (4-ounce) jar fresh oysters, drained well and chopped
- 4 large radishes, cut into fine julienne or shredded
- 2 scallions, white and light green parts, very thinly sliced
- 1 tablespoon finely chopped fresh dill, plus a few whole sprigs
  About ¼ cup crème fraîche or sour cream
  Caviar, preferably high-quality sturgeon (optional)

Preheat the oven to 400°F. Reserve 4 pieces of salmon to garnish the stuffed potatoes and coarsely chop the rest. Set aside.

Oil the potatoes well and place them on the oven rack. Bake until soft, about 1 hour. Remove from the oven (but leave the oven on) and, using hot pads to protect your fingers, cut a lid lengthwise off the potatoes. Scoop the flesh into a warm bowl, leaving a shell about ¼ inch thick. Try to keep the potato pieces as large as possible and keep the potatoes warm. Reserve the lids.

Brush the potato shells and lids inside and out with oil and season with salt and pepper. Put them on a baking sheet and bake until crisp, about 15 minutes. Remove and keep warm.

While the potatoes bake, make the vinaigrette: In a small bowl, whisk together the vinegar and 6 tablespoons of the olive oil and salt and pepper to taste. Add more oil if the dressing is too tart. Set aside.

In a medium bowl, whisk the eggs with a good pinch each of salt and pepper. Heat a medium saucepan over medium heat. Add 1½ teaspoons of the butter and then pour in the eggs. Lower the heat to very low and cook the eggs very slowly, whisking them continuously until they are thick, creamy, and still very moist, about 5 minutes. When done, remove from the heat and whisk in the remaining 1 tablespoon of butter and the chopped oysters. Set aside and keep warm.

Add the chopped salmon, radishes, scallions, and dill to the warm potato flesh. Toss gently. Add just enough vinaigrette to moisten and flavor the potatoes. Toss carefully so you do not end up with mashed potatoes. You want a chunky, warm salad.

To serve, divide the warm scrambled eggs among the baked potato shells. Top with the potato salad, mounding it above the edge of the shells. Arrange a curl of smoked salmon on top of each; add a spoonful of crème fraîche, caviar, and a dill sprig. Serve immediately.

Notes

♣ The method I use for scrambled eggs is one of the first things I learned during my apprenticeship at L'Auberge de L'Ill and is called *oeufs brouillés aux truffes*. We cooked the eggs by whisking them in a little copper *sauteuse* and then added chopped black truffles. You don't need to use a double boiler if you control the heat and cook the eggs very slowly.

Mac and Cheese with Shrimp

♣ You can use either cream or half-and-half in the macaroni-and-vegetable mixture, but use cream for the *glaçage*, the cream-and-egg-yolk enrichment spooned on top of the dish and browned just before serving. The *glaçage* gives more richness without adding more cheese. But more cheese will give more gooeyness, which often makes dishes like these better. If that is your preference, up the amount of Gruyère to ¾ or 1 cup grated cheese from the ½ cup I call for.

THIS IS THE DISH THAT WON ME A CHALLENGE on one episode of *Top Chef Masters*. We were to prepare a three-course dinner for twelve people, spending $120 or less, and we'd be cooking in a college dorm room with a hot plate, a microwave oven, and a toaster oven. I had to first cool off and rinse my pasta in the shower! And then a little later, when I needed to reheat it, I went back in the shower and used hot water.

Serve this dish for supper with a salad or serve smaller portions as an appetizer. It would make a great dish for Christmas Eve—simple and comforting. You can make it very festive by adding lobster, crab, or truffles.

Serves 4

- 8 ounces elbow macaroni or small pasta shells
  Sea salt
- 2 tablespoons extra-virgin olive oil, divided
- 1 pound peeled, deveined large shrimp (16-20 count), cut into ½-inch pieces
- ⅓ cup finely chopped shallots
- ¼ cup finely chopped carrot
- ¼ cup finely chopped celery
- 1 bay leaf
- 1 teaspoon finely chopped fresh tarragon
- 1 teaspoon finely chopped fresh flat-leaf parsley
  Freshly ground white pepper
- 1½ cups plus ½ cup heavy cream or half-and-half
- 1 tablespoon cognac or brandy
- 2 tablespoons ruby port
- 2 tablespoons finely sliced fresh chives, divided
- 2 large egg yolks
- ½ cup coarsely grated Gruyère cheese

Bring a large pot of water to a boil and add salt. Add the macaroni and cook, stirring occasionally, until tender, about 8 minutes. Drain and set aside.

In a large saucepan, heat 1 tablespoon of the olive oil over medium heat. Add the shrimp and stir and cook until the shrimp have turned pink and opaque throughout, about 3 minutes. Scrape the shrimp onto a plate and set aside.

Add the remaining 1 tablespoon of olive oil to the pan and return to medium heat. Add the shallots, carrot, celery, bay leaf, tarragon, and parsley and season with salt and pepper. Cook, stirring, until the vegetables have softened, about 5 minutes. Add the 1½ cups of the cream, the cognac, and the port. Bring to a simmer and cook, uncovered, until the mixture has thickened slightly, about 7 minutes. Discard the bay leaf, stir in the shrimp and 1 tablespoon of the chives, and then cover and keep warm.

Preheat the broiler to high. Arrange the rack about 4 inches below the heat.

To make the glaçage: In a small bowl, whisk the remaining ½ cup of cream with the egg yolks and set aside.

Stir the reserved macaroni and the cheese into the warm vegetable-shrimp mixture. Divide it among 4 (1½-cup) individual gratin dishes and set them on a baking sheet. Divide the yolk mixture evenly over the gratins and broil until lightly browned, about 1 minute. Watch carefully; the *glaçage* browns quickly. Sprinkle with the remaining tablespoon of chives and serve immediately.

Wild Mushroom Mac and Cheese

Omit the shrimp and just use mushrooms. Use the recipe and ingredients as directed in the main recipe, adding the few additional ingredients and steps below.

- 1 ounce dried wild mushrooms (such as porcini, black chanterelles, morels, or a mix of all three)
- 2 tablespoons extra-virgin olive oil
- ¾ pound fresh mushrooms (such as ¼ pound each shiitake, baby portobello, and button mushrooms), cut into ⅓-inch-thick slices
- 1 tablespoon truffle oil or porcini oil

Quickly rinse the dried mushrooms and place them in a small bowl. Pour 1 cup boiling water over them. Set aside to let them soak until soft, about 20 minutes. Drain the mushrooms, reserving them and the soaking liquid separately. Chop the mushrooms and set them aside.

Heat 1 tablespoon of the olive oil in a large skillet over medium-high heat. Scatter half the fresh mushrooms in the pan without crowding them and cook, without moving until they brown, 1 minute. Then stir and cook until the mushrooms are browned and tender, about 5 minutes. Scrape them into a bowl and repeat with the remaining oil and fresh mushrooms. When they have fully cooked, add the chopped dried mushrooms and carefully decant the mushroom soaking liquid into the pan, leaving any solids behind. Bring to a boil and cook until only a few tablespoons of liquid remains. Transfer them to the bowl with the other mushrooms and toss to mix evenly. Set aside.

When the cream sauce has thickened, stir in the mushrooms with the chives.

Whisk the truffle oil with the ½ cup cream and egg yolks for the *glaçage* and set aside. Finish the recipe as directed.

Red-Wine-Braised Beef Cheeks
with Ginger and Lemongrass

Notes

♣ At the restaurant I use American *wagyu* for this braise. The meat has lots of marbling and is very tender, juicy, and flavorful. If you do not use *wagyu*, do buy another high-quality beef such as organic grass-fed beef.

THIS PRESENTATION TURNS A PLATE OF BEEF CHEEKS into a dish so attractive and appealing that I serve it at Fleur de Lys. Beef cheeks have a wonderful, rich flavor, but when cooked they tend to fall apart. I've come up with a technique to shape the cheeks so they stay together and stand up. It's an elegant dish and a great way to introduce beef cheeks to your guests. And almost all the preparation is completed ahead of time. For a simple presentation, serve the cheeks over polenta or wide-cut noodles. For a more elegant presentation, serve the cheeks with blanched spinach sautéed in butter, slices of roasted winter squash, and poached sweetbreads. You may need to special-order beef cheeks, which really are the cheeks of the cow.

Serves 6 to 8

Braise

4   pounds beef cheeks
    Sea salt and freshly ground
    black pepper
3   tablespoons extra-virgin olive oil
2   small yellow onions, thinly sliced
2   medium carrots, peeled and
    coarsely chopped
2   medium stalks celery,
    coarsely chopped
1   (2-inch) piece fresh ginger, peeled and
    thinly sliced

2   cloves garlic, finely chopped
1   stalk lemongrass
1½   cups dry red wine
3   cups low-salt beef broth
1   cup canned diced tomatoes
     with their juice
3   tablespoons tomato paste
2   tablespoons brown sugar
2   tablespoons finely chopped fresh
     flat-leaf parsley
1   sprig fresh sage

HOW TO ROLL BEEF CHEEKS

Lay a portion of the cooked, cooled, and cleaned beef cheeks in the middle of a large sheet of plastic wrap. Restaurant-style wrap makes the process much easier.

Fold the plastic over the meat and pull it tight to force all the air out of the meat and form a sausage about 2½ inches in diameter and 6 to 7 inches long.

Assembly and Reheating

1 cup dried breadcrumbs, preferably from brioche

1½ tablespoons finely chopped fresh flat-leaf parsley

1½ teaspoons finely chopped fresh thyme

Sea salt and freshly ground black pepper

About 2 tablespoons Dijon mustard

To braise the beef: Preheat the oven to 350°F. Season the beef on all sides with salt and pepper. Heat the olive oil in a large sauté pan with a lid or a Dutch oven over medium-high heat. Add the cheeks and sear them on both sides until well browned, about 5 minutes per side. As they are done, use tongs to transfer the cheeks to a baking sheet or platter and set aside.

Add the onions, carrots, celery, ginger, and garlic to the sauté pan and return to medium-high heat. Smash the lemongrass stalk with the back of a knife, thinly slice the stalk, and add it to the pan. Sauté the vegetables until

softened and slightly browned, about 10 minutes.

Add the wine and bring to a boil while stirring and scraping all over the bottom and sides of the pan with a wooden spoon. Add the broth, diced tomatoes, tomato paste, brown sugar, parsley, and sage. Bring to a simmer and return the cheeks to the pan. Cover and place in the oven to braise for 1½ hours. Check occasionally to make sure the liquid just simmers gently. Remove the lid and continue to cook at a slow simmer until the meat is very tender, about 1 hour.

Using tongs, transfer the meat to a platter or baking sheet and let cool. Pour the cooking liquid through a fine sieve into a clean bowl; press against the solids to get as much of the rich sauce as possible and then discard the solids. Cover and refrigerate the sauce to allow the fat to rise to the surface. Defat the sauce by skimming it off the top.

♣ When you buy beef cheeks, sometimes they arrive well trimmed and sometimes not. Check them over and trim out large pieces of fat and membranes before you braise them, but don't worry about getting everything. You have a second opportunity after the cheeks have cooked.

To make the roll really compact, pull the ends taut while rolling the sausage on the counter away from your body.

Tie the ends off and refrigerate the roll for 1 hour. This allows the natural gelatin in the beef to firm up the roll.

Notes

♣ Like many braises, this dish develops more flavor if you start a day or two ahead of time. Plus you need the extra time to shape the beef cheeks and let them firm up in the refrigerator.

♣ If you do not want to go the extra step of shaping the cheeks, you can simply reheat them in the sauce and serve them in generous soup plates. This is the usual, rustic presentation.

When the cheeks are cool enough to handle, clean them of any remaining fat and ligaments. Moisten a work surface and smooth a long (about 20 inches) sheet of plastic wrap down. The moisture will stick it to the counter. Place a fourth of the meat on the plastic wrap and use the wrap to force the meat into a fat sausage about 6 or 7 inches long and about 2½ inches in diameter. Roll the plastic around the meat very tightly to form an even roll, tie the ends tightly against the roll so it keeps its shape, and refrigerate for at least 1 hour. The natural gelatin in the beef will stiffen the meat into a single piece. Repeat with the remaining meat, making 3 or 4 sausages total.

To assemble and reheat the dish: Preheat the oven to 450°F. Place the defatted sauce in a saucepan and bring to a simmer over medium-high heat. Simmer until slightly thickened, about 5 minutes. Taste and adjust the seasoning. In a medium bowl, mix the breadcrumbs

with the parsley, thyme, and salt and pepper to taste.

Unwrap the meat and, while still cold, cut the rolls crosswise into disks 2 to 2½ inches thick. You should have about 4 slices per roll. Each roll will serve 2. Arrange the slices, standing up on end and close together, in a large, ovenproof sauté pan. Let sit at room temperature for about 15 minutes. Brush the top of each piece of meat with mustard and then sprinkle on a light layer of the breadcrumbs. Carefully pour in enough sauce into the pan to come a third of the way up the slices. Cover the pan tightly with a lid or with aluminum foil, but don't let the cover touch the meat. Warm in the oven until just heated through, about 5 minutes. Do not let the meat get too hot or the disks will fall apart. Use a spatula to carefully transfer 2 slices of meat per person to warm, rimmed soup plates. Spoon some sauce around the meat and serve immediately.

When ready to finish the dish, cut one end off a roll. Use the flat of your knife to push the meat out of the wrapping.

Cut the rolls crosswise into disks about 2 to 2½ inches thick.

Tarte Flambée Alsacienne

THESE TARTS ARE AN ALSATIAN VERSION OF PIZZA and have been part of our regional cuisine for generations. Instead of an airy crust, this tart has a shatteringly crisp, cracker thin crust. And tarte flambée has a creamy, rich topping of fromage blanc and crème fraîche. Today in Alsace, our tarte flambée is being rediscovered and updated in local restaurants. As it cooks, the topping and the dough bubble and brown—getting quite dark in places along the edges where the crust bubbles up. That's where the name, *flambé*, comes from. At Fleur in Las Vegas we do both sweet and savory variations.

Serves 4

Dough

Makes 4 tarts
(about 1 pound of dough)

- 1½ teaspoons (4 grams) active dry yeast
- ⅔ cup warm water (105° to 115°F)
- 2 cups (10 ounces) unbleached bread flour
- ½ teaspoon sea salt
- 1½ teaspoons sugar
- 1 tablespoon extra-virgin olive oil
  Unbleached all-purpose flour for dusting the bowl and work surface

Topping

- 4 slices bacon, cut into ½-inch pieces
- 1 medium yellow onion (about 6 ounces), very thinly sliced
  Sea salt and freshly ground black pepper
- ½ cup fromage blanc
- ½ cup crème fraîche
- ½ teaspoon sherry vinegar
  Pinch of piment d'Espelette
- 1 cup coarsely shredded Gruyère cheese (optional)

To make the dough: In a small bowl, stir the yeast into the warm water. Let it sit in a warm place until bubbly and active, about 15 minutes.

Meanwhile, measure the bread flour, salt, sugar, and olive oil into the bowl of a stand mixer fitted with the dough hook attachment. Turn the machine on low for a few seconds to combine the ingredients. With the mixer on low, gradually add the yeast mixture.

Knead the dough for 5 minutes, let the dough rest in the bowl for 20 minutes, and then continue kneading for another 5 minutes. You should have a stiff, very elastic, nonsticky dough. Round the dough into a ball, dust a bowl with flour, add the dough, cover with plastic wrap, and let rise in a warm place until doubled, about 1 hour. Punch the dough down, divide into 4 portions of about 4 ounces each, and roll each into a tight ball. Set them aside on a lightly floured counter covered with a kitchen towel. Let rise about 30 minutes.

When ready to bake, preheat the oven to 500°F or as high as it will go. Line 2 baking sheets with parchment paper.

To make the topping: In a large skillet over medium heat, cook the bacon until most of the fat has been rendered but the bacon is not yet crispy. With a slotted spoon, transfer the bacon pieces to a plate lined with paper towels to drain. Discard all but 1 tablespoon of the fat in the skillet.

Add the onion, a pinch of salt, and ½ cup of water to the skillet and place it over medium heat. Stir well, cover, and cook until the onions are very soft and tender, about 7 minutes. Uncover and continue to cook until any liquid left in the pan has cooked away. Remove from the heat, cover, and set aside until needed.

In a small mixing bowl, combine the fromage blanc, crème fraîche, vinegar, ½ teaspoon salt, ¼ teaspoon pepper, and piment d'Espelette. Whisk until smooth and then set aside.

To make the tarts: Pat each dough ball flat. On a lightly floured work surface, roll each into an oval (about 5 inches wide and 15 inches long, as we do at Fleur) or into a circle. Work sequentially, allowing one crust to relax a bit while you work through the others. Then return to the first. This way, the dough will eventually stretch as thin as it needs to be without fighting you. The dough should be very, very thin, less than 1/8 inch thick. Transfer the crusts to the prepared baking sheets.

Spread the cream mixture evenly over the dough, leaving a 1/2-inch border all around. Divide the onions and bacon evenly between the tarts. Sprinkle them with the cheese. Bake until the crust has browned and the topping is browned and bubbling, about 7 minutes. Serve immediately.

Asparagus and Roasted Portobello Mushroom Tarte Flambée

If you want to make this tart very fancy, add chopped truffle to the vinaigrette or add a little truffle oil to it. Even chopped black olives or halved cherry tomatoes would add nice contrasting color and good flavor.

Serves 4

6 to 8 medium asparagus spears, trimmed
    Sea salt and freshly ground black pepper
5 tablespoons extra-virgin olive oil, divided, plus more for drizzling
1 tablespoon sherry vinegar
1/2 teaspoon Dijon mustard
1/2 teaspoon finely chopped fresh thyme

2 large or 4 medium portobello mushrooms (about 12 ounces), sliced about 1/4 inch thick (or use shiitakes, very well-cleaned morels, or black chanterelles)
1 recipe Tarte Flambée dough (page 116), through the second rise

Fromage Blanc and Crème Fraîche Topping

1/2 cup fromage blanc
1/2 cup crème fraîche
1/2 teaspoon sherry vinegar
1/2 teaspoon sea salt
1/4 teaspoon freshly ground black pepper
    Pinch of piment d'Espelette

    Handful of microgreens and mixed flower petals

Cut the asparagus stalks on a sharp diagonal to form slices about 1/8 inch thick and about 3/4 inch long. Leave the tips whole. In a saucepan over high heat, bring about 1 inch of water to a boil. Prepare an ice-water bath. Add a good pinch of salt to the boiling water and add the asparagus. Cover and cook just until bright green, about 1 minute. Immediately drain the asparagus and plunge it into the ice bath. Drain well, transfer to a bowl, toss with a little olive oil, and set aside. The asparagus can be cooked up to several hours ahead of time.

In a medium bowl, whisk together the vinegar, mustard, 3 tablespoons of the olive oil, the thyme, and salt and pepper to taste. Set aside.

In a large skillet over medium-high heat, add the 2 remaining tablespoons of olive oil and the mushrooms. Sprinkle with salt and pepper and cook without stirring them until they brown, 1 to 2 minutes. Stir and cook until tender and well browned, 5 to 8 minutes. Scrape the mushrooms onto a cutting board and let them cool. Chop the mushrooms coarsely and toss them with the vinaigrette. Cover and set aside until needed.

"At Fleur we turn classic Tarte Flambée Alsacienne from savory to sweet with this Caramelized Apple Tarte Flambée."

♣ When fennel is in season, slice the bulbs thinly on a mandoline as a substitute for the onions.

When ready to bake, preheat the oven to 500°F or as high as it will go. Line 2 baking sheets with parchment paper. Follow the main recipe recipe (page 116) to shape the tarte dough. Transfer the crusts to the prepared baking sheets.

To make the topping: In a small mixing bowl, combine the fromage blanc, crème fraîche, vinegar, salt, pepper, and piment d'Espelette. Whisk until smooth. Spread the cream mixture evenly over the dough, leaving a half-inch border all around. Scatter the asparagus and mushrooms evenly over the tartes. Bake until the crust has browned and the topping is browned and bubbling, about 7 minutes. Transfer the tartes to serving plates. Scatter the microgreens and flowers over the tarts and serve immediately.

Prosciutto and Arugula Salad Tarte Flambée

Serves 4

The quality of the prosciutto is important here, so buy a good-quality artisanal domestic or an imported brand. This is a very simple tart but pretty with the pink ham and vibrant green arugula. And the salty, bitter flavors play well against the rich, creamy background of the topping.

- 1 recipe Tarte Flambée dough (page 116), through the second rise
- 1 recipe Fromage Blanc and Crème Fraîche Topping (page 117)
- 2 large handfuls arugula
- ½ teaspoon sherry vinegar
- 1½ teaspoons extra-virgin olive oil
  Sea salt and freshly ground black pepper
  About 4 very thin slices prosciutto (about 3 ounces)
  Small wedge of Parmesan cheese

When ready to bake, preheat the oven to 500°F or as high as it will go. Line 2 baking sheets with parchment paper. Follow the main recipe (page 116) to shape the tart dough. Transfer the crusts to the prepared baking sheets. Spread the topping evenly over the dough, leaving a half-inch border all around. Bake until the crust has browned and the topping is browned and bubbling, about 7 minutes.

While the tarts bake, in a medium bowl, toss the arugula with the ½ teaspoon vinegar, the olive oil, and salt and pepper to taste. When the tarts come out of the oven, transfer them to serving plates, arrange the salad on top of the tarts, and ruffle up a slice of prosciutto on each. With a vegetable peeler, cut curls of Parmesan over the tarts and serve immediately.

Caesar Salad Tarte Flambée

Serves 4

At Fleur de Lys we make our Caesar dressing with white anchovies, also called *boquerónes*. They are pickled instead of salted and have a mild anchovy flavor that we love.

Ceasar Dressing

- 1 clove garlic, very finely chopped
- 2 white anchovy fillets (boquerónes), or more to taste
- ¼ cup mayonnaise
- 2½ tablespoons freshly squeezed lemon juice
  Sea salt and freshly ground black pepper
- ¼ cup extra-virgin olive oil

Tarts

- 1 recipe Tarte flambée dough (page 116), through the second rise
- 1 recipe Fromage Blanc and Crème Fraîche Topping (page 117)

4 large eggs

About 4 cups thickly sliced romaine lettuce

About ¼ cup Caesar dressing

12 white anchovy fillets (*boquerónes*)

Freshly grated Parmesan cheese

To make the dressing: Whirl the garlic, anchovies, mayonnaise, lemon juice, and salt and pepper to taste together in a blender or food processor. With the machine running, add the olive oil in a slow stream. Taste and adjust the seasoning with salt and pepper. It will taste distinctly lemony. If you love the taste of anchovy, add more. Makes about ½ cup dressing. Store in a clean jar in the refrigerator for up to a week.

To make the tarts: When ready to bake, preheat the oven to 500°F or as high as it will go. Line 2 baking sheets with parchment paper. Follow the main recipe (page 116) to shape the tart dough. Transfer the crusts to the prepared baking sheets. Spread the topping evenly over the dough leaving a half-inch border all around. With the back of a spoon, make a slight depression in the middle of the cream. Break an egg into the depression and season it with salt and pepper. To keep the eggs in place, very carefully transfer the baking sheets to the oven while keeping the eggs level. Bake until the crust has browned, the egg has cooked, and the topping is browned and bubbling, about 7 minutes.

While the tarts bake, in a medium bowl toss the romaine with enough of the dressing to coat it well. When the tarts come out of the oven, transfer them to serving plates. Surround the egg with the anchovies and top with a quarter of the salad. Dust the tarts generously with the Parmesan and serve immediately.

Caramelized Apple Tarte Flambée

Serves 4

In a few minutes you can serve individual fresh, hot apple tarts for dessert. And you want to serve these very hot. Have all your ingredients ready and your crusts rolled out. Preheat the oven when you sit down to dinner and then assemble—you may need to neaten the crusts if they have waited an hour—and bake the tarts during the lull afterward.

1 recipe Tarte Flambée dough (page 116), through the second rise

4 large tart apples, peeled, quartered, cored, and very thinly sliced crosswise

Freshly squeezed lemon juice

About 2 cups Vanilla Pastry Cream (page 128)

About 3 tablespoons unsalted butter, melted

2 tablespoons cinnamon sugar

1 cup heavy cream or 1 pint vanilla ice cream

About 1½ teaspoons powdered sugar

121

Notes

♣ If you are working ahead, you can knead the dough, wrap it well in plastic wrap, and refrigerate for at least 1 hour and up to 12 hours. Or freeze for up to 1 month. Time permitting, you can also cut the yeast by half and let the dough ferment slowly in the refrigerator overnight. Take it out a few hours before you want to bake it to allow the dough to come to room temperature.

When ready to bake, preheat the oven to 500°F or as high as it will go. Line 2 baking sheets with parchment paper. Follow the Tarte Flambée recipe (page 116) to shape the tart dough. Transfer the crusts to the prepared baking sheets. Toss the apple slices with a little lemon juice to prevent discoloration. Whisk the pastry cream until smooth. Spread the pastry cream mixture evenly over the dough, leaving a ½-inch border all around. Arrange the apple slices in a nice pattern over the pastry cream, drizzle the tarts with the melted butter, and sprinkle lightly with cinnamon sugar. Bake until the crust and pastry cream have browned, about 7 minutes.

While the tarts bake, whip the cream with the powdered sugar (add more to taste if necessary) in a large bowl until it holds soft mounds. Stop here if you want to spoon the cream onto the tart. If you want to pipe it, continue to whip the cream just until it's firm.

As soon as the tarts come out of the oven, transfer them to large plates, spoon on the whipped cream, and serve immediately with forks and knives. The cream will begin to melt and puddle in a delicious way.

Berries and Cream Tarte Flambée

Serves 4

When I was back in Alsace recently, I had a strawberry tarte flambée and thought I had gone to heaven. Try it for yourself.

2   pints ripe berries (such as strawberries, raspberries, or blueberries, or a combination)

1   recipe Tarte Flambée dough (page 116), through the second rise

About 2 cups Vanilla Pastry Cream (page 128)

Granulated sugar, for dusting

1   cup heavy cream, or 1 pint vanilla or strawberry ice cream

About 1½ teaspoons powdered sugar

Dark Chocolate Sauce (page 174, optional)

¼   cup coarsely chopped pistachios (optional)

If you use large strawberries, slice them very thinly. When ready to bake, preheat the oven to 500°F or as high as it will go. Line 2 baking sheets with parchment paper. Follow the Tarte Flambée recipe (page 116) to shape the tart dough. Transfer the crusts to the prepared baking sheets. Whisk the pastry cream until smooth.

Spread the pastry cream mixture evenly over the dough, leaving a ½-inch border all around. Arrange the berries nicely over the pastry cream, dust with granulated sugar, and bake until the crust and pastry cream have browned, about 7 minutes.

While the tarts bake, whip the cream with the powdered sugar (add more to taste if needed) in a large bowl until it holds soft mounds. Stop here if you want to spoon the cream onto the tart. If you want to pipe it, continue to whip the cream just until it's firm.

When the tarts have baked, transfer them as quickly as possible to large warm plates and spoon or pipe the whipped cream onto them. Drizzle lightly with the chocolate sauce, and sprinkle with pistachios. Serve immediately with forks and knives.

Maple Syrup and Fromage Blanc Ice Cream

Notes

♣ Use very good maple syrup for the ice cream. If you like a strong maple flavor, use Grade B; for more subtle flavor, choose Grade A.

I REALLY ENJOY COMBINING typically American ingredients with classic French techniques and then presenting guests with something hopefully new and interesting. We serve a very smooth fromage blanc ice cream at both Fleur in Las Vegas and Fleur de Lys in San Francisco. The taste has an intriguing hint of something other than what you'd expect. Many people ask me if I like pancakes and waffles. I do, especially when they have a scoop of this ice cream on top. You can also serve it with the Meringues Glacées (page 50), and for sure make a milkshake with it.

Makes about 2 quarts

4 cups whole milk
¾ cup plus 6 tablespoons high-quality maple syrup (12 ounces total by weight)
8 large egg yolks
1 generous cup fromage blanc (8 ounces by weight)

Prepare an ice-water bath. In a large saucepan, heat the milk and the ¾ cup of maple syrup over medium heat just until it begins to steam and bubbles appear around the edges.

In a large mixing bowl, whisk the egg yolks with the remaining 6 tablespoons of maple syrup until smooth. While whisking vigorously, very slowly pour the hot milk into the eggs. Then return the mixture to the saucepan and place over low heat. Cook, while whisking and reaching all over the bottom and sides of the pan, until the mixture thickens enough to coat the back of a spoon, about 5 minutes. If you have an instant-read thermometer, it should read 180° to 185°F. Do not let your custard boil, or it will break. Whisk in the fromage blanc until fully melted and incorporated into the custard.

Immediately strain the custard through a fine sieve into a large bowl. Place the bowl over the ice bath and whisk occasionally until the mixture is quite cold. Refrigerate the custard for several hours or put it in the freezer until very well chilled. Freeze in an ice-cream maker according to the manufacturer's instructions. The ice cream can be completed a day ahead of time.

Chantal in downtown São Paulo.

124

Learning to Make Do: Brazil

Roger Vergé's new restaurant, La Cuisine du Soleil in São Paulo, Brazil, would be strictly a restaurant *gastronomique*, housed in a brand-new hotel tower, the Maksoud Plaza, built and owned by Henry Maksoud. He was a great fan of M. Vergé and had often stayed at Moulin de Mougins with his wife. Everything was so new in Brazil when we arrived in 1979. But there were no systems in place for supplying the demand—for trained staff, for equipment, for ingredients.

Normally, we would have brought our equipment—the stoves, the pots and pans—from France, but the 500 percent import tax made it too expensive. We had locally made stoves from places that had never made stoves before. Literally, after two months, the doors fell off. This is when I earned my graduate degree in improvisation. It would make my move to the United States a few years later much easier. I could not worry about wanting a particular brand of fryer. It was more a case of, Do you have a fryer? Does it work? Let's go!

And the language! Everything I said to anyone required a translator. I quickly started learning Portuguese, and communication improved. After a while, I realized that many of the staff could not read or write. In those days, that was the reality, and coming from France, I had assumed everyone could read. That was a real learning experience.

I did not like to complain, so when M. Maksoud would come through the kitchen and ask, "Chef? How is everything?" I would say, "Everything is good." But I was also representing M. Vergé, and he would want to see things running well. If I were unsuccessful, there were ten chefs behind me who would want to take over. Finally, one night I just lost it.

A special finish had been put down in the walk-in refrigerators by installers who did not know how to apply it. When we cleaned the floor after a few weeks, the water drained underneath the finish—where it stayed, creating bubbles and fermenting. If you stepped on one, it released a horrible smell.

M. Maksoud came with his question, "So, Chef, how is everything?" "M. Maksoud," I said, "it's really hard." I took him into the walk-in and stepped on one of the bubbles. Then he was on the telephone. By 2 a.m. every executive was there, and he tore into them. I couldn't understand everything he said, but I got the message.

The men we hired as cooks had never touched a pot or pan before. But they were smart, and once we taught them, they could do the job. After a while, we had a really good crew going. Then as we got even busier and more successful, M. Maksoud and M. Vergé suggested bringing in another sous chef from France. But I felt I could promote some of our Brazilian cooks instead, that these men, with more responsibility and a higher salary, would go through fire for us. But it was not so simple and, in the end, I had to bring in another sous chef from France after all.

When we said good-bye after two years, the cooks all came to the airport to see Chantal and me off. We were so touched to see that each one had some kind of gift that cost maybe a month's salary and would make their living tighter.

Brioche Bretzels

FOR MY FIRST TWO MONTHS IN THE ARMY I was based outside Toul. In the town was a pâtisserie that made the best brioche with pastry cream. I would go to the shop whenever I could. The baker spread pastry cream over the dough, and then rolled it up like a *biscuit rolé* (jelly roll). My father made a brioche-and-pastry-cream roll, too, but shaped it like a bretzel. Chantal still remembers them from the first time I brought her home to meet my parents—to do that you had to be serious. When I told my father I planned to put them in this book, he was so pleased.

Makes about 12 brioche bretzels (about 2½ ounces each; about 2 pounds of dough), or 1 (12-inch) galette plus 3 or 4 rolls

¼ cup whole milk, lukewarm (105° to 115°F)

1 envelope (¼ ounce) active dry yeast

2½ cups (12½ ounces) plus ¼ cup (1¼ ounces) unbleached all-purpose flour, plus more for dusting the work surface

7 tablespoons (2.6 ounces) sugar

¼ teaspoon sea salt

3 large eggs

3 tablespoons whole milk, at room temperature

½ cup (1 stick or 4 ounces) unsalted butter, at room temperature

1 recipe (about 2 cups) Vanilla Pastry Cream (page 128)

1 egg yolk

¼ cup powdered sugar or about ½ cup Vanilla-Mint Tart Glaze (page 129, optional)

Pour the lukewarm milk into a small bowl. Add the yeast and the ¼ cup of flour and whisk until smooth. Cover with plastic wrap and leave in a warm place until the mixture gets puffy and active, at least 15 minutes.

Meanwhile, in the bowl of a stand mixer fitted with the dough hook attachment, combine the remaining 2½ cups flour, the sugar, and the salt. Add the eggs and the room-temperature milk to the bowl and knead on low speed until the dough is a smooth mass (it may not form around the dough hook), 5 to 8 minutes.

While the dough is kneading, cut the butter into about 12 pieces. With the machine running on low, gradually add the butter, a few pieces at a time, until thoroughly incorporated. Continue kneading on low for about 8 minutes. The dough may still not form around the dough hook. Scrape the dough off the dough hook and add the yeast mixture. Knead on low speed until the dough feels smooth and elastic, yet still fluffy and soft, about another 10 minutes. It will remain sticky.

On a lightly floured work surface, shape the dough into a ball, dust a large bowl lightly with flour, and add the dough. Cover the bowl with plastic wrap and leave in a warm place to rise until doubled in size, about 2 hours. When ready, the dough will not spring back when poked gently with a finger.

Punch the dough down and turn it out onto a lightly floured work surface. Cut the dough into 12 evenly sized pieces (about 2½ ounces each). Under cupped palms with stiff fingers, roll the pieces into tight balls. They should stick a little bit to the counter to create tension, so use very little to no flour on the countertop. Cover with a kitchen towel and let rest for about 15 minutes.

To shape the bretzels, work sequentially, completing each step with all the dough. This allows the dough to rest and makes it easier to work. As you work, if the dough seems to fight you and doesn't stretch out, just let it rest for a few minutes and then continue. Line 2 baking sheets with nonstick baking mats or parchment paper.

Preheat the oven to 350°F. Roll each ball into a log about 6 inches long. Then roll each of these into a long, thin rope about 30 inches long, tapering the ends to points, and immediately shape it and arrange it on the prepared baking sheet.

To make the classic twisted pretzel shape, pick up the tapered ends of the 30-inch-long roll and cross your hands, right over left. The end that was on the right is now on the left. Repeat for a second twist. To complete the classic pretzel shape, lift the tapered ends and drape them over the sides of the bretzel, at 10 o'clock and 2 o'clock. You can leave the tips on top or flip the bretzel over, covering the ends with the sides of the bretzel. Either is correct. Your finished bretzel should be about 5 inches wide with very large openings to fill with the pastry cream.

Meanwhile, scrape the warm pastry cream into a pastry bag fitted with a large round tip. As soon as you have shaped a bretzel, pipe the pastry cream into the open spaces of the bretzels, overfilling them so the cream mounds above the dough. This helps prevent the dough from springing back on itself. With a wet finger, smooth any points left by the piping. Set the bretzels aside in a warm place to rise, about 30 minutes.

To finish and bake the bretzels: In a small bowl, whisk the egg yolk with 1/2 teaspoon water. With a pastry brush, brush the dough only with the egg wash. Bake until medium brown, about 20 minutes, rotating the pans front to back and top to bottom about halfway through. Let the bretzels cool for a few minutes on the baking sheets.

Mix the powdered sugar in a bowl with just enough water to make a thin sugar glaze and brush it onto the breads. Or brush with the tart glaze. It makes the pastries very shiny and a little sticky but also even more irresistible. Let the bretzels continue to cool on the baking sheets until the pastry cream has firmed up. I like them best still warm from the oven (a privilege of living above a pastry shop), but they taste very good for the whole day.

Five Pounds of Dough for a Larger Batch

This dough is so practical that I suggest you make this larger batch of dough and freeze half for up to a month. Let it defrost and rise in a warm place and you will have your treat in half the time it would take otherwise. Or bake bretzels for your family and a loaf of brioche to give to your neighbors. Use the following amounts and prepare as directed in the main recipe.

1/2 cup whole milk, lukewarm (105° to 115°F)

2 envelopes (1/2 ounce) active dry yeast

5 cups (25 ounces) plus 1/2 cup (2 1/2 ounces) unbleached all-purpose flour, plus more for dusting the work surface

3/4 cup (5 1/4 ounces) sugar

1/2 teaspoon sea salt

5 large eggs

6 tablespoons whole milk, at room temperature

1 cup (2 sticks or 8 ounces) unsalted butter, at room temperature

Vanilla Pastry Cream

HERE'S THE FLEUR DE LYS PASTRY CREAM. There are richer versions, but I learned richer is not necessarily better. This one strikes a nice balance. If you want to use the pastry cream to fill pastries and then bake them (like the Brioche Bretzels, page 126), your pastry cream needs to be a bit "tighter." Otherwise it cooks too quickly and "pops" in the oven, leaving you with tasty but not very good-looking pastries. See the variation at the end of this recipe for the right proportions to use.

Makes about 2 cups

2 cups half-and-half

¼ cup (1¾ ounces) plus ¼ cup (1¾ ounces) sugar

Pinch of sea salt

1 vanilla bean, split lengthwise, or 1 teaspoon vanilla extract

2 large eggs

3 tablespoons cornstarch

1 tablespoon unsalted butter, at room temperature

Place the half-and-half, ¼ cup of the sugar, and the salt in a large saucepan over medium heat. Scrape the vanilla bean seeds into the milk and then drop in the pod. Bring to a boil, remove from the heat, and let the vanilla infuse into the milk while you work with the eggs.

In a medium bowl, whisk the eggs with the remaining ¼ cup of sugar. Whisking some of the sugar into the eggs helps prevent lumps later when you whisk in the hot cream. Whisk in the cornstarch until smoothly incorporated.

Remove the vanilla bean, rinse, dry, and reserve for another use. While whisking vigorously, pour the hot milk into the eggs a little at a time. Then pour the mixture back into the saucepan and place over medium heat. Bring to a boil, whisking all the while and making sure to scrape the bottom and sides of the pan. Boil until the pastry cream thickens, about 1 minute. Remove the pan from the heat. If the cream looks lumpy, pass it through a sieve into a bowl. Otherwise, whisk in the butter and vanilla extract, if using, and then transfer the pastry cream

onto a sheet pan to cool for about 5 minutes. Lay a piece of plastic wrap directly on the surface to prevent a skin from forming. Let cool to room temperature and then chill.

Thick Vanilla Pastry Cream for Brioche Bretzels

Makes enough to fill 12 large brioche bretzels

For this use, the pastry cream needs to be thicker and tighter so that it bakes up like a custard. It has extra yolks and a little extra cornstarch to accomplish this. Plus, as my brother explained when he visited San Francisco in 2011, the pastry cream should be warm when it is piped into the bretzels. Make it right before you shape your bretzels and, whatever you do, do not stir the cream to loosen it before transferring it to a pastry bag. This will break the cream and it will not bake properly. For convenience, I've included a complete ingredient list; follow the preceding method. But once it is made, keep the pastry cream in the saucepan or transfer it to a bowl. This will help it stay warm until you need it.

4 cups half-and-half

½ cup (3½ ounces) plus ½ cup (3½ ounces) sugar

¼ teaspoon sea salt

1 vanilla bean, split lengthwise in half, or 1 teaspoon vanilla extract

4 large eggs

4 large egg yolks

½ cup cornstarch

1 tablespoon unsalted butter, at room temperature

Vanilla-Mint Tart Glaze

THIS GLAZE GIVES FRUIT TARTS A NICE SHINE and adds a little flavor without detracting from the main ingredients. We use it at Fleur de Lys for our mini fruit tartlets, which are part of our petits fours presentation after dinner. You can dip big, ripe strawberries and bunches of grapes in the glaze and make them part of a cheese or dessert presentation.

Makes about 1¾ cups

1½ tablespoons powdered pectin
1 cup (7 ounces) sugar
½ vanilla bean, split lengthwise
5 fresh mint leaves

In a small bowl, mix together the pectin and sugar until evenly blended. Measure 2 cups of water into a large saucepan. Scrape the seeds from the vanilla bean into the water and then drop in the pod. Add the mint leaves and bring to a boil over high heat. Whisk in the pectin-sugar mixture and boil rapidly for 5 minutes. Remove from the heat and let cool uncovered. Store extra glaze, covered, in the refrigerator. Take out what you need and melt it in the microwave.

Notes

♣ Use a clean spoon to dip what you need out of the glaze so the remainder does not get contaminated. Then it will keep, covered and refrigerated, for up to a month.

Laurent Pillard, our corporate executive chef, and I discuss photographing the Poached Pear Brioche Galette (page 132).

THE POWER OF GETTING ORGANIZED
Working with Gaston Lenôtre

When I was coming up, Gaston Lenôtre was the most well-known and innovative pastry chef. Through his books and school and shops, he restructured French pastry. We all learned from him. I worked with him two separate times. The first was when Chef Haeberlin sent me to Paris to help Lenôtre run the food concessions for the International Paris Air Show at Le Bourget in 1973. M. Lenôtre had thought out our needs completely. Each morning the food arrived with the menus and everything we had to cook. If the menu said béarnaise, the butter would have been clarified, the eggs separated, the tarragon measured out, and everything packed separately. He thought of every detail down to the broom, dustpan, and a small toolbox. That convinced me that he was someone who was really thinking. He knew that things go wrong and that a toolbox might be just what you needed when you were off site and on your own.

I would put that experience to work later when it came my turn to do parties and events. Other chefs would tease me for how I had packed everything, had sketched pictures of my dishes, and had thought every detail through. But I knew it worked.

I worked with M. Lenôtre again while preparing for the opening of the Chefs de France restaurant in the French Pavilion at Epcot Center, a joint venture by Paul Bocuse, Roger Vergé, and Gaston Lenôtre. It amazed me to see how M. Lenôtre's production facility worked. His values and those of M. Bocuse and Chef Haeberlin were the same—consistency and the highest quality. But he had all these ideas for ways to expedite making complex items. A machine turned out thousands of perfect croissants a day. Too perfect. The machine could not put the characteristic curve to the tips of the croissant. So Lenôtre stationed a man on each side of the belt who hand-curved those tips. And he invented the pastry guitar cutter, a tool for cutting cakes into perfect squares.

Another thing that stayed with me was the way M. Lenôtre had thought out the design of his ice-cream production. One wall of the production facility was a rank of refrigerators that opened on their opposite side to the shipping facility. Once packed, the ice-cream containers were loaded onto the correct shelves. When you picked one out to ship, the next slid into place in a natural rotation. On a smaller scale, I have used this idea for Burger Bar's on-premise butcher shops.

Honey-Caramel Sauce with Lavender

WE USE A LOT OF HONEY AT HOME IN ALSACE—both a pine forest honey and wild-flower honey—and my uncle was an apiarist. Originally he apprenticed as a butcher but was shot in the arm in World War II. My grandpa was a *garde champêtre*, a sort of ranger who looked after the village common-held fields. There were separate guards for the forest and the fields. He got my uncle his new trade. Hermenegildo "Gilberto" Banuelos Villarreal, Fleur de Lys's pastry chef, created this honey caramel for this book. Slather it on Brioche (page 126) or pour it over the Maple Syrup and Fromage Blanc Ice Cream (page 124).

Makes about 1 cup

- 1 cup heavy cream
- 2 (3-inch) strips orange zest
- ½ teaspoon sea salt
- ¾ teaspoon dried lavender flowers, 1 small rosemary sprig, or a pinch of herbes de Provence (optional)
- ¾ cup (12 ounces by weight) honey

Heat the cream in a small saucepan with the orange zest, salt, and lavender. Bring the cream to a boil, remove from the heat, and set aside.

In a large saucepan, bring the honey to a boil over medium heat. Boil rapidly until it turns very dark, 3 to 4 minutes.

When the honey is ready, add the cream, whisking until smooth and being careful to avoid getting splattered as the mixture foams up. Whisk until the sauce is smooth, strain into a bowl, and let cool to room temperature. Scrape into a piping bottle and store in the refrigerator for up to a week. The sauce will thicken as it cools. Rewarm gently, if needed, by holding the bottle in simmering water or heating in a microwave oven.

Notes

♣ Warm the honey to make it easier to measure, or buy a 12-ounce container and then you will not have to measure at all.

Chantal and me in Rio.

131

Poached Pear Brioche Galette

YOU DO NOT OFTEN SEE THIS RUSTIC GALETTE EVEN IN FRANCE with its crust of brioche dough. When we were working with my dad's brioche bretzel dough, I remembered those old-fashioned tarts and created this one. Serve it for dessert, of course, or as a breakfast pastry. Change the fruit with the seasons. Apricots are really good and do not need to be poached first—the same goes for plums.

Serves 8

Unbleached all-purpose flour for dusting the work surface

1 recipe Brioche Bretzel dough (page 126), through the first 2-hour rise

About 1 cup Vanilla Pastry Cream (page 128)

4 Poached Pears

1 large egg yolk

Granulated sugar, for sprinkling

About ½ cup Vanilla-Mint Tart Glaze (page 129)

About 2 tablespoons coarsely chopped pistachios (optional)

Vanilla ice cream or softly whipped cream

Preheat the oven to 350°F. Line a large baking sheet with parchment paper. On a lightly floured work surface, roll out about three-quarters of the dough into a 12-inch circle a little less than ¼ inch thick. Spread the pastry cream over the dough to a depth of about ⅛ inch, leaving a 1-inch border all around.

Drain the pears well. Halve and core them, then slice them very thinly on a diagonal. Lay them on a counter and gently pat them to fan out the slices. With a large, thin spatula, arrange the halves evenly on the pastry cream with narrow ends to the center. Make sure to leave space between the halves.

In a small bowl, whisk the egg yolk with ½ teaspoon water. With a pastry brush, brush the border with the egg glaze and let the galette rest just until the dough begins to relax and rise, 30 minutes. Sprinkle the pears lightly with sugar. Bake until the pastry

cream has firmed and the brioche has browned underneath, about 35 minutes. Lightly brush the tart all over with the glaze and sprinkle with the pistachios. Serve warm with vanilla ice cream or whipped cream.

Notes

♣ You will have a little more dough than you need for the galette. Divide the extra dough into 3 or 4 (2- to 3-ounce) pieces and roll into balls. Let them rise for about 30 minutes while you work on your galette. Brush them with egg wash. With wet scissors, cut a + into the top of the dough and sprinkle with coarse sugar, such as turbinado. Bake for about 15 minutes and reserve as a cook's snack! Or roll out the dough balls into narrow strips about ¼ inch thick. Spread with pastry cream, sprinkle generously with brown sugar and either raisins or chopped nuts or both, and then dust with cinnamon. Roll the strips up into a neat spiral and bake for about 20 minutes.

Poached Pears

Makes 4

The secret to poached pears is counterintuitive. Poach them in water and only add the sugar once they are tender to avoid the pears turning brown. Then let them sit in the syrup for a day to soak up the flavors. And don't throw the flavorful cooking liquid away, either. You can make a drink of it with carbonated water or boil it down until very reduced and use it to glaze the galette.

4   large ripe but firm pears, peeled
    Juice of 1 lemon
1   vanilla bean, split lengthwise
2   cups (14 ounces) sugar

Place the pears in a saucepan large enough to hold them in a single layer. Add only enough water to just float the pears, about 5 cups. Add the lemon juice; scrape the seeds from the vanilla bean and add them along with the pod.

Bring the pears to a boil over medium-high heat. Simmer gently, uncovered, until a sharp knife easily pierces them to the center, about 25 minutes. Using 2 large spoons, turn the pears occasionally while they cook, being careful not to nick them. As soon as the pears are tender, add the sugar and remove them from the heat. Let the pears cool to room temperature in the syrup, cover, and refrigerate overnight.

Spiced Chocolate Quinoa Pudding with Fresh Berries

♣ You can create a pretty presentation by serving the dessert in martini glasses. Garnish simply with the whipped cream, coconut, and a scattering of ripe fresh berries such as raspberries or sliced strawberries, or let your imagination go wild and layer the pudding with whipped cream, raspberry jam, fresh berries, orange segments, caramelized bananas (page 176), and then top with mint leaves and a mango fan.

♣ This amount of hot paprika will give you just a little heat in the back of your throat. If you want more heat than that, double the amount.

I STARTED WORKING WITH QUINOA IN BRAZIL. Its fluffy, light texture and delicate, nutty flavor as well as its powerhouse nutritional profile all interested me. I was inspired to include quinoa by a chocolate-rice pudding I had made when I was younger. It's fun to make this dessert for friends who are unfamiliar with quinoa. They will be so surprised to discover how delicious it is.

Serves 6 to 8

About ¼ cup coconut flakes (sweetened or unsweetened)
1 cup heavy cream
1 tablespoon plus ½ cup sugar (3½ ounces)
Sea salt
5 tablespoons quinoa, well rinsed
1 cup whole milk
1 cup coconut milk
6 tablespoons Dutch-process cocoa powder
1 teaspoon ground cinnamon
¼ teaspoon Spanish hot paprika
1 tablespoon unflavored gelatin
2 ounces bittersweet chocolate (at least 60% cacao), coarsely chopped
Sweetened whipped cream for serving
½ pint fresh raspberries or strawberries, thinly sliced (optional)

Preheat the oven to 350°F. Spread the coconut on a baking sheet and toast it in the oven, stirring occasionally until light gold, about 10 minutes. Coconut can burn easily, so be sure to watch carefully as the flakes begin to brown. Pour the coconut into a bowl and set aside until needed. You can toast the coconut several days ahead and store it in a clean glass jar.

Whip the cream with 1 tablespoon of the sugar in a cold mixing bowl until it holds firm peaks. Refrigerate the whipped cream until needed.

Bring 8 cups of water to a boil in a large heavy saucepan over high heat. Add a pinch of salt and whisk in the quinoa. Simmer vigorously, uncovered, for 10 minutes. Drain the quinoa and

then return it to the saucepan. Add the milk, coconut milk, ½ teaspoon salt, and the remaining ½ cup of sugar. Bring the mixture to a simmer over medium-high heat. Turn the heat to low, cover, and cook very slowly until the quinoa is very tender, about 20 minutes. Stir occasionally to make sure the quinoa does not stick to the bottom of the pan. Remove the pan from the heat and whisk in the cocoa powder, cinnamon, and paprika.

In a small saucepan, soften the gelatin in ¼ cup cold water for several minutes. Melt the gelatin by setting the pan over low heat. Stir with a rubber spatula until melted. While the gelatin softens, in a small microwave-safe bowl, melt the bittersweet chocolate on low power. Prepare an ice-water bath in a large bowl and set it in the sink.

Transfer the quinoa mixture to a large mixing bowl. With a rubber spatula, stir the gelatin and chocolate into the quinoa. Set the bowl in the ice bath and stir occasionally until the mixture is cool to your touch and has begun to thicken. (Don't wander off; the mixture will set quickly once it's cool.) Immediately remove the bowl from the ice bath and rapidly but thoroughly fold in the whipped cream. Pour the mixture into dessert glasses or bowls and refrigerate until firm, about 1 hour or overnight.

To serve, add a dollop of whipped cream, and some berries, then sprinkle the top with the toasted coconut.

CHAPTER

4

*Modern
French Cooking*

Hits American Shores

"Our philosophy is to cater to our clientele and to accommodate their needs and wishes."

ADAPTING TO THE USA

When Chantal and I went to Brazil, the move was paid for; we had a translator and a driver every day; and we had a beautiful furnished apartment in the best corner of São Paolo. We thought that our welcome in the United States to open Roger Vergé's Sutter 500 restaurant on the corner of Sutter and Powell would be even more extraordinary.

Pages 136 and 137: Two of the fantastic spoon towers we used to build when Fleur de Lys was invited to participate in grand tasting events. Each row of spoons held just a taste of a different vegetable puree.

And it was. Chantal, Dominique Lemercier (our general manager in São Paolo who came with us as part of the opening team), and I were met at the airport by Jean Gabriel, a Frenchman. Only M. Gabriel spoke French and English; we had no English. M. Gabriel owned a bookshop on Larkin Street and was one of the partners in Sutter 500. He was driving a sort of hippie VW van with no seats in the back. Chantal sat in the one seat in front while Dominique perched on a dining chair (a risk when M. Gabriel braked!) and I sat on a pile of newspapers. He dropped us at the Star Motel on

From left: The original dining room at Fleur de Lys, about 1986. Me with Julia Child in 1989. She was in town during the earthquake and came to dinner, sitting at table 31, just a few days after the quake. We felt an aftershock that night and the dining room fell silent for a moment. *Above:* The three Fleur de Lys partners—me, Chantal, and Maurice Rouas—at my birthday party in a private home.

Lombard Street, told us to settle in, and said he'd be back to take us to dinner on Union Street. The first morning in the United States, M. Gabriel picked us up at 7:00 a.m. to go to the restaurant. After that it was the number 45 bus to work for quite a while.

When I spoke with San Francisco's French chefs in the early '80s (I arrived in the U.S. in 1982), they would tell me that if I wanted shallots or haricots verts (and so much else), I would have to order from France. I almost began to think: *Am I in the same boat as in Brazil?* Then I put to use what I had learned there: If what I need isn't available, it's not a big deal. What is available? Instead of shallots I might use torpedo onions. In place of haricots verts I might substitute brussels sprouts or spinach. I was already happy that when I ordered zucchini I got them and all the same size. I think many of my dishes still reflect this cross-cultural mix. We play with American ingredients and present them in a French context—

139

In the kitchen at
Fleur de Lys soon
after I arrived there.

for instance, the corn madeleines (page 155). Or we add chocolate to an Alsace-inspired marinated game dish (page 167).

Sutter 500 was open for breakfast, lunch, dinner, and in between, as well as for takeout. To help me write the breakfast menu, M. Vergé gave me a couple of San Francisco menus he had collected, but I didn't read English then. I looked at them and compared. If an item appeared on all of them, I put it on my menu. We had no clue; it was wild. Times were different then—the global expansion of restaurants created by a single chef was all new. We were just figuring out how to do it.

Before arriving in the United States, I had planned a menu but didn't know how it would be received. I knew I couldn't serve fish with the head on, and I knew organ meats wouldn't go over well. I knew that cockscombs and sweetbreads might taste good but that they would not fly here. Still I made mistakes, some big ones. At Moulin de Mougins we made a molded gelatin dish of rabbit. The meat and little vegetables were suspended in a clear, delicious gelée. We thought it was a great dish and put it on Sutter 500's menu. Instead, it was a disaster. One night a lady cried when she learned she'd eaten rabbit, and I took it off the menu. I did not create my ballotine of rabbit (page 148) to disguise the rabbit, but

A Fleur de Lys menu and cover from the 1970s before I joined the restaurant.

as a warm version of a cold dish I served first at Le Prieuré, where I earned my first Michelin star.

In the early 1980s small producers began to knock on our kitchen doors to offer us foraged mushrooms, artisanal cheeses, and baby vegetables. Two brothers with big beards (I had one, too) brought us the most beautiful lettuces arranged in little baskets and garnished with edible flowers. After a while, I noticed that just one brother arrived with our delivery, and I asked what had happened. It turned out the missing brother was in jail. They were lettuce-and-marijuana growers. I wrote a character reference for him, hoping it would help.

A year or two into the Sutter 500 project, M. Vergé pulled out of the restaurant and offered us new jobs in France. But Chantal and I liked it here and wanted to stay. Because of the terms of my visa, I could not leave the restaurant and remain in America without a green card—unless I was offered a position that required a French chef. Chantal and I felt that we were on our own. We loved San Francisco, but we did not know if we could make it work. Nothing seemed to work in our favor. After a while, it seemed that the harder our situation became, the more stubborn we became.

White Gazpacho with Vanilla Oil

WE CREATED THIS REFRESHING SOUP for our summer menu a few years ago. We often improvise around a gazpacho theme and hope to surprise our guests. The ingredients are not classic gazpacho flavors but are still Spanish in feel. The presentation brings immediate satisfaction to the eye, and then comes the moment when you taste the soup—the layers of flavors in the grapes, cucumbers, yogurt, and almonds. Blending them together with vanilla oil really closes the circle with a final surprise.

Serves 6 to 8

Vanilla Oil

½ cup grapeseed or other neutral-flavored oil

3 Tahitian vanilla beans

White Gazpacho

2 cups seedless green grapes plus about 18 more whole grapes for garnish

1 English cucumber, peeled and seeded

¾ cup (2½ ounces) finely ground almonds

½ cup extra-virgin olive oil

¼ cup whole-milk plain yogurt

2 tablespoons sherry vinegar

1 small shallot, coarsely chopped

1 clove garlic, coarsely chopped

Sea salt and freshly ground white pepper

To make the vanilla oil: With a small sharp knife, cut the vanilla beans in half lengthwise. Then, using the back of the knife, scrape out the seeds and put them in a clean glass jar. Add the grapeseed oil, cover, and shake well. Set the jar aside in a cool, dark place for 3 days to allow the vanilla seeds to perfume the oil. Shake the jar several times a day. When the oil is ready, transfer it to a small squeeze bottle and store it in the refrigerator.

To make the garnish: Thread 3 or 4 grapes onto each of 6 decorative cocktail skewers and freeze. This can be done several days ahead of time. Remove the skewers a few minutes ahead of serving to allow them to soften a bit.

To make the soup: Put the 2 cups of grapes, the cucumber, almonds, olive oil, yogurt, ¼ cup water, vinegar, shallot, and garlic into a blender or food processor and process until very smooth. Taste for seasoning and adjust with salt and pepper. Transfer the soup to a container, cover, and refrigerate for 1 or 2 hours or up to a day before serving.

Just before serving, stir well and pour into chilled martini glasses. Shake the bottle of vanilla oil and carefully squeeze out a few drops on top of each portion. Add a frozen grape skewer and serve immediately.

A drawing for the tomato gazpacho presentation with details of cutting below it. These clear line drawings—sometimes I color them—are easier for my cooks to follow than a photograph.

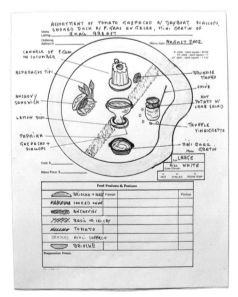

Notes

♣ I like to use plump, aromatic Tahitian vanilla beans for the oil. Keep the oil refrigerated and shake it well before each use to disperse the seeds in the oil. The recipe does make more than you need, but you can find all sorts of ways to use it—on grilled fish, shellfish, lobster, chicken breasts, and summery salads. A small bottle of it would also make a much-appreciated hostess gift.

Fresh Crab and Black Truffle Cappuccino

AT FLEUR DE LYS WE HAVE BEEN MAKING savory cappuccinos for a long time, and I think we were among the first to introduce the idea. We were playing with trompe l'oeil, having fun with the mania for cappuccinos and specialty coffee drinks. The soup is served in a cappuccino cup, and the foam is dusted with porcini powder and looks like cinnamon on a coffee drink. And the soup even comes with a corn madeleine just the way you would get a cappuccino with a madeleine on the side in France. When diners dig underneath the foam, they discover chunks of crab and truffle.

Serves 6

Cappuccino

- 1 tablespoon extra-virgin olive oil
- 1/3 cup and 2 tablespoons finely chopped shallots
- 2 large cloves garlic, finely chopped
- 1½ cups dry white wine
  Juice of 1 lemon
  Sea salt and freshly ground black pepper
- 2 tablespoons finely chopped fresh flat-leaf parsley
- 2 tablespoons chopped fresh cilantro
- 3 pounds fresh mussels, scrubbed and debearded
  About 2 cups clam juice or shellfish broth
- 1 large live Dungeness crab

Assembly and Serving

- 1 small leek, white and pale green parts
- ½ ounce black truffle
- 1 tablespoon extra-virgin olive oil
- 1 small red potato, cut into ¼-inch dice (about ¼ cup)
- 2 tablespoons finely chopped shallots
- 1½ teaspoons black truffle oil
- 2 tablespoons freshly squeezed lemon juice, plus more for seasoning
  Sea salt and freshly ground black pepper
- ½ cup heavy cream
- 1 medium tomato, peeled, seeded, and chopped
  Dried porcini powder
- 6 to 12 Corn Madeleines with Cracked Black Pepper (page 155)

To make the cappuccino: Heat the olive oil in a large saucepan over medium heat. Add the shallots and garlic and cook them until soft but not brown, about 5 minutes. Add the white wine, lemon juice, a good pinch of salt, the parsley, cilantro, and mussels. Cover the pan and bring to a boil over high heat. Cook, shaking the pan occasionally until the mussels open, about 5 minutes. With a large slotted spoon, scoop the mussels into a bowl and let cool. Remove the meat from the shells and reserve for another use; discard the shells.

Measure the mussel cooking liquid and add enough clam juice to make 4 cups. Bring the broth to a boil in a large saucepan over high heat. Prepare an ice water bath. Lower the crab into the pot headfirst, cover, and poach at a gentle simmer for 20 to 25 minutes. Transfer the crab to the ice water and let cool. Strain the broth through a fine sieve and set aside. Crack and clean the crab, pick out the meat, cutting any large pieces into ¼-inch dice, and set aside.

To prepare the soup garnishes: Julienne the leek by cutting it into 1-inch lengths and then, carefully cutting lengthwise, slice just to the center of each piece. Open these out flat and cut into strips ⅛ inch wide and 1 inch long. Cut the truffle into very thin slices; cut the slices into very thin strips.

Notes

♣ Périgord black truffles are considered the highest quality and have the best flavor when freshly harvested in the colder weather. Summer truffles have less flavor. You can substitute wild mushrooms such as morels, porcini, chanterelles, and black chanterelles for the truffles. Use about 2 medium mushrooms for each person.

♣ If you happen to have shellfish stock on hand, you can skip the first part of the recipe here in which you cook mussels to make a poaching broth for the crab. Save your shrimp, lobster, and crab shells in the freezer and make stock when you have a little extra time in the kitchen.

Heat the olive oil in a large saucepan over medium heat and add the julienned leek and truffle, diced potato, and shallots. Cook, without browning the vegetables, until softened, about 5 minutes. Add the reserved broth and bring to a gentle simmer. Cook for 5 to 6 minutes to meld the flavors. Stir in the truffle oil and lemon juice. Taste. It should be flavored strongly with lemon and be seasoned assertively so that the flavors do not become diluted with the addition of the frothy cream. Add salt, pepper, and more lemon as needed.

To serve: In a small bowl, whip the cream just until it begins to mound softly. Do not overwhip. Divide the tomatoes and crabmeat among 6 warm cappuccino cups that hold at least 1 cup. Top with a spoonful of the whipped cream. Immediately ladle the broth, including some of the solids, into the cappuccino cups, filling them almost to the rim. Within a few seconds the foam builds up from the contact of the hot broth with the cream. Dust the foam with the porcini powder and serve immediately with a corn madeleine on the side.

The First Thrill of Ownership

When I first came to Fleur de Lys in 1986, it was a totally new and exciting feeling to open the door in the morning to our restaurant with my key. Everything I touched—if I straightened something on the wall—I would think, That is mine. Suddenly I had a bigger picture; I was the owner of a restaurant. It was not doing well, but still, it was a thrill. So then, of course, Chantal and I put everything into it—not just the cooking, but painting, plumbing, wiring, tiling. All that came with it.

Every morning Chantal came to work with me and we painted and cleaned. Then, while I started with the desserts and pastries, she worked to organize the office. She inventoried office supplies, and we discovered we didn't even have stationery. After we got the place a little bit settled, I taught Chantal to make the desserts and she became the pastry chef. When the press started kicking in, we realized we needed a press kit and Chantal took that on.

Very quickly, we realized that our weakness was in the back office and administration. I was cooking, Maurice Rouas was in the front of the house, and Chantal took over the third leg of our business: all the administration from payroll to reservations to press relations to staff training. When I lost Chantal to the office, I had to train another pastry chef.

Over the years we did our own promotion by doing charity events and personal appearances around the world. We realized that meeting and greeting people in their own cities was very important. Then, whenever they would visit San Francisco, they would come to visit us at Fleur de Lys. We were able to do that because Maurice remained at the restaurant, making sure everything ran smoothly. People joked about Chantal and me that if you saw one of us, you always saw the other as well.

Roasted Maine Lobster with Artichoke Puree, Citrus Salad, and Orange Butter Sauce

Notes

RICK RICHARDSON, CHEF DE CUISINE, CREATED THIS DISH for the first New Year's Eve after the fire (see page 154). It became one of our most long-lasting menu items. "The secret to the dish," says Rick, "is the citrus butter sauce and the citrus salad." He changes these with the season. In March, when blood oranges come in, we use those; and in the fall, when pomegranates arrive, we scatter some of their seeds into the salad and on the plate. When tangerines are at their best, we use them instead of oranges.

Serves 4 as an appetizer or 2 as an entrée

♣ The drizzle of porcini oil "adds a taste and a look," says Rick. When the oil comes in contact with the warm lobster, its aroma is released. But in the mouth the flavor is not too strong because we use so little. It's one of those combinations that, when you marry them, it really works. You wouldn't be able to say, "I taste wild mushroom." The flavored oil gives you more depth of flavor rather than an identifiable flavor.

1	tablespoon plus 1 tablespoon freshly squeezed lemon juice
2	lemons
4	to 5 large artichokes
	Sea salt and freshly ground white pepper
¼	cup heavy cream or crème fraîche
¼	cup white wine vinegar
1	bouquet garni (page 65)
2	live lobsters (about 1½ pounds each)
3	tablespoons unsalted butter, chilled and cut into pieces, plus 2 tablespoons for brushing on the lobsters
1	large orange
1	lime
1	scallion, white and pale green parts, very finely sliced
½	teaspoon Dijon mustard
1	tablespoon extra-virgin olive oil
	About 1 cup freshly squeezed orange juice
	Porcini oil, for drizzling (optional)
	Pinch of toasted cracked coriander (optional)
1	heaping tablespoon finely chopped fresh chervil

To make the artichoke puree: Put a large saucepan of water on to boil. Prepare a medium bowl of cold water and add 1 tablespoon of the lemon juice. Cut 1 of the lemons in half; while you work on the artichokes, rub all the cut surfaces with the halved lemon to prevent discoloration. Trim the artichokes: Cut off the stems and the top third of the vegetables. Snap off the outer leaves until you reveal pale, tender green. Then, with a sharp paring knife, trim the artichoke bottoms, removing all the hard green skin. Drop the artichoke bottoms into the lemon water when done trimming to prevent oxidation.

Add a teaspoon of salt and the remaining 1 tablespoon of lemon juice to the boiling water and drop in the trimmed artichokes. Simmer until tender, about 25 minutes. Drain and let cool.

A poster drawn by Jacques Pépin for the James Beard Awards French evening in New York City in 1994.

146

Halve the artichokes lengthwise and scoop out and discard the fuzzy chokes. Slice the hearts into thin slices and put them in a small saucepan with the cream. Season with a pinch each of salt and pepper and bring to a simmer. Cook gently to meld the flavors, about 3 minutes. Scrape the mixture into a small food processor and puree until very smooth. Taste and adjust the seasoning. Return to the small saucepan and set aside.

To cook and clean the lobsters: While the artichoke hearts cook, prepare the lobsters. Bring a large stockpot of water to a boil. Add the vinegar, a good handful of salt, and the bouquet garni and simmer together for several minutes. Prepare an ice-water bath big enough for the lobsters. Add them to the stockpot headfirst, cover tightly, and poach for 9 minutes. The shells will have turned bright red and the meat will still be a little underdone. Remove the lobsters and immediately plunge them into the ice water to cool. Drain and break the lobsters in two, twisting where the tail meets the body. Turn the lobster belly up and, using scissors, cut through the shells down the length of the tails to remove the meat in one piece. Cut the tails in half lengthwise and remove the intestinal tube. Break off the claws, carefully crack the shells, and remove the meat in one piece.

Melt 2 tablespoons of the butter in a large ovenproof sauté pan over low heat. Remove from the heat and arrange the lobster meat in the pan, brushing it all over with the butter until well coated. Season lightly with salt and pepper. Set aside.

To make the citrus salad: Peel the orange, lime, and remaining lemon. With a small, sharp knife, first cut off the stem and flower ends, cutting through to the flesh. Stand the fruit up on one of the cut ends and cut off the remaining skin, again cutting down to the flesh. Working over a bowl to catch the juices, put the peeled fruit in the palm of one hand and cut between the membranes to loosen the segments. Cut the segments crosswise into 2 to 3 pieces each and place them in a separate bowl. Stir in the scallion. In a small bowl, whisk together 1½ teaspoons of the reserved citrus juices, the mustard, the olive oil, and a pinch each of salt and pepper. Gently toss the dressing with the citrus segments and set aside. Preheat the oven to 375°F.

To make the orange butter sauce: Pour the 1 cup orange juice into a small nonreactive saucepan and cook over medium-high heat until you have about 2 tablespoons remaining. Add 1 teaspoon of the reduction to the citrus salad. Remove the pan from the heat and whisk in the remaining 3 tablespoons of butter, a few pieces at a time. Return the pan to very low heat, if needed, and whisk until all the butter has been incorporated. It's important to regulate the heat so the butter emulsifies into the orange juice but does not completely melt. Season with salt and pepper and keep warm.

To serve: Rewarm the artichoke puree over low heat and pop the lobster into the oven just until warm through, about 3 minutes. Divide the artichoke puree equally among 4 warm dinner plates and arrange the lobster on top, giving each person half a tail and a claw. Spoon a little of the citrus salad over the lobster and the orange butter sauce all around. Add a few drops of porcini oil to the plate and finally sprinkle each plate with the coriander and chervil. Serve immediately.

Rabbit Ballotine
with Coconut-Piquillo Pepper Sauce

FOR FLEUR DE LYS, I ADAPTED A COLD RABBIT ballotine I used to do at La Prieuré in the Loire Valley, where I earned my first Michelin star as a very young chef. When we served it there, it was cut into thin slices, glazed with a thickened consommé, and accompanied by a frisée or celery salad. In this warm version, the rabbit is tender, sweet, and rosy. For the sauce I borrowed the flavors of a soup I created for the queen of Thailand, who booked our entire dining room during a visit to San Francisco.

Serves 4

2 large rabbits
1 tablespoon extra-virgin olive oil
1 stalk celery, chopped
1 medium carrot, peeled and chopped
1 small yellow onion, chopped
  Sea salt and freshly ground white pepper
½ cup dry white wine
4 cups low-salt chicken broth
1 cup coconut milk
½ stalk lemongrass, bashed and finely chopped (about 3 tablespoons)
2 (¼-inch-thick) slices peeled fresh ginger
1 large clove garlic, very finely chopped
1 tablespoon chopped fresh cilantro
1 tablespoon freshly squeezed lemon juice
2 teaspoons cornstarch (optional)
¼ cup ⅛-inch diced piquillo peppers
10 fresh basil leaves
1 tablespoon unsalted butter

Mousse

4 ounces rabbit leg meat
1 large egg, chilled
½ cup heavy cream, chilled
  Sea salt and freshly ground white pepper
2 dark green large leek leaves, about 10 inches long
¼ cup very small dice of carrot
1 large or 2 small piquillo peppers, drained and patted dry

To bone the rabbits: Save all the trimmings and bones in a bowl. You will need them for the sauce. First remove the back legs, then the forelegs and reserve these. With the rabbit belly up, cut through the backbone just above the hip sockets. Notice the loins running along each side of the backbone between the hips and the rib cage. With your knife, reach inside the rib cage and cut through the backbone to free the saddle.

Spread the saddle out in front of you. If the floating ribs are still attached to the saddle, cut them out. Make a shallow cut between the loins to free the tenderloins. Set the tenderloins aside. Then very carefully follow along the spine, freeing it from the meat without cutting through the skin side. It is very thin, and the spine nearly goes through the flesh in several places, so this is tricky work. Don't rush. Once you have freed one side of the backbone, turn the saddle around and free the second side. Lift the backbone out and add it to the bowl of trimmings.

To make the mousse: Bone 2 hind legs and remove any tendons. Cut the meat (you should have about 4 ounces by weight) into chunks and transfer it to the bowl of a small food processor. Add the bones to the other trimmings. Chop the carcass into pieces, put it in the bowl of trimmings, and set aside. Reserve the remaining hind legs for another use such as the Rabbit in Mustard Sauce (page 36).

Process the rabbit leg meat until finely ground. Season generously with salt and pepper and pulse in the egg until incorporated. Process until the mixture firms and holds against the sides of the bowl without slumping. With the machine running, very slowly drizzle in the cream. Scrape the mixture into a chilled mixing bowl, cover well with plastic wrap, and refrigerate for at least 15 minutes and for as long as a day.

Bring a medium pot of water to a boil and add a good pinch of salt. Prepare an ice-water bath. Add the leek leaves to the simmering water and cook until very tender but still very green, about 6 minutes. Pluck them out with tongs and immediately submerge them in the ice bath. Drain well, pat dry with paper towels, trim each to a 6-inch length, and set aside. Add the carrot to the boiling water and blanch briefly, just enough to soften it but not cook it all the way through, about 1 minute. Fish the carrot out and put in the ice-water bath to cool. Drain well and set aside.

Moisten a work surface and smooth out a long (about 12 inches) sheet of plastic wrap on it. Very finely chop and mash the piquillo peppers until you have 4½ teaspoons. Put them in a small bowl, add ¼ cup of the mousse, and mix until evenly incorporated. You should now have a pink mousse with red flecks.

Arrange a leek leaf lengthwise in the center of the plastic wrap. Spoon about half the pink mousse in a line down the length of the center of the leek. Use the plastic wrap to help you roll the leek around the filling until you have a tight "cigar" about ½ inch in diameter. Seal

the wrap tightly, tying the ends closed, and freeze for about 30 minutes or for up to 2 days. Repeat with the second leek leaf to make a second roll. Freezing them helps them hold their shape when the ballotine is cooked.

To make the sauce: Heat the olive oil in a medium Dutch oven over medium heat. Add the trimmings and bones and brown them well, stirring occasionally, about 10 minutes. Add the celery, carrot, and onion to the pan with a good pinch each of salt and pepper. Sear over medium to medium-low heat until nicely browned, 7 to 10 minutes. Add the wine and stir and scrape all over the bottom and sides of the pan to loosen any browned bits. Add the broth, bring to a simmer, and cook slowly, partially covered, for 1 hour. Add the coconut milk, lemongrass, ginger, garlic, cilantro, and lemon juice. Return the liquid to a simmer and cook gently, uncovered, until the flavors have melded, about 30 minutes. Strain the sauce into a clean saucepan; you should have about 1 cup. If you have more than that, boil and reduce to 1 cup to concentrate the flavors. Set aside.

To form the ballotine: With the point of a sharp knife, prick the belly flaps of the rabbit loins again and again to tenderize them. Moisten the counter again and spread another long (at least 20 inches) sheet of plastic wrap on it. Lay a rabbit saddle out on the wrap, with one belly flap coming toward you and the other away. The loin meat will then form 2 longer mounds parallel to the table edge. Take the tenderloins and place them next to the loins, positioning the thicker end of the tenderloin next to the thinner end of the loin so the mounds are more even along their lengths. Season with salt and pepper.

♣ Here in California, it is fairly easy to buy Meyer lemons. If you have access to them, use their juice for the sauce. Since they are less acidic than Eureka lemons, you can double the amount of lemon juice called for in the recipe.

♣ If you have leftover stuffing, you could shape it with a teaspoon into little quenelles and poach them gently in simmering water. They would be good garnishes for a soup.

♣ Perhaps the most important advice I could give you for this recipe is to make sure that your ballotines are wrapped watertight. Restaurant plastic wrap and aluminum foil are both wider than consumer wraps, so it is easier to wrap things watertight. To achieve this at home, you might consider wrapping the rolls in wrap both lengthwise and crosswise. Or invest in a roll of restaurant plastic wrap, available at restaurant supply houses and big-box stores. The aluminum foil is an essential step; the foil holds the ballotine's shape during poaching.

Mix the blanched carrot into the remaining rabbit mousse. Spread a little less than half of the mousse over the loins but not the belly flaps. Unwrap a leek cigar, trim it to match the length of the saddle, and lay it between the loins where the backbone was. Dab a little more mousse over the leek cigar to cover it. Lift up the belly flaps to the center so they overlap and nicely enclose the mousse. Wrap the plastic wrap tightly around the ballotine and tie the ends closed. The ballotine will be a sausage about 6 inches long and 2½ inches in diameter. Wrap the ballotine in a second layer of plastic wrap, tie closed, and then wrap in a tight layer of aluminum foil. Twist the ends of the foil so the sausage looks like a New Year's popper. Tie the ends tightly with string. Repeat with the second rabbit saddle and leek cigar. Try to roll the ballotines the same size so they cook through in an equal amount of time. The ballotines may be prepared ahead to this point in the morning before serving in the evening. Refrigerate. Let them sit at room temperature for 30 minutes before cooking.

To cook the ballotines: Bring a large pot of water to a very gentle simmer. It should barely bubble. Lower the ballotines into the water and poach for 15 minutes. If you are worried that your ballotine may not be watertight,

you might also seal the completely wrapped ballotines with a vacuum sealer and bag if you have them, or a heavy-duty resealable bag with all the air pushed out.

When ready to serve, reheat the sauce: Bring the sauce to a simmer over medium-low heat. Thicken the sauce a little, if needed; you want a silky, creamy texture, not a thick sauce. Place the cornstarch in a small jar with twice as much water, shake well, and dribble into the simmering sauce while whisking and watching for signs of thickening. Taste and adjust the seasoning. Stir in the remaining ¼ cup piquillo peppers. Stack 5 of the basil leaves, roll them up, and cut crosswise into a fine chiffonade. Repeat with the remaining 5 leaves and stir the chiffonade into the sauce. Keep warm.

To finish the ballotine: Peel the foil off the ballotines and trim off one end. Hold the second end of the wrap in one hand and pull while pushing the ballotine out of the wrap with the back of your knife. Heat the butter in a large skillet over medium heat. Transfer the ballotines to the skillet and roll them in the butter to color them a little, about 5 minutes. Slice each into 4 slices. Spoon some of the sauce onto 4 warm dinner plates and arrange 2 slices of the ballotine on top. Serve immediately.

Forty-One Years and Counting

MAURICE ROUAS AT FLEUR DE LYS, THE PERFECT PARTNERSHIP AS THE PERFECT MARRIAGE

One day I called him and asked him if he would stop by for a drink after work so we could talk. He walked the three blocks up Sutter to Fleur de Lys, and we sat in the corner of the little private dining room. I said, "I want you to join me not just as chef but as a partner." And Hubert was always very humble and polite. He said he needed to talk with his wife and that he didn't have any money to invest.

In 1970 my brother Claude Rouas and I took over Fleur de Lys. It had been opened by Charles and Sherry le Bougle in about 1960. The society decorator Michael Taylor did the decor, creating the signature tented dining room, and the restaurant became a great success because of it. Then, around 1973 or 1974, Claude decided to give me Fleur de Lys while he concentrated on L'Étoile and his new resort project in the Napa Valley, Auberge du Soleil.

But the French restaurant business had started going down in about 1982. Before that nearly every corner had a French restaurant. Now it was 1985. My business was not doing well. I had to do something. Then a chef came to San Francisco and started making noise. And that guy was Hubert Keller at Sutter 500. We became friends, and I wondered if I could get him for Fleur de Lys. But I knew that everyone in San Francisco wanted him to be their chef. Since they could offer salaries I could not afford, I had to offer him something else.

I answered, "You don't have any money, and I don't have any business. So let's stick together as equal partners and see what happens." When word got around that Hubert was coming to Fleur de Lys and that I had given him fifty percent of the business, some of my colleagues asked if I was crazy. But I said, "Together we are building something, and I would prefer to have fifty percent of something than one hundred percent of nothing." From the beginning we trusted each other so much. Hubert was the star here. And I give credit to Chantal and Hubert. They have wonderful taste. It was their ideas that lightened and refreshed Michael Taylor's original dining-room design.

In 2011 it was forty-one years since Claude and I opened a bottle of champagne to celebrate taking over Fleur de Lys. The same year Hubert and I celebrated our twenty-fifth anniversary. We are like an old married couple now.

—*Maurice Rouas, San Francisco, 2011*

Chestnut Soup with Pear, Walnut Oil, and Rabbit Loin

Notes

♣ You need only a single poached pear as the garnish for this recipe, but if you go to the trouble to make it, you might think about poaching 4 and serving them as a quick dessert on another night with a dollop of crème fraîche or ice cream.

♣ You will use just the loins of the rabbit for this recipe. Use the legs for the Rabbit in Mustard Sauce (page 36) and save any extra bones and trimmings for stock. See page 148 for instructions on boning a rabbit, if needed. You could also substitute chicken tenders for the loins, cooking them just as you do the rabbit.

MANY OF OUR REGULAR CUSTOMERS come every New Year's Eve. That night, everything on the menu is new. In this dish I wanted to push a little beyond a traditional chestnut soup. I thought to introduce rabbit; you would not automatically put rabbit and chestnut together. We fanned the loins in the bottom of soup plates. We added a little round of puff pastry, just the size of a single bite and stuffed with a surprise of celery root puree. We poached pears in red wine, cut them vertically into wedges, and then fanned one out in each plate as well. Pears are so good with chestnuts. The waiters put the garnished soup plates in front of the diners, poured in the soup, and drizzled toasted walnut oil over the top. For this version, I've streamlined the garnishes a bit.

Serves 4 to 6

Poached Pear

1 cup fruity, dry red wine such as a pinot noir
1 star anise
1 small cinnamon stick
1 ripe but firm pear, peeled, halved, and cored
3 tablespoons sugar

Soup

2½ tablespoons unsalted butter
1 medium onion, chopped (about 1 cup)
1 large leek, white and light green parts, finely chopped (about 1 cup)
Sea salt and freshly ground black pepper
1 cup dry white wine
4 cups low-salt chicken broth
1½ pounds prepared packaged chestnuts
1 large pear, peeled, cored, and diced
1 large clove garlic, crushed
1 teaspoon ground cardamom
¾ cup heavy cream
1½ tablespoons toasted walnut oil

Rabbit

2 boneless rabbit loins (about 2 ounces each and ¾ inch diameter)
Sea salt and freshly ground black pepper
1½ tablespoons unsalted butter

To poach the pear: In a small nonreactive saucepan, bring the wine, star anise, and cinnamon stick to a boil over high heat. Simmer gently for 5 minutes to meld the flavors. Add the pear and cook very gently, turning the halves occasionally, until the pear is tender, about 15 minutes. Remove from the heat, add the sugar, and transfer the pear and cooking liquid to a bowl or container and let cool. Cover and refrigerate overnight so the pear can soak up flavor and color.

To make the soup: Heat the butter in a large sauté pan over medium heat. Add the onion and leek, season with salt and pepper, and cook until the vegetables are very soft, about 10 minutes. Do not let them color. Add the wine, broth, chestnuts, pear, garlic, and cardamom and bring to a boil. Simmer, uncovered, until the flavors have melded and the chestnuts are very soft, about 45 minutes. Let cool.

Puree the soup in a blender or food processor until very smooth. Pour it through a fine sieve into a clean saucepan and whisk in the cream and walnut oil. Heat over medium heat to just below a simmer and taste for seasoning. Keep hot. Just before serving, pour the soup into a warm pitcher.

When ready to serve, slice the pear very thinly crosswise. Season the rabbit loins well with salt and pepper. Heat the butter in a medium skillet over medium heat. Add the loins and roll them gently in the butter just until they are lightly colored and cooked through, about 3½ minutes. Transfer the loins to a cutting board and let rest for a minute. Then slice on the diagonal into nice ¼-inch-thick slices.

Have your soup plates warm and fan some of the pear slices in the bottom of each with some of the rabbit loin slices. Present each diner with a garnished soup plate and pour the soup over.

Fire!

By 2001, after years of our hard work, we owned the restaurant and our building. That year we completely remodeled Fleur de Lys, including an earthquake retrofit. We put everything we had back into the business. Then that fall, one night after service was over and everyone had gone home, a fire started. It destroyed the restaurant entirely.

The first night after the fire, Chantal and I sat together at home. We didn't really know what had happened to us. The second night, we were home. The third night we were home. On the fourth night we were at home. For the first time since we had known each other, we had eaten at home four days in a row. We realized that we had to get out; we couldn't continue sitting at home and thinking of what had happened.

We had never been as deeply in debt as we were then. Because of the remodeling, we had zero reserves. After the fire, we hoped that in two months we would reopen. Then it was three, four, five, six, seven, and more. We paid our employees for the entire time. Then the process stretched on so long that we exhausted the insurance. We had to dig into our pockets as deeply as we could.

During the eleven months it took to reopen, we were sometimes pressed so hard against the wall that we knew we could not pull it off. But each time, we found a solution. Still, we were running out of steam. There were a few times when we said to ourselves, "Let's quit the whole thing and move to an island; it would be easier." We wondered if customers would come back after so long. Finally, ready or not, we had to open. At 4 p.m., the drills and lots of equipment were still lying around everywhere. We opened up the construction chute to the outside and slid everything down, because at 6 p.m., guests would be walking in.

Local television news had covered the fire, so we contacted them to see if they might want to cover our reopening. And we were lucky— nothing happened in the news that day to preempt us. And our loyal clientele arrived; everybody came back. It was a long and very busy day. But we were so happy. Then Chantal went home and I stayed on. Later I drove home. It was really late. I was in my car and I had the most amazing feeling: *Yes! We are part of something again.*

During all those months at home, Chantal and I decided we needed to branch out. To no longer pour everything we had into the one restaurant. And that's when Mandalay Bay came to us and asked us to open a Fleur de Lys in its resort in Las Vegas. And that led to Burger Bar. And Burger Bar led to the next thing.

Corn Madeleines with Cracked Black Pepper

AT FLEUR DE LYS WE BAKE SWEET AND SAVORY VERSIONS of madeleines. To accompany the crab and truffle cappuccino (page 144), I wanted to play with the idea of having a madeleine on the side of a cup of cappuccino as we do in France. To make it American, we thought to use corn; cornbread is definitely not French. We also serve these madeleines with our New York Strip Buffalo Steaks with Coffee Spice Rub (page 165).

Makes 24 to 30 (3-inch) madeleines or about 36 mini muffins

- 1 generous cup (6 ounces) cooked corn kernels
- 2 tablespoons extra-virgin olive oil
- 3½ tablespoons sugar
- 2 large eggs
- 1 teaspoon sea salt
- ½ cup and 2 tablespoons heavy cream
- ½ cup and 3 tablespoons (3½ ounces) fine cornmeal
-    Scant ½ cup (2 ounces) unbleached all-purpose flour
-    Unsalted butter for buttering molds, melted, or nonstick cooking spray
-    About 2 teaspoons cracked black pepper

Preheat the oven to 375°F. Place the corn kernels in a food processor with the oil, sugar, eggs, and salt. Process until the mixture is fairly smooth. Add the cream and pulse briefly. Pour the batter into a large mixing bowl and whisk in the cornmeal and flour just until smooth. Do not overmix. Cover and refrigerate for at least 15 to 20 minutes and for as long as several hours.

Brush the madeleine molds with butter and drop a few grains of the cracked pepper in the bottom of each. Fill each mold entirely with the corn mixture. Place the molds on one or two baking sheets and bake until the madeleines are firm and light gold, about 15 minutes. Rotate the pans halfway through baking. Let the breads cool in the molds and then carefully push and pry them out with your thumb. Serve them warm. Rewarm, if necessary, in a slow oven before serving.

Spiced Corn Madeleines

At Fleur de Lys we add a house spice mix to the cracked black pepper corn madeleines. If you feel adventurous, I encourage you to give it a try. Mix the 1½ teaspoons spice mix with the cornmeal and flour, then add the dry ingredients to the wet as directed.

- ½ teaspoon Spanish hot paprika
- ½ teaspoon ground cinnamon
- ¼ teaspoon curry powder
- ¼ teaspoon freshly grated nutmeg

Notes

♣ Piping the batter into madeleine molds is the easiest way to fill them, especially if you're using the 1½-inch molds. If you don't have madeleine molds, use mini muffin pans and sprinkle the cracked pepper over the cornbread instead of in the bottom of the molds.

155

Spicy Sesame Kettle Corn

RICK RICHARDSON, CHEF DE CUISINE, OFTEN CHANGES THE MENU offerings in early spring. "I wanted something new to serve as part of the vegetarian menu canapé," said Rick. He worked with Antonio Gonzales, Jr., a second-generation cook at the restaurant. His father, Antonio Gonzales, Sr., also worked for us at Fleur de Lys and now owns his own pizza restaurant in San Francisco. Rick continued, "For some reason, I had a lot of white sesame seeds in house and wanted to use them up. Antonio and I would brainstorm ideas, taste, brainstorm, and Antonio would try again, until we came up with this assertively spicy, sweet corn."

Makes about 12 cups

¼ cup extra-virgin olive oil

½ cup raw popcorn

4 tablespoons (½ stick or 2 ounces) unsalted butter cut into pieces

1½ cups (10½ ounces) sugar

½ cup sesame seeds (preferably a mixture of black and white)

1 teaspoon red chili flakes, or more for heat

Sea salt

Heat the oil in a large, deep pot over high heat. Add the popcorn, cover, shake the pot well, and pop the corn.

When the pot is quiet, working quickly over medium-high heat, add the butter and then sprinkle the sugar little by little over the popcorn, stirring all the while with a very large spoon. The sugar will melt and caramelize, coating the popcorn. Keep moving the pan off and on the heat to regulate the temperature. You want the sugar to caramelize but not burn. Keep adding sugar until the popcorn is evenly coated with a medium-brown caramel. While continuing to stir, add the sesame seeds.

Remove the pot from the heat and immediately sprinkle the chili flakes and salt to taste over the popcorn, stirring and tossing all the while. Taste and adjust the heat with more chili flakes if you like. Scatter on a baking sheet to cool. The kettle corn tastes best the same day, but because of the sugar coating, if kept well sealed in a container it will stay crisp for a couple of days.

Chicken-Liver Mousse with Smoked Duck Ham and Pineapple-and-Vanilla Consommé

Notes

♣ You can find both styles of duck ham at specialty food shops and online. One source I found for smoked duck breast is Marky's (www.markys.com).

♣ In order to be most like a real consommé, the pineapple and vanilla mixture must be strained twice. You will lose some of the vanilla seeds, but they will also be well dispersed.

♣ You can bake the mousse in individual 2- or 4-ounce molds. Turn them out and serve them warm as a side dish with a chicken breast, for instance. Our testers loved leftovers as a sandwich filling. Give it a try.

THIS STYLIZED, MODERN PRESENTATION of chicken-liver mousse is a play of textures and flavors. The combination of sweet pineapple with its undercurrent of tartness and the salty ham really works with the rich liver. For the elegant restaurant presentation shown, we put the mousse on top of a layer of duck geleé. There are two kinds of duck ham: one more like prosciutto (dry-cured) and one more like ham (brined and then smoked). We use the ham-style duck breast at Fleur de Lys. But you can also substitute prosciutto very successfully.

Serves 10 to 15 as an appetizer

Mousse and Presentation

Unsalted butter, for buttering baking mold and aluminum foil
1 slice white bread, crusts removed
2 tablespoons cognac
5 ounces whole chicken livers, trimmed of connective tissue
2 large eggs
2 large egg yolks
¾ cup heavy cream
1½ cups low-salt chicken broth reduced to ¾ cup and cooled
1 tablespoon finely chopped fresh flat-leaf parsley
2 teaspoons finely chopped fresh thyme
2 cloves garlic, very finely chopped
1 teaspoon sea salt
½ teaspoon freshly ground black pepper
½ fresh pineapple, peeled but not cored, and cut lengthwise into slices about ¼ inch thick
Sugar, for sprinkling on pineapple slices
10 to 15 thin slices smoked duck ham or prosciutto (see Notes)
10 to 15 small pineapple leaf tips
30 or more Marcona almonds, blanched and toasted

Consommé

1 fresh pineapple, peeled but not cored
4 teaspoons unseasoned rice vinegar
½ teaspoon sea salt
Sugar, for sweetening pineapple if needed
1 vanilla bean, preferably Tahitian

To make the chicken-liver mousse: Preheat the oven to 350°F. (Do not use convection.) Butter a 3-cup glass or ceramic mold such as a terrine or loaf pan. Bring a kettle of water to a boil. Break the bread into pieces and place it in a bowl. Pour the cognac over and let it soak for several minutes. Transfer the mixture to a blender or food processor with the chicken livers, eggs, egg yolks, cream, reduced broth, parsley, thyme, garlic, salt, and pepper. Blend until very well pureed and push through a fine-mesh sieve into the prepared mold.

Place the mold in a larger pan that is deeper than the baking mold. Place it on the oven rack and pour the boiling water into the large pan until the water reaches about halfway up the mold. Bake for 20 minutes.

Meanwhile, butter a sheet of aluminum foil large enough to cover the baking pan. When the 20 minutes are up, place the foil, buttered side down, on top of the pan, making sure the foil does not touch the mousse, and do not seal the foil around the larger pan. You want the steam to be able to escape; the foil prevents a skin from forming. Continue to bake until the mousse feels firm to the touch and a tester inserted in the middle of the mousse comes out clean, about another 20 minutes. Uncover, let cool, and refrigerate.

To make the pineapple-and-vanilla consommé: Cut the pineapple into chunks

158

and puree it in a blender with the rice vinegar, salt, and 2 tablespoons of water until very smooth. Taste and add sugar to taste if needed. You should have about 3 cups. Transfer the puree to a bowl. Scrape the seeds from the vanilla bean into the puree and drop in the pod. Cover and refrigerate for at least 1 hour and preferably 2 hours. Push the puree through a fine-mesh sieve into a bowl and repeat. You should have about 2½ cups. Cover and chill until needed.

To prepare the pineapple garnish: Cut 30 to 40 small decorative shapes such as small circles or diamonds from the pineapple slices. Sprinkle them lightly with sugar and caramelize the tops with a pastry torch or under the broiler. Watch carefully so the pineapple does not char. Set aside until needed.

When ready to serve, arrange a slice of mousse in each rimmed soup plate. Ruffle up the duck ham slices and arrange them on top of the mousse. Tuck a pineapple leaf tip into the mousse so it stands up. Lay the caramelized pineapple pieces and the almonds in a pattern around the mousse and then carefully ladle in some consommé. Serve. The mousse will keep, covered well and refrigerated, for about 5 days.

Three Strong Guys in the Kitchen

The three of us—Chantal, Maurice Rouas, and I—run Fleur de Lys like a family business. And I am proud that we have been partners for more than twenty-five years. But two of my chefs have been with me for even longer. Rick Richardson (shown with me, below) and Remberto Garcia have worked with me since our years at Sutter 500. And in the kitchen, it's a family business, too. None of us really have titles. But Rick, who has been with me since 1983, could be called the chef de cuisine. Usually, he is just "Rick" or "Chef."

By 1984 Rick had become my chef at Sutter 500. Shortly after I moved to Fleur de Lys, I brought him over because I needed one strong person who knew by heart the cuisine I was doing. Soon I brought over Remberto Garcia, my sous chef, from Sutter 500 as well. We were then overstaffed, but we were gambling that once I started introducing my new dishes and the restaurant kicked in, we would need them. At the beginning, for the little income we had, Maurice, Chantal, and I decided to invest in these two chefs. We personally did not pay ourselves.

And the best part? It worked. We couldn't know that both local and national press articles would line up like they did. It was not even a dream. But when they were published and the restaurant took off, I had my two strong chefs overseeing the kitchen. And I was always there, too, so we were three solid guys in the kitchen.

Halibut Cheeks on a Bed of Basquaise, Red Wine Essence, Fingerling Potatoes, and Speck

Notes

♣ If you make this dish with halibut fillets or steaks instead of cheeks, increase the cooking time to about 3 minutes per side. Do not overcook; halibut can so easily dry out.

THERE ARE LOTS OF BIG, BOLD FLAVORS HERE that combine the earthiness of Alsace cuisine and the colorful, aromatic qualities of Mediterranean cooking. When Chef Rick Richardson puts together a new dish, he often adds ingredients that are characteristic of Alsace. For instance, he added speck to the potatoes here. Speck is a sort of smoked prosciutto. Like prosciutto, it is made from a pig's back leg; but unlike prosciutto it is boned before it is salt-cured with spices, and it is cold-smoked. In this recipe, the final touch of a quail egg is also a reminder of traditional French cuisine, where it is common to have a sunny-side-up egg on dishes (see the frisée salad with poached egg, page 60), so the yolk blends with the ingredients to make a rich sauce.

Serves 4

Red Wine Essence

- 2 small to medium heads garlic, unpeeled and halved crosswise
- Sea salt and freshly ground black pepper
- 1½ teaspoons extra-virgin olive oil, plus more for drizzling
- 3 tablespoons very finely chopped shallots
- 2 cups pinot noir
- 1 cup ruby port
- 1½ teaspoons finely chopped fresh thyme
- 3 cups low-salt chicken broth or beef broth, boiled until reduced to 1½ cups
- 1 tablespoon unsalted butter

Halibut and Potatoes

- 1¼ to 1½ pounds fingerling potatoes (about 14)
- 6 tablespoons extra-virgin olive oil, divided
- Sea salt and freshly ground black pepper
- 2 thin (1/16-inch-thick) slices speck or prosciutto, cut into small squares (about ¼ cup)
- 1 small yellow onion, thinly sliced
- 1 bay leaf
- 1 to 2 cloves garlic, thinly sliced
- 1 (10-ounce) jar piquillo peppers, cut into strips about 1½ inches long and ¼ inch wide (9 or 10 peppers)
- 2 tablespoons nonpareil capers
- 1 tablespoon liquid from caper jar

- 1 teaspoon finely chopped fresh thyme
- 12 halibut cheeks, halibut steaks, or large sea scallops (about 1¼ pounds)
- Unbleached all-purpose flour, for dusting
- 4 quail eggs (optional)
- Spicy Paprika Oil (page 192), for garnishing plates

To prepare the sauce: Preheat the oven to 400°F. Put the garlic in a small baking dish, season with salt and pepper, and drizzle with olive oil. Cover tightly and bake until the garlic cloves have begun to pop out of their skins, about 30 minutes. Uncover and continue to bake until the garlic is very soft and browned, about another 15 minutes. Let cool and squeeze the pulp out of the skins. Try to keep at least half of the roasted garlic intact. Set aside.

Heat the olive oil in a medium saucepan over medium heat, add the shallots, and cook until tender but not browned, about 2 minutes. Add the pinot noir, port, and thyme. Bring to a boil and cook until reduced to about ¼ cup, about 15 minutes. Add the broth and continue to boil until reduced to ½ to ¾ cup, about 20 minutes. Scrape the liquid into a blender, add half the roasted garlic, and blend until smooth.

Push the sauce through a sieve into a clean saucepan, place over low heat, and whisk in the butter. The butter should soften and emulsify into the sauce. Whisk in the remaining roasted garlic cloves and taste for seasoning. If the sauce is too thick, stir in a little water to thin. Keep the sauce warm.

To make the potatoes: Slice the fingerling potatoes into small disks the thickness of a nickel. Wash the sliced potatoes, drain, and dry them with kitchen towels. Heat 2 tablespoons of the olive oil in a large nonstick skillet over medium-high heat. Add the potatoes, season with salt and pepper, and cook—stirring and tossing—until they are tender and well browned, about 25 minutes. Taste and adjust the seasoning with salt and pepper. Toss with the speck and keep warm.

Meanwhile, prepare the basquaise: Heat 1½ tablespoons of the remaining olive oil in a skillet over medium heat. Add the onion, bay leaf, and a pinch of salt and cook until tender but not browned, about 10 minutes. Add the garlic for the last minute or two. Add the piquillo peppers, season with salt and pepper, and cook, stirring, for about 3 minutes. Add the capers, caper juice, and thyme. Stir well and cook just until all is hot, about 30 seconds. Be careful to keep the *basquaise* warm or hot, but don't let it overheat; the oil would start frying the ingredients, and you would not end up with the same result.

To cook the halibut: Season the fish with salt and pepper. Dredge the fish in flour and shake off any excess. Heat 2 tablespoons of the remaining olive oil in a large nonstick skillet over medium-high heat. Add the fish and cook until golden brown, about 1 minute. Turn over and cook the second side until browned and the fish is just cooked through, another 1 to 2 minutes.

While you cook the fish, put another nonstick pan over medium heat and add the remaining ½ tablespoon of olive oil. Crack in the quail eggs, lower the heat, and fry the eggs gently until the whites are just set but the yolk remains runny.

Arrange the potatoes in the centers of 4 warm dinner plates. Place the halibut on the potatoes. Spoon the *basquaise* on top of the fish and then spoon the red wine sauce all around the fish. Top the *basquaise* with the quail eggs. Dot the plates with the paprika oil and serve immediately.

Pepper-Flecked, Slow-Roasted Swordfish with a Cardamom-Carrot Infusion

JACQUES MAXIMIN FIRST INTRODUCED ME to vegetable-based sauces such as this one when we worked together at Le Chantecler on the Côte d'Azur. I've streamlined his recipe a little. This is a very clean, simple dish with the sparkle of pepper on the fish and a pretty, delicious yet healthy, low-fat sauce made from reduced carrot juice infused with cardamom. You could use the same sauce with sautéed chicken breasts, a veal medallion, or grilled sea scallops.

Serves 4

- 2 teaspoons extra-virgin olive oil, plus more for brushing
- 4 skinless swordfish steaks (about 5 ounces each and ¾ to 1 inch thick)
  Sea salt
  About ½ teaspoon cracked black pepper
- 1 cup fresh carrot juice
- 1½ teaspoons unseasoned rice vinegar
- ½ teaspoon cracked green cardamom pods (about 6)
  Freshly ground white pepper
  Sugar, for sweetening the sauce
- 1½ teaspoons cornstarch
- 2 cloves garlic, very finely chopped
- 1 pound fresh pea shoots or baby spinach

Preheat the oven to 250°F and oil a baking dish or sheet pan that will fit the fish in a single layer. Brush the swordfish with olive oil and let sit in the prepared pan at room temperature for a few minutes. Season the swordfish on both sides with salt and sprinkle the top with the black pepper. Cover with parchment paper and then seal tightly with aluminum foil. Bake until the fish is just cooked through and the flesh begins to flake, about 45 minutes.

Swordfish is a delicious and expensive fish, so you want to be careful with your timing. Check your fillets first at about 30 minutes, because ovens always vary and you do not want to overcook your fish. Also, swordfish dries out quickly once cooked, so have your sauce ready, the pea shoots sautéed, and your plates warm so you can serve immediately.

Meanwhile, place the carrot juice in a small nonreactive saucepan. Add the vinegar, cardamom, a pinch each of salt and freshly ground white pepper, and a pinch of sugar. Bring to a boil, lower the heat, and simmer very gently, uncovered, for 10 minutes. The juice may separate while it simmers, but it will come back together when you thicken it into a sauce. Cover the pan and let the cardamom infuse the carrot juice for another 10 minutes. Strain through a fine-mesh sieve into a clean small saucepan and return to a gentle simmer. Put the cornstarch in a small lidded jar with twice as much water and shake well. Add the cornstarch mixture little by little while whisking and watching for signs of thickening. Shake before each addition. The finished sauce should have the consistency of heavy cream. Taste for seasoning and sweetness and add more salt, white pepper, and sugar as needed. Keep the sauce warm. If the sauce gets too thick, thin it with the cooking juices from the pan.

Heat 2 teaspoons of olive oil in a large skillet over medium heat. Add the garlic and cook just until the garlic is soft and fragrant, about 1 minute. Add the pea shoots to the skillet with the garlic. Toss and cook just until the shoots have wilted and turned bright green, about 1 minute. Season with salt and pepper.

Divide the pea shoots among 4 warm dinner plates and arrange the fish on top. Spoon the cardamom-carrot sauce around and serve immediately.

Notes

♣ If you have the time and curiosity, make the carrot sauce the way we did originally: Braise carrots in a covered pot over low heat with salt, pepper, a little butter, and a very small amount of broth, white wine, or water. Cook until the carrots are very, very tender. Uncover and cook off any remaining liquid. Then puree the carrots in a blender with just a touch of cream until very smooth. You will have to work to get the mixture to puree. Put the puree through a fine-mesh strainer and add a few tablespoons to the carrot juice to thicken it.

Building a Clientele

The transition from the old Fleur de Lys customers to a newer audience had its ups and downs. We didn't know if we were going to succeed. But Maurice always supported and encouraged me. He never suggested that I go back to this or that dish that had been customer favorites. He proudly introduced me to all of his customers as the new chef. One evening, shortly after I started changing the menu and implementing my own dishes, Maurice introduced me to one of his best customers. The man barely looked at me and said directly to Maurice—as if I were not standing there—"Let me tell you something. If you want to make sure your business continues, you better buy a couple of cookbooks. Because your chef doesn't know how to cook."

Laurent's Creamed Corn with Parmesan

LAURENT PILLARD, our corporate chef, came up with this simple and delicious corn dish to accompany meats and roast chicken. We used to serve a seared tuna over a creamed corn like this at Fleur de Lys. When we made the creamed corn then, we infused the cream with fresh ginger and then folded tomato and thinly sliced scallions into the finished dish. I suggest serving this more streamlined version with the buffalo steak with coffee spice rub on the opposite page.

Serves 4

- 4 large ears fresh corn
- 1½ cups low-salt chicken broth
- ⅓ cup heavy cream
  Salt and freshly ground white pepper
  Pinch of sugar (optional)
- ½ small bunch chives, cut into 1-inch sticks
- ½ cup freshly grated Parmesan cheese

One by one, stand the corn up in a bowl and slice the kernels off with a chef's knife. You should have about 4 cups. In a large sauté pan, bring the chicken broth to a boil over medium-high heat. Add the corn and cook, uncovered, until the pan is nearly dry, about 10 minutes. Add the cream and simmer until thick, about 5 minutes. Season with salt and pepper and perhaps a pinch of sugar. Stir in the chives. Scrape the corn into a warm serving dish and sprinkle with the Parmesan. Serve immediately.

New York Strip Buffalo Steaks with Coffee Spice Rub

IN 2010 CHEF DE CUISINE RICK RICHARDSON started thinking about a new buffalo dish for Fleur de Lys. "I free-associated: *buffalo, cowboy coffee, Wild West flavors.*" We serve the steak with the Corn Madeleines with Cracked Black Pepper (page 155) and a red wine sauce flavored with a little of the spice rub and a very small amount of bittersweet chocolate. At home, especially in the summer, serve the steak with creamed corn (page 164) and a sliced tomato salad. Use the rub on red meats that can stand up to the coffee and spice, including beef or buffalo roasts, steaks, and burgers; lamb; venison; and elk.

Serves 4

Spice Rub

Makes ¾ cup rub

- ½ cup finely ground or high-quality instant espresso
- 2 tablespoons ancho chili powder
- 1 teaspoon ground chili árbol powder or hot Spanish paprika
- 1 teaspoon dark brown sugar
- 1 teaspoon dry mustard
- 1 teaspoon Spanish sweet smoked paprika
- 1 teaspoon ground coriander
- 1 teaspoon ground cumin
- 1 teaspoon kosher salt
- 1 teaspoon freshly ground black pepper

- 4 New York boneless buffalo strip steaks (about 8 to 10 ounces each and 1¼ inches thick), well trimmed
- ¼ cup extra-virgin olive oil
- 2 tablespoons unsalted butter
  High-quality extra-virgin olive oil, for drizzling

To make the spice rub: In a medium bowl, whisk together the espresso powder, the ancho and árbol chili powders, and the sugar, mustard, paprika, coriander, cumin, salt, and pepper. Store in a tightly sealed jar, preferably in the freezer.

To cook the steaks: Have your steaks at room temperature. Rub the meat all over with a generous coating of rub. Make sure the rub seals the steaks well. Tap off any excess. Let them sit for about 15 minutes before cooking.

I cook these steaks on top of the stove instead of grilling them to protect the rub from burning. So have your pans hot enough to sear the meat, but don't allow the pans to get so hot that they smoke. Heat 2 large heavy skillets over medium heat. Add 2 tablespoons of olive oil to each skillet, then add 2 steaks to each. Let them sear on the first side until browned, about 3 minutes. Then turn, add a tablespoon of butter to each pan, and sear the second side for another 3 minutes. Baste the steaks with the fat in the pan. Remove from the heat and let rest for 5 minutes before serving. This timing should give you medium-rare meat. Buffalo is so lean that if you cook it longer it can easily get too dry. Serve the steaks on warm dinner plates and drizzle each with a little high-quality olive oil.

Notes

♣ You can use any chili powder in place of the ancho chili powder, including New Mexican, pasilla, or California chili powder. If you want even more heat and spice, add some chipotle chili powder.

Marinated Venison Chop with Cacao-Nib Sauce and Cacao-Nib Tuile

THE INSPIRATION FOR THIS DISH from Fleur de Lys dates back to my apprentice-ship. It's an updated variation on *le lièvre à la royale*, a complicated and rich wild rabbit preparation that is part of the classic French repertoire and very popular in Alsace. L'Auberge de L'Ill was well known to have one of the best versions of the dish. One of the secrets was that at the end of cooking a little chocolate was added to the sauce—just enough to add depth and complexity. By infusing the sauce for the venison with cacao nibs you get a hint of chocolate, but it is not overpowering. It's only when you bite into the cacao-nib tuile that you can recognize the slightly bitter and nutty chocolate flavor. Cacao nibs are unsweetened, fermented, and roasted cocoa beans. I think Pierre Hermé of Fauchon was one of the first chefs to launch the popularity of cacao nibs about a dozen years ago. They are used basically as you would any nut—in salads and desserts. When you cook with cacao nibs, you get a chocolate flavor, but if you bite one it is not like biting into choco-late. At first it's sort of nutty, and then when you crack it between your teeth you think: *Oh, it tastes sort of like chocolate.*

Serves 4

Tuiles

Makes 60 or more cookies, depending on the size

- 9 tablespoons (4½ ounces) unsalted butter, at room temperature
- 10 tablespoons (4½ ounces) sugar
- 1 cup and 2 tablespoons (4½ ounces) cake flour
- 6 tablespoons (4 ounces by weight) corn syrup or liquid glucose
- ¼ cup (1 ounce) cacao nibs, crushed

Venison

- 1 venison rack (about 2½ pounds) (see Note)
- 1 large carrot, cut into ½-inch dice
- 1 medium yellow onion, cut into ½-inch dice
- 1 stalk celery, cut into ½-inch dice
- 2 cloves garlic, peeled and crushed
- 2 large sprigs fresh thyme
- 2 bay leaves
- 5 whole juniper berries, lightly crushed
- 1 (750-milliliter) bottle dry red wine (preferably low-tannin)
  About 4 tablespoons extra-virgin olive oil, divided
- ¼ cup (1 ounce) cacao nibs, lightly crushed

About 2 cups low-salt beef broth
- 1 tablespoon tomato paste
  Sea salt and freshly ground black pepper
- 1 tablespoon cornstarch

To make the tuiles: In the bowl of a stand mixer fitted with the paddle at-tachment, beat together on low speed the butter, sugar, and flour until evenly incorporated. On low speed, mix in the corn syrup, 1 tablespoon of water, and the cacao nibs until evenly combined. Cover and refrigerate the dough for at least 30 minutes and up to several days. When cold, the dough is easier to handle. If it is too stiff, let it soften at room temperature for a few minutes. The dough can also be frozen for up to several months.

Preheat the oven to 350°F. Line 2 bak-ing sheets with baking mats or parch-ment paper. Pinch off a nut of dough about 1½ inches in diameter. With wet hands, pat the dough onto one of the prepared baking sheets into an evenly flat disk about 4 inches in diameter. Place only 2 disks on each sheet, be-cause the dough spreads in the oven to 6 or 7 inches across or more. Bake the

Notes

♣ Farm-raised venison is available year-round. The meat became popu-lar about fifteen years ago. It was the leanest red meat available other than ostrich. The flavor is very mild, and the meat is very tender. When purchased, some venison racks are very clean and well trimmed, and others are not. Have your butcher remove the silver skin for you, but ask for it and any other trimmings (for instance, from frenching the rib bones) so you can use them for your sauce. If you do not have a butcher who can order the venison, it can be found on the In-ternet from Broken Arrow Ranch (www. brokenarrowranch. com).

Notes

♣ Make sure the wine you choose for the marinade is not too tannic. The wine will be greatly reduced for the sauce, and reducing will emphasize bitter tannins.

♣ The lacy tuiles are a sort of cross between a candy and a cookie. Once you've made the dough, you can make just as many cookies as you need and freeze the remaining dough. We have made many versions over the years incorporating poppy seeds, peanuts, cracked black pepper, cubeb pepper, and almonds. You could add orange zest or a teaspoon of ground ginger. Have fun!

cookies until very brown and caramelized, about 10 minutes. Remove from the oven and let the cookies sit very briefly on the baking sheets to firm up. Then quickly lift them off to a work surface and cut them into desired shapes. At Fleur de Lys we cut them into narrow triangles about 6 inches tall. If the cookie gets too hard to cut and starts to shatter, simply return it to the oven briefly to soften.

You can also drape the still-warm cookies over rolling pins to give them an attractive curled shape; wrap them around a dowel to form a cigarette shape; or fit them over the backs of muffin cups and pinch them into basket shapes. If you want to form small rounds, use a nut of dough about ⅓ inch in diameter.

Once the cookies have cooled, store them in a covered container. They will stay crisp for several days.

To prepare the venison: Trim the rack by first removing any silver skin. Save the skin in a bowl. If the rib bones are not completely clean, scrape them clean with the back of a knife and save those trimmings with the silver skin. If the meat is ragged and uneven at either end, trim it and add the meat to the trimmings bowl. Turn the rack bone side up with the bones facing away from you. At the base of each rib you will find a small triangular knuckle bone. Cut them loose and add them to your trimmings. Cover and refrigerate your trimmings. Place the rack in a nonreactive container or heavy-duty plastic bag. Add the carrot, onion, celery, garlic, thyme, bay leaves, juniper berries, and enough wine to

cover the meat. Cover and refrigerate overnight. If using a plastic bag, turn it over occasionally.

The next day, drain, dry, and cut the rack into 4 double chops. You can simply cut between each two-rib section, or, because the rack tapers slightly from one end to the other, I eyeball the portions to even their size. I might cut, for example, a single-rib chop on the thicker end or cut closer to the bone of one chop instead of dead center. Remove one of the rib bones from each chop by cutting it out near the knuckle. Add these bones to your trimmings. Now each portion looks like a very thick single chop.

Strain the marinade, reserving the vegetables and the liquids separately. Place the liquid in a nonreactive saucepan and bring to a rapid simmer over medium-high heat. Skim well for several minutes, remove from the heat, and set aside. Simmering and skimming the wine marinade allows the blood to coagulate and rise to the surface so you then have a clear liquid as the base for your sauce.

In a skillet over medium-high heat, add a tablespoon of oil and brown the bones and meat trimmings, 5 to 10 minutes. Add the reserved vegetables to the skillet and another tablespoon of oil, if needed. Cook and stir until the vegetables have browned, about 10 minutes. Add the cacao nibs and the skimmed marinade, bring to a boil over high heat, and boil until the liquid has reduced by two-thirds. Add enough beef broth so that the vegetables and bones are generously covered. Return to a simmer, stir in the tomato paste, and cook until the sauce has reduced to about 1 cup. Strain the sauce into a large measuring cup and discard the solids. Defat the sauce if needed.

♣ The volume amounts may not be exact equivalents of the weight measures, but they are easier to measure. When the dough is baked on nonstick baking mats, the holes will be quite small. The mats insulate the cookies a bit as they bake. On parchment paper the holes will be larger as the dough spreads more than it does on baking mats.

Pat the chops dry and season well on both sides with salt and pepper. Heat a large heavy skillet over medium-high heat and add the remaining 2 tablespoons of oil and the chops. Lower the heat a little and sear the chops nicely on one side, about 4 minutes, and then turn and sear the second side for another 4 minutes. Transfer them to a plate and let rest for 3 to 4 minutes. Pour off the fat, if any, from the skillet, add the reserved sauce, and stir and scrape all over the bottom of the pan to loosen all the browned bits. Because the pan will be very hot when the sauce is added, it may reduce too much very quickly. You can simply add a little more broth until you have at least ½ cup of sauce.

Put the cornstarch and 2 tablespoons of water in a small lidded jar and shake it well. Drizzle about half the mixture into the sauce and simmer gently while whisking and watching for signs of thickening. Continue adding more of the cornstarch—shaking before each addition—and then simmering, until you have a glossy, smooth sauce with the thickness of heavy cream. Taste the sauce and adjust the seasonings with salt and pepper.

To serve, pour some of the sauce in the center of each warm dinner plate. Center the chop on top, place a cacao-nib tuile to the side, and serve immediately.

Individual Peach Strudels
with Lavender Crumble

ONE DAY I WAS PLAYING AROUND WITH PHYLLO DOUGH and came up with this fun technique for wrapping fillings. It's not complicated to do, but it looks good and the pastry gets, and stays, really crisp all over. This is a twist on strudel, and you could make a cool little apple strudel, too, stuffed with sautéed apples and raisins. But with this technique, you can make your pastries any size and fill them with savory fillings, too—for instance, a fish mousse (perhaps scallops studded with lobster chunks) or choucroute, as we've done at Fleur de Lys.

Serves 6

Peach Filling

- 1 tablespoon unsalted butter
- 1½ pounds ripe peaches (3 to 4 good-sized fruits), peeled, pitted, and chopped, or apricots, unpeeled and chopped
- 1 tablespoon freshly squeezed lemon juice
- ⅓ cup sugar, or more or less, depending on the sweetness of the fruit
- 1 tablespoon Amaretto almond liqueur (optional)

Lavender Streusel

- ¼ cup (1¼ ounces) unbleached all-purpose flour
- ¼ cup (¾ ounce) finely ground almonds
- ¼ cup (1¾ ounces) sugar
- ½ teaspoon dried lavender flowers, crumbled
  Pinch of sea salt
- 5 tablespoons (2½ ounces) unsalted butter, chilled and cut into about 10 pieces

Caramel Sauce

Makes 1 cup sauce

- ½ cup heavy cream
- 1 large strip fresh lemon zest
  Pinch of sea salt
- 1 cup (7 ounces) sugar
  Freshly squeezed lemon juice

Assembly

- 8 tablespoons (1 stick or 4 ounces) unsalted butter, plus more for buttering the molds
- 9 sheets phyllo dough (about 18 by 13 inches)
- 6 individual brioche à tête molds (3½-inch diameter at the rim) or jumbo muffin cups

To prepare the filling: Melt the butter in a large skillet over medium heat. Add the peaches and lemon juice and bring to a boil. Simmer to cook off the juices the peaches release, stirring all the while so the peaches do not scorch. Sprinkle the sugar over the peaches and continue to cook and stir until the peaches are tender and the mixture is thick. Add the liqueur for the last minute of cooking. Set aside and let cool.

To make the streusel: Place the flour, almonds, sugar, lavender, salt, and butter in a food processor. Pulse quickly until the mixture resembles coarse crumbs. Scrape into a bowl and set aside.

To make the sauce: In a small saucepan, heat the cream, lemon zest, and salt just to a boil. Set aside. In a large heavy saucepan, heat the sugar and ¼ cup water together over medium-high heat, stirring, until the sugar has dissolved. Boil, watching the pan carefully, until the mixture turns a medium golden color. Immediately remove the pan from the heat and, standing back to avoid being splattered, add the cream. Return the pan to the heat and stir until the sauce is smooth and returns to a boil. Remove the lemon zest and discard. Taste the sauce and add a squeeze of lemon juice if you like. Pour the sauce into a bowl or pitcher and set aside until needed. Cover and refrigerate if made a day ahead. Reheat over very low heat or in the microwave.

To assemble the strudels: Preheat the oven to 375°F. Butter the molds. Clarify the 8 tablespoons butter: In a small saucepan or skillet, melt the butter over low heat. Skim off any foam, let cool slightly, and pour the clear liquid portion off the milky solids into a bowl.

Lay a sheet of phyllo on a work counter and brush it generously with some of the butter. Lay another sheet of phyllo on the first and butter it. Repeat with a third sheet. Trim the edges and cut the sheet into 6 (5-inch) squares. You will need 3 triple-ply squares per strudel. Lay 1 triple-ply square on top of another, rotating the top one by 45° so that you have an 8-pointed star. Fit the pastry into one of the molds to form a cup. The corners should stick up above the top of the mold by about an inch or so. Repeat until all the molds are lined.

Spoon ¼ to ⅓ cup filling into the center of a third triple-ply square and fold the pastry over the filling to enclose it. Carefully fit the little packages, seam side down, into the phyllo-lined molds. Repeat until you have 6 individual strudels. Sprinkle each with a generous tablespoon or more of the streusel. Bake until browned and very crisp, 15 to 20 minutes. To serve, warm the caramel sauce gently and pour a circle of it onto the dessert plates. Lift the strudels out of their molds and center them on the sauce. Serve immediately while still warm.

The Power of the Press

Herb Caen, the powerful columnist at the *San Francisco Chronicle*, used to come into Sutter 500 and sit in a corner because he didn't want attention. But whatever he ordered, even a sandwich, I dropped everything, made it for him, and brought it to him. I think his grandfather was from Lorraine (Lorraine, like Alsace, is now a *département* of France; the two areas used to be called Alsace-Lorraine and have gone back and forth between Germany and France for centuries), so maybe he felt some kinship for us. And he liked Maurice, too. Maurice tells me that his brother Claude and Herb Caen were best friends, and Mr. Caen was in L'Étoile (owned by Claude) nearly every night.

Everyone read Herb Caen's daily column, and a mention there meant a lot. When he heard from Maurice that I would be moving to Fleur de Lys, he reported it. That was really big news for us. Then, two months later, out of the blue on a Friday morning Mr. Caen wrote, "Since Hubert Keller has been cooking at Fleur de Lys, it is hard to get a table." The telephone started ringing, and that was the first Friday we were packed.

Make-Ahead Dark Chocolate Soufflé

SOUFFLÉS ARE ONE OF THE OLDEST RECIPES IN FRENCH PASTRY, and they have always made a statement. You can imagine how chefs sweated over their egg whites, beating them into the proper lofty volume, before the invention of electric mixers. I think many home cooks are afraid to make a soufflé, fearing that their spectacular height and airy texture are too hard to achieve. But a soufflé can be a practical dessert for a dinner party: The base may be prepared in advance and refrigerated. Before you sit down for dinner, preheat the oven, have your egg whites in a covered mixing bowl, and have your molds prepared and lined up on a counter. Then during a break for dessert—this will heighten your guests' anticipation—all you need to do is whip the whites, fold them into the room-temperature soufflé base, divide the mix between the molds, and slip them into the oven. We serve soufflés at both Fleur and Fleur de Lys. It's such an old dessert that it's new again. And it is one of our most popular desserts.

Makes 8 (6-ounce) individual soufflés or 1 (1½-quart) soufflé

Soufflé Molds

About 4 tablespoons (½ stick or 2 ounces) unsalted butter, softened
Sugar, for dusting

Soufflés

8 tablespoons (1 stick or 4 ounces) unsalted butter

10 tablespoons all-purpose flour

2 cups whole milk

6 ounces semisweet chocolate (at least 60% cacao), chopped into small pieces

2 ounces unsweetened chocolate, chopped into small pieces

1 cup (7 ounces) plus 1 teaspoon granulated sugar

2 tablespoons vanilla extract

2 tablespoons dark Jamaican rum (optional)

8 large egg yolks

10 large egg whites

½ teaspoon cream of tartar

¼ cup (1 ounce) powdered sugar, for dusting

1 pint premium vanilla ice cream (optional)

Dark Chocolate Sauce for serving (page 174)

To prepare the molds: Preheat the oven to 375°F and place an oven rack at the lowest level. Butter the molds well with the softened butter and dust the bottoms and sides evenly with sugar: Pour about 2 tablespoons of sugar into each, then tilt and tap the mold so the sugar covers all the surfaces. Tap out excess sugar into the next mold. Continue, adding more sugar as needed, until all are coated. Arrange the molds on a baking sheet and set aside until needed.

To make the soufflé: In a medium saucepan over medium heat, melt the butter. Whisk in the flour and whisk and cook for about 3 minutes to cook the flour. Do not let it brown. The roux should be very smooth. Remove the pan from the heat and set aside.

In a small saucepan, heat the milk over low heat just until it comes to a slow simmer. Whisk in the semisweet chocolate and the unsweetened chocolate until melted. Add the 1 cup sugar, vanilla, and rum, and whisk until smooth.

While whisking, gradually pour the chocolate mixture into the roux in the saucepan. Return the saucepan to low heat and cook, whisking continuously, until the mixture thickens and begins to bubble, 5 to 7 minutes. Off the heat, whisk in the egg yolks one at a time until fully incorporated.

Notes

♣ If you want to save yourself a little work, omit the chocolate sauce and use ice cream. Melt half of it for your sauce to pass at the table, and then give each guest a generous scoop of ice cream on the side of the soufflé.

173

Scrape the soufflé base into a large mixing bowl. If you are preparing it ahead of time, press a piece of plastic wrap directly onto the surface and refrigerate until later. When you are ready to finish the soufflés, put the base in a warm place in the kitchen so it can soften and warm to room temperature or about lukewarm. This will ease folding the whites into the base.

In the bowl of a stand mixer fitted with the whisk attachment, beat the whites with the remaining 1 teaspoon of sugar and the cream of tartar. Start on low speed until the whites are frothy and then gradually increase the speed to high. Beat until soft peaks form.

With a large rubber spatula, scrape about one-fourth of the whites into the soufflé base. Stir until the whites are evenly combined with the base. Add half of the remaining whites and fold them gently into the soufflé base, using big strokes and rotating the bowl with your other hand to maintain the airiness of the whites. Fold in the remaining whites using the same technique.

Divide the mixture evenly among the molds, filling them three-fourths full. Bake the soufflés until they have risen high over their rims and the tops have browned lightly, 12 to 14 minutes.

As soon as the soufflés are done, dust them lightly with the powdered sugar, place them on dessert plates, and add a generous scoop of ice cream to each plate. At table, have the guests poke a small hole in the middle of their soufflés and pass the chocolate sauce.

Dark Chocolate Sauce

Makes about 2 cups

This is a deeply flavorful sauce that is simple to make. It keeps very well in the refrigerator, so you can always have it on hand for your milkshakes (page 226), the dark chocolate soufflé, and, if you dare, the Sweet Pea Ice Cream (page 192).

- ¾ cup heavy cream
- ½ cup (3½ ounces) sugar
  Finely grated zest of ½ orange
- 8 ounces semisweet chocolate (at least 60% cacao), chopped

Place the cream, sugar, ½ cup of water, and the orange zest in a small saucepan and bring to a boil. Place the chocolate in a small bowl and pour the hot cream over it. Cover and let sit for a few minutes until the chocolate has softened. Whisk it until smooth and then keep it warm. When ready to serve, pour the sauce into a warmed pitcher to pass at the table. The sauce can be made up to several days ahead and rewarmed on low in a microwave oven.

174

Espresso-Chocolate Mousse
with Caramelized Bananas

Notes

♣ Chocolate
mousse is a classic
of French cuisine.
The eggs are not
cooked, so if this
concerns you,
you might skip
this recipe or use
pasteurized egg
products to make
it. I recommend
buying very fresh
eggs, preferably
pasture-raised eggs.
Their rich flavor
will enhance the
mousse.

♣ If you plan to
serve the mousse in
glasses or ramekins
and not shaped
into quenelles, you
don't need to add
the gelatin.

AT FLEUR DE LYS WE MAKE THIS MOUSSE nearly every day. Chantal frequently treats herself to a spoonful of it; I think she uses it as her afternoon pick-me-up instead of a cup of coffee. The recipe calls for gelatin and belonged to Mr. Chen, one of the chefs my partner Maurice Rouas had hired before my arrival at the restaurant. It's a wonderful mousse, and that's why we've kept it all this time. The only change was to add the espresso.

Serves 8

1½ tablespoons powdered gelatin
¼ cup fresh espresso or coffee
8 ounces bittersweet chocolate, chopped (at least 60% cacao)
1⅓ cups heavy cream
5 large eggs, separated
⅓ cup plus 2 tablespoons sugar
4 bananas (optional)
   Brown sugar for sprinkling (optional)
   Lightly sweetened whipped cream (optional)
8 organic fresh rose petals

Place the gelatin in a small saucepan and pour the espresso over it. Let the gelatin soften for a few minutes. Place the pan over low heat and whisk until the gelatin melts and the mixture is smooth.

Heat a pan filled with an inch of water to a very gentle simmer. Put the chocolate in a heatproof bowl and place it over, but not touching, the water. Let the chocolate soften and then stir it with a rubber spatula until smooth. Set it aside.

Whip the heavy cream in a large bowl until it forms soft mounds. Be careful not to overwhip it. Cover and refrigerate until needed.

In a stand mixer, whisk the egg yolks on high speed until they have doubled in volume and become thick and nearly white, about 8 minutes. While the yolks are beating, bring the ⅓ cup of sugar and 2 tablespoons of water to a boil in a small saucepan. Cook until

the sugar syrup reaches the soft-ball stage (235°F). With the mixer running, very slowly pour the syrup into the yolks. Continue to whisk on high for 2 minutes. Turn the machine to low and whisk in the melted gelatin and then whisk in the chocolate until smooth.

Scrape the mixture into a large mixing bowl. Whisk the egg whites in another large mixing bowl until frothy. Add the remaining 2 tablespoons sugar and whisk on high until they form soft peaks. With a large rubber spatula, stir about one-third of the egg whites into the egg-yolk mixture to lighten it. Then gently fold in the rest. Gently and carefully fold the whipped cream into the egg mixture until evenly combined. Cover and refrigerate for at least 1 hour or until serving time. The mousse tastes best when just made—you can serve it even before it has completely set—but will keep, well covered and refrigerated, for about 3 days.

When ready to serve, cut the bananas in half crosswise and on a diagonal. Without cutting all the way through to the end, slice the halves lengthwise into thin slices. Fan them out on a baking sheet and sprinkle with brown sugar. With a pastry torch, melt and caramelize the sugar. Carefully transfer a banana to each dessert plate and scoop a quenelle of mousse next to it. Add a dollop of whipped cream and a rose petal.

A Wine List Anchored by 1947 Cheval Blanc

In 1986, when I came to Fleur de Lys, we didn't have money to invest in wine. But as a high-quality French restaurant, we had to have a good wine list. We had a couple of top vintages that had been sitting in the cellar forever, and even now I remember some of them—for instance, a Cheval Blanc 1947. We had only enough money to buy wines we expected to sell immediately, or as we say in French, *les vins du bataille*—that means they come in, they go out. For the remainder of the list, I turned to the wine and liquor store that used to be across the street from us. They were into wines and had a good selection. We worked out a deal so that I could put my list together from what they had on their shelves. Then, when a guest ordered one of those wines, either Maurice or another of us would go over to the shop and get the bottle.

But for many years running now, *Wine Spectator* has given Fleur de Lys's wine program a Best of Award of Excellence. In the late '80s and '90s, we invested in a serious wine program, buying and cellaring wines. Now we focus on classic regions such as Bordeaux and Burgundy and California and feature all the great wines of Alsace. Under the guidance of Marcus Garcia, our dining room manager and sommelier, our list has become more expansive and flexible. Marcus has been with us for about a decade now, so I will let him describe our wine program and how he works with our guests.

Marcus Garcia: "We complement the notable French and California wines with international selections from up-and-coming wine regions as well as wines from very small wineries whose winemakers are so full of passion. Many of our wines are grown and made using organic, sustainable, and even biodynamic methods. Some are from friends and neighbors. Usually we feature these wines as part of our wine-pairing program.

"We love showcasing Alsace wines as part of our wine-pairing program, too, because they work so well with Chef's cuisine. It's a nice introduction, to be able to say: 'This is from Chef's home region.' We even carry wines from Ribeauvillé.

"When planning wine pairings, whether the dish is vegetarian, vegan, or whatever, my rule is 'flavor first.' Each element of the dish should bring out something in the wine, and vice versa. I want to create excitement around the pairings; the flavors should pop. For instance, we have a petrale sole on the menu with Dungeness crab, caviar, sea urchin, and a little spice component. A white Burgundy would be a great match, but this is also an opportunity to be able to incorporate a wine from Alsace. A classic gewürztraminer has a richness and a touch of sweetness that brings a refreshing balance to the spicy elements of the dish. The combination explodes flavor-wise because of the contrast of the saltiness of the caviar and the slight sweetness of the wine.

"That's what our pairings try to do: to hit on all cylinders. And people want to be surprised. We don't want to lose that element of surprise, because it is part of the adventure our guests take when they dine here."

We offer nonalcoholic pairings even to nondrinkers and children, so no one needs to feel like an outsider. Sometimes we'll have a couple come in and the wife will be very pregnant. You can tell this is probably the last time they will be going out before the baby arrives, so it is a special night for them. Here in the U.S. women don't usually drink during pregnancy and are accustomed to drinking water. But imagine how she feels when we say, "Let us surprise you with a pairing for your meal tonight." And then, with each course a different concoction of juices and purees arrives made especially for the menu and for her.

Gilberto's Beignets

GILBERTO VILLARREAL, PASTRY CHEF OF FLEUR DE LYS, and I have been teaching and learning from each other for years. This is his version of *boules de Berlin*, a delicious, tender doughnut my father used to make only at Carnaval time, just before Lent begins. Gilberto gives his dough a Latin flavor and richness with sweetened condensed milk and evaporated milk. He bakes the dough to use as buns for our dark-chocolate dessert burger (included in my cookbook *Burger Bar*). When fried, the breads are called *beignets*. At home when my dad made them, my brother and I would fill them with raspberry or orange jam. That was definitely something special for when we got off from school.

Makes about 20 beignets or mini buns to serve 6 to 8 (about 20 ounces of dough)

- ½ cup and 1 tablespoon warm evaporated milk (105°F)
- 1 envelope (¼ ounce) active dry yeast
- 2 tablespoons (0.7 ounce) sugar, plus more for sprinkling
- 2 cups (10 ounces) unbleached all-purpose flour, plus more for dusting the work surfaces
- ⅓ cup sweetened condensed milk
- 1 large egg
- 4 tablespoons (½ stick or 2 ounces) unsalted butter, cut into pieces
- 1 egg yolk, beaten lightly with 1 teaspoon water if baking
- Turbinado sugar, for dusting if baking
- 1 cup granulated sugar mixed with 1 teaspoon ground cinnamon if deep-frying
- 6 cups vegetable oil if deep-frying

Place the evaporated milk, yeast, and 2 tablespoons sugar into the bowl of a stand mixer and whisk well. Cover and set aside in a warm place until the mixture begins to foam, about 15 minutes.

Add the 2 cups flour, the condensed milk, egg, and butter to the mixing bowl and fit the mixer with the dough hook attachment. Knead until the dough is very stretchy and slaps against the side of the bowl, 15 to 20

minutes. It may remain sticky and not entirely form a ball around the dough hook. Cover the bowl with plastic wrap and leave it in a warm place for the dough to rise until doubled in size, about 1 hour. When ready, the dough will not spring back when poked gently with a finger.

Punch the dough down and turn it out onto a floured work surface. Line two baking sheets with parchment paper. Divide the dough into 1-ounce pieces and shape them roughly into balls: Hold each piece of dough beneath your cupped palm. Rotate your hand in quick circles until the dough forms a nice, smooth ball. Let the dough stick very slightly to the counter to help pull it into a tight ball. Arrange the balls on the baking sheets, leaving plenty of space between the balls. Let them rest in a warm place to rise until fully risen and puffy, about 1 hour.

To bake the beignets: Preheat the oven to 350°F. Press the dough balls down lightly to form 2-inch circles. Brush the tops with the beaten egg yolk and then dust with turbinado sugar. Bake until medium gold, about 10 minutes. Rotate the pans front to back and top to bottom halfway through the baking time. Cool on a rack. The buns are best eaten the same day they are baked, but they keep—wrapped in a paper or plastic bag—for a day or two at room temperature. They also freeze very well.

To fry the beignets: Heat the 6 cups of vegetable oil to 320°F. Line a sheet pan with paper towels and put the cinnamon-sugar in a large bowl or paper bag. Fry the beignets, a few at a time. Cook until brown on their undersides, about 2 minutes. Carefully turn them over with a skimmer and fry until the second side is brown, about 1 minute. Cook, turning the beignets occasionally, until they are medium brown, about 5 minutes total. Regulate the heat so the beignets do not brown too quickly and form a crust before they properly expand. They do not puff much in the fryer because they will have fully risen before frying. Briefly drain the beignets on the prepared sheet pan. Toss them, while still warm, with the cinnamon-sugar and serve immediately.

Pioneer

Seeking Adventure & Finding My Own Path

UPENDING EXPECTATIONS

A NEW MODEL FOR
FRENCH RESTAURANTS IN AMERICA

WHEN I FIRST ARRIVED IN SAN FRANCISCO, I felt I was fighting against the belief in America that French cuisine was rich, heavy, and full of eggs, butter, and cream. Unfortunately, it was true of most of the French food in the city. But in France, there had been the whole movement toward *nouvelle cuisine* and *cuisine légère*. Roger Vergé, Jacques Maximin, and Michel Guérard, the chefs who had trained and inspired me, had led the way, removing cream and the classic roux from sauces and using vegetables in new ways.

In San Francisco, I continued to cook in this "new style" while remaining true to my classic French training. I wanted to prove

"I remain true to my classic French training while cooking in a light, naturally healthy style."

From left: Chantal and me running on the beach in San Francisco. That's Alcatraz behind us. In the kitchen at Fleur by Hubert Keller, Las Vegas. Desert flowers outside the city.

Pages 180 and 181: Riding my old bike out into the Nevada desert at sunup.

to my guests that they could enjoy a French twelve- or fourteen-course dinner (that was what we did then) and not feel over-stuffed. Although I created the Crab and Avocado Salad with Watermelon Gazpacho (page 188) years later, it demonstrates this idea of reimagining dishes in a new, lighter presentation.

I wanted to change our guests' experience in the dining room, too. In those days when people ate at a French restaurant, they expected to get a bit of an attitude from the maître d' and waitstaff. Maurice, Chantal, and I wanted to cut out all that pretension, because for us it is all about making people feel good. One of my favorite quotes that captures our philosophy is this one from

Left to right: The entrance to Fleur inside the Mandalay Bay casino. Saucepans ready on the stove. In the Oval Office with President Clinton. Making Mini Tuna Tacos with Avocado-Lime Cream (page 216).

Maya Angelou: "I've learned that people will forget what you said, people will forget what you did, but people will never forget how you made them feel."

Back then, every French restaurant had a beautiful menu written in French and translated extremely poorly into English. For example, the translation for the dish Filet Henri IV—filet mignon with béarnaise sauce served in a hollowed-out artichoke heart—would simply read "Filet Henri IV." You had to know what that meant or ask. So the first thing we did at Fleur de Lys was to write our menu only in English. Then people could understand what they were ordering.

And at every French restaurant, the waiters were dressed formally in tuxedos. We cut that out and put the waiters in a relaxed-but-elegant uniform with long, fitted aprons, vests, and shirts with white sleeves. At the time, a female was not the proper person to be on the floor. Guests expected a waitress at a coffee shop but not in an upscale restaurant. Fleur de Lys was the first to put female staff on the floor. And behind the bar, too. Those waiters and waitresses were Americans; they could explain to our guests in a friendly and clear manner what we were trying to do.

Creating All-Vegetable Tasting Menus

When I started cooking in the U. S., if you were a vegetarian, from a French chef's perspective, you were not very welcome. The chef

would be upset because you wouldn't try one of his dishes. But I could feel that being vegetarian was taking root. I felt it was not just a trend, but becoming a permanent lifestyle choice. As soon as I got to Fleur de Lys, I created a multi-course vegetarian menu, on the same level as the regular menu degustation. It had the same attention to detail in taste, creativity, and presentation, the same care in wine pairings.

At Fleur de Lys the customers could order and eat exactly what they wanted. Our philosophy is to cater to our clientele and to accommodate their needs and wishes. Back then—and it is still true today—if a party of six arrived and one was a vegan, one was on the Atkins diet, and another followed Dr. Ornish's regimen, while the rest preferred the regular menu, all of them could have exactly what they wanted. The waiters were trained; the kitchen was trained. It was not a surprise. We were ready for it. I applied all my skills and creativity to the vegan menu so the guest could say,

"I never had a vegan menu like that before." We always want the customers to be happy, to be impressed by their experience, but not intimidated. That's why we feature both a veggie burger and a vegan burger at our Burger Bars.

In this chapter, I've included a number of recipes—some with their roots in my apprenticeship and some with a more current inspiration—that could be assembled into a vegetarian menu.

You could start with the deeply flavored Truffled Onion Velouté Shooters (page 201), then clear your palate with a raw vegetable salad of asparagus, radishes, and mushrooms (page 204), and then move on to the surprise of a creamy burrata cheese paired with a cool, elegantly green sweet pea ice cream (page 192). One of my favorites is a dish that reminds me of the smells and flavors of the south of France, a turnip confit with orange, ginger, and rosemary (page 197).

Many people come to Las Vegas and never see the spectacular desert scenery outside the city. The colors are subtle and vibrant at the same time. Sunrise and sunset are the best times to be in the desert.

Crab and Avocado Salad
with Watermelon Gazpacho

THIS IS ONE OF THE FIRST DISHES WE CREATED for Fleur by Hubert Keller's opening in Las Vegas. But its roots go back to my apprenticeship at L'Auberge de L'Ill, where we had Salade de Langouste Paul Haeberlin on the menu. It was an avocado and lobster salad with a sauce Andalouse. No one had seen an avocado before. At that time featuring an avocado at a three-star restaurant was the most exotic thing, and then with lobster! Nobody knew what the sauce was, either. It was mayonnaise, ketchup, a little lemon juice, a big dice of black truffle, and quartered tomato.

Serves 4

1 pound ripe seedless watermelon
Sea salt and freshly ground white pepper

1 teaspoon sherry vinegar, plus more for seasoning

1 cup fresh lump crabmeat

1 teaspoon finely chopped fresh flat-leaf parsley

¼ cup peeled and seeded cucumber in ⅛-inch dice

¼ cup peeled and seeded sweet red bell pepper in ⅛-inch dice

¼ cup red onion in ⅛-inch dice

1 tablespoon extra-virgin olive oil, plus more for brushing
Juice of about 2 large lemons

3 ripe but firm avocados
Handful of microgreens, finely sliced fresh chives, or smoked sea salt flakes (optional)

Scoop the watermelon flesh into a blender and puree. Season the puree with a good pinch each of salt and pepper and 1 teaspoon of sherry vinegar. Taste and adjust the seasoning with more salt, pepper, and vinegar as needed. The flavor should have a very slight acidic edge to it. Chill well.

In a mixing bowl, toss the crabmeat with the parsley, cucumber, bell pepper, onion, olive oil, and a splash each of sherry vinegar and lemon juice. Season to taste with salt and pepper and adjust with more vinegar or lemon juice as needed. Chill well.

Cut the avocados in half lengthwise and scoop out the flesh in one piece. Slice the avocado halves on a diagonal into very thin slices. Cutting on a diagonal gives longer pieces to work with. Moisten the work surface and spread out a piece of plastic wrap about 10 by 12 inches. Brush the wrap lightly with olive oil and drizzle with lemon juice. In the center of the plastic wrap, arrange 2 slices of avocado in a wide, upside-down V. The ends at the point of the V should overlap by about ½ inch. Arrange another 2 slices below these, slightly overlapping the ones above and again overlapping their ends by a ½ inch. Repeat twice more to form a rough square with a sort of herringbone pattern.

Arrange a heaping tablespoon of crab salad in the center of the avocado slices. Pick up the corners of the plastic wrap so the avocado encloses the crab. Twist the ends together, tighter and tighter, until you have a tight little purse. Repeat until you have 8 little balls. You can keep the balls wrapped and refrigerated for several hours.

When ready to serve, get ready 4 shallow soup plates. Twist the plastic wrap around each ball so tightly that it snaps out of the wrap at the base. Stir the watermelon gazpacho and ladle ½ inch or so into each bowl. Add 1 or 2 avocado balls. Top with microgreens, chives, or sea salt flakes and dot the gazpacho with olive oil. Serve immediately.

HOW TO SHAPE THE CRAB & AVOCADO SALAD

Cut the avocado halves into very thin, steep
diagonal slices.

Arrange the avocado in a herringbone pattern,
overlapping the slices in the middle by about ½ inch.

Pick up the corners of the plastic wrap. As you twist
them, the avocado forms a ball around the crab.

Keep twisting; the wrap stretches so tightly that the
ball pops out of the wrap into your hand.

Burrata with Sweet Pea Ice Cream, Pickled Cherry Tomatoes, and Spicy Paprika Oil

Notes

♣ Burrata is a small ball of mozzarella cheese filled with cream. *Burrata* means "buttery." It's just delicious, and best when eaten very fresh. It is beginning to appear in retail stores as more is imported and American artisanal cheese makers start production. Call your specialty cheese store and ask if they carry it and, if so, when deliveries are scheduled. Then plan your menu. A good substitute would be very high-quality, fresh and creamy mozzarella.

♣ If you have a garden, experiment with various mints in the ice cream. I like the delicate texture and sophisticated flavor of Persian mint.

AT FLEUR IN LAS VEGAS, we serve burrata with pickled tomatoes. But for this recipe, I thought to add another element to make this a special dish for a vegetarian menu or a surprising appetizer for a dinner party. If you add more frisée salad, you could serve this for lunch with a freshly baked baguette. To add crunch, I used the potato crumbs I have used before to encase a fillet of sea bass. Here the crumbs make a crisp, salty nest for the creamy, sweet ice cream. I've not tried the ice cream with Dark Chocolate Sauce (page 174), but something tells me it would be good.

Serves 4

Spicy Paprika Oil

Makes 1 cup oil

1   cup grapeseed or other neutral-flavored oil
1   tablespoon Spanish hot paprika
1   tablespoon ground chipotle chili

Pickled Cherry Tomatoes

¾   cup apple cider vinegar
4   teaspoons kosher salt
1   tablespoon sugar
3   to 4 sprigs fresh thyme
2   cloves garlic, thinly sliced
1   lemon
1   pint cherry tomatoes, grape tomatoes, or pear tomatoes, or a mixture

Sweet Pea Ice Cream

Makes 5 cups

1½   pounds sweet green peas, shelled (about 1½ cups or 8 ounces), defrosted if frozen
¾   cup whole milk
     Sea salt
1¼   cups heavy cream
3   large eggs
½   cup (3½ ounces) sugar
1   packed teaspoon very finely chopped fresh mint, such as Persian mint

Presentation

1   large Russet potato, peeled
     About 3 cups canola oil, for deep-frying
     Sea salt and freshly ground black pepper
2   tablespoons extra-virgin olive oil

1½   teaspoons freshly squeezed lemon juice
     Large handful baby frisée lettuce
4   balls (about 4 ounces each) burrata cheese
     Fleur de sel or other coarse-grain salt
1   teaspoon finely chopped fresh mint, such as Persian mint
     Edible flowers (optional)

To make the paprika oil: Place the grapeseed oil in a small saucepan over low heat. Heat until very warm, 1 minute. Remove from the heat and whisk in the paprika and chipotle. Set aside for 45 minutes to let the flavors infuse the oil. The paprika and chipotle will settle to the bottom of the pan. Decant the oil into a small piping bottle. Store in a cool, dark place. It will keep for at least several weeks.

To pickle the tomatoes: Pour the vinegar and ¾ cup water into small nonreactive saucepan. Add the salt, sugar, thyme, and garlic. Using a vegetable peeler, zest the lemon, dropping the strips into the saucepan as you go. Bring to a boil over medium-high heat while stirring to dissolve the salt and sugar. Remove from the heat, transfer to a medium bowl, and let cool for 20 minutes. Meanwhile, pierce each tomato twice with the tip of a sharp knife or a skewer. Add the tomatoes to the brine, cover, and let sit at room temperature for at least 2 hours and up to 8 hours. Refrigerate. The tomatoes can be made 1 to 2 days ahead of time.

To make the sweet pea ice cream: If using frozen peas, do not cook them but move directly to pureeing them with the milk. Bring a large saucepan of water to a boil over high heat and add a teaspoon of salt. Meanwhile, prepare an ice-water bath. Add the peas to the boiling water, lower the heat, and simmer until just bright green and tender, about 8 minutes. Drain and then plunge them immediately into the ice bath to stop the cooking. Drain well and transfer the peas to a blender with the milk and a good pinch of salt. Puree until very smooth and then push through a fine-mesh sieve to obtain a fine puree. Scrape it into a bowl, cover, and refrigerate.

Prepare an ice-water bath and set a medium mixing bowl in it. Place the cream in a medium saucepan and bring just to a boil over medium-high heat. Turn off the heat. Meanwhile, in another medium bowl, beat the eggs and sugar together until foamy. While whisking vigorously, slowly pour the hot cream into the eggs. Pour the mixture back into the saucepan, place over low heat, and cook while stirring continuously until the custard is thick enough to coat the back of a spoon (about 175°F), 5 to 7 minutes. Do not let the custard boil. Immediately strain the custard through a fine sieve into the mixing bowl in the ice bath. Let cool, stirring occasionally, until chilled.

When the custard is cold, stir in the pea puree until smooth. Transfer the mixture to an ice-cream maker and freeze according to the manufacturer's instructions. While the ice cream is freezing, finely chop the mint leaves. Stir them into the ice cream while still soft and then transfer it to a shallow container. Cover and freeze until needed.

For the presentation: Begin by making the potato crumbs. Cut the potatoes with a mandoline into 1/16-inch julienne strips. Rinse very well under cold running water to remove the starch. Drain and dry thoroughly, squeezing the potatoes in kitchen towels. Line a baking sheet with paper towels.

Pour the canola oil into a medium deep pan to a depth of 2 inches and heat to 360°F. When hot, add the potatoes in 2 or 3 batches and fry until golden brown, about 4 minutes. Transfer the potatoes with a large skimmer to the prepared baking sheet and season well with salt. When cool enough to handle, coarsely chop them and store in an airtight container.

In a small bowl, whisk together the olive oil, lemon juice, and salt and pepper to taste. Place the frisée in another small bowl, drizzle a little of the vinaigrette over it, and toss well. Taste for seasoning.

Arrange a burrata on each plate. Season with fleur de sel and arrange a small mound of frisée on top of the cheese. Spoon the remaining vinaigrette over and around the cheese. Top the frisée with a small pinch of the mint and add a few edible flowers. Drizzle some of the paprika oil over and around the cheese. Next to it arrange the pickled cherry tomatoes. Make a small bed of potato crumbs on each plate and top with a quenelle or nicely shaped scoop of the sweet pea ice cream. Don't wait before serving.

♣ Make the paprika oil ahead of time and keep it in a small squeeze bottle. We use it at our restaurants more for color than for flavor. But it is spicy and good, so if you like heat use it on eggs, drizzle over fresh cheeses, or add to tomato sauce or sautéed greens. Filtering flavored oils such as these can be messy and slow. The solids settle out of the oil, so we simply decant the oil off the solids.

"We love to surprise our guests with unexpected combinations as in this Burrata with Sweet Pea Ice Cream, Pickled Cherry Tomatoes, and Spicy Paprika Oil (page 192) served on a petrified wood slab."

Turnip Confit Enhanced with Orange, Ginger, and Rosemary

CHANTAL AND I BOTH LOVE TURNIPS, so I was interested when I saw this combination of flavors in a book of vegetable recipes from French chefs. It is a confit, so yes, there is butter, but the combination of brown butter, orange, and rosemary tastes so good. You can use large turnips or sweet little Tokyo turnips. They are turning up more and more often at farmers' markets and good produce shops and have the advantage of not needing to be peeled. You can serve this as a separate course in a vegetarian menu or as a side dish for meat or poultry.

Serves 4 as a separate course or 6 as a side dish

2 tablespoons unsalted pistachios

½ cup (1 stick or 4 ounces) unsalted butter

1¼ pounds turnips, peeled and sliced ¼ inch thick, or 4 bunches Tokyo turnips, stems trimmed to about ½ inch

2 teaspoons honey

Sea salt and freshly ground white pepper

1 cup freshly squeezed orange juice

1½ teaspoons freshly grated peeled fresh ginger

2 teaspoons finely chopped fresh rosemary

1 teaspoon freshly grated orange zest

1 tablespoon finely chopped fresh flat-leaf parsley or finely sliced chives (optional)

Place the pistachios in a small dry pan and toast the nuts over medium to medium-low heat, stirring and tossing so they cook evenly, until fragrant and lightly browned, about 5 minutes. Pour onto a small plate to cool. Set aside.

Heat the butter in a large sauté pan over medium-high heat. Add the turnips and cook, stirring once or twice, 3 to 4 minutes. They will brown a little, but don't worry about browning them all over. Stir in the honey and cook for another 2 minutes, season with a good pinch each of salt and pepper, and add the orange juice. Cover, reduce the heat to a gentle simmer, and cook until the vegetables are about half tender, about 5 minutes. Add the ginger and rosemary, re-cover, and continue to simmer until the vegetables are fork-tender, about another 6 minutes. Transfer the turnips to a warm serving dish and cook the juices, if needed, until reduced to a syrupy consistency. Stir in the orange zest and then pour the pan juices over the vegetables, toss gently, and taste for seasoning. Adjust with salt and pepper. Sprinkle with the pistachios and parsley. Serve immediately with good crusty bread for soaking up the buttery juices.

Celery Root and Potato Pancakes
with Shallot Relish

Notes

♣ I prefer using a mandoline to the shredding blade of a food processor for these. The cleaner cuts of the mandoline give the pancakes a spiky look, which is half the fun.

♣ These pancakes do not have much potato starch to hold them together. If you are confident of your technique, try them without the small flour addition. If you would like a little help, add the flour. You really cannot tell the difference in taste.

THIS IS A VARIATION on the *Pommes Paillasson* (page 82) I first learned at L'Auberge de L'Ill. The addition of the celery root gives the pancake a lighter feel and a rounder, more complex taste. The pancakes can form part of a vegetarian menu: Start with a soup, then a raw vegetable dish such as the asparagus salad (page 204), and then these crispy pancakes made luxurious with crème fraîche and shallot jam. Top them with a poached egg (page 60) or a generous spoonful of caviar for a brunch or a dinner party first course. They make a good side dish for roasts, too.

Serves 4 to 6 (2 to 3 pancakes per person)

½ pound shallots
About 3 tablespoons extra-virgin olive oil, divided
1½ teaspoons brown sugar
¾ teaspoon finely chopped fresh thyme
Sea salt and freshly ground black pepper
4 tablespoons finely sliced fresh chives, divided
1 lemon, halved
½ small celery root (about ½ pound)
1 teaspoon freshly squeezed lemon juice
1 Russet potato (about ½ pound), peeled
2 tablespoons all-purpose flour
2 to 3 tablespoons unsalted butter
¼ cup crème fraîche

Preheat the oven to 375°F. Place the shallots in a bowl of water and let soak for about 2 minutes. Drain and trim off the root and stem ends. Place the shallots on a small baking sheet and roast until they are very tender, about 40 minutes. Remove them from the sheet, let cool, peel, and chop very finely.

Heat 1 tablespoon of the olive oil in a small skillet over medium heat. Add the shallots, sugar, thyme, ½ cup water, and a pinch each of salt and pepper. Stir well, cover, and cook, stirring occasionally until the shallots have completely softened, 5 to 10 minutes. Uncover, and cook off excess

liquid, stopping when the shallots are still very moist. Stir in 1 tablespoon of the chives, taste, and adjust the seasoning. Set aside and keep very warm. The shallot relish can be made a day or two ahead of time and even frozen.

Fill a medium bowl halfway with water. Squeeze the juice from 1 lemon half into the water and drop in the peel. Working as quickly as you can, peel the celery root and rub the cut edges with the second lemon half to prevent discoloration. When finished, drop this lemon half into the bowl of water, too.

Cut the celery root into several pieces and drop them into the lemon water as you go. Shred the chunks on a mandoline or with the coarse shredding disk of a food processor. You should have about 2 packed cups. Transfer the celery root to a baking sheet and toss with the lemon juice to prevent discoloration.

Shred the potatoes and add them to the celery root with 2 tablespoons of the remaining chives. Season well with salt and pepper and toss to combine. Let sit for a minute or two. The salt will begin to wilt the vegetables and draw out liquid. Have your pan on a tilt so that some of the water naturally drains away.

Line a baking sheet with paper towels. Preheat the oven to 200°F. Gather handfuls of the vegetables and press firmly, squeezing out any excess water that has accumulated. Add the flour and toss gently until evenly combined. As you go along, you may need to squeeze the vegetables again before cooking.

You will need to cook the pancakes in batches or use 2 large skillets. Heat a large nonstick skillet over medium heat. Add 1 tablespoon of the oil and 1 tablespoon of the butter. Swirl the pan until the butter and oil have melted and mixed. Lightly pile about ¼ cup vegetables in the skillet into a 3-inch disk. Neaten the edges with the back of a spoon and press down lightly to coax them into holding together. Cook over medium to medium-low heat until the pancakes have browned around the edges, about 5 minutes. Place a little nut of butter in the center of each pancake and then turn them carefully with a thin-bladed spatula. Cook—turning occasionally, neatening the edges as needed, and adding more oil and butter to prevent sticking—until the pancakes are very browned and crispy outside and soft within, 10 to 15 minutes total.

When the pancakes are done, transfer them to the prepared baking sheet to drain and keep them warm in the oven. When ready to serve, pat the tops with paper towels, if necessary, to remove excess oil, and transfer the pancakes to a warm serving platter. Spoon some of the hot shallot relish and a dollop of crème fraîche on each, sprinkle with the remaining tablespoon of chives, and serve immediately.

Looking down into Fleur by Hubert Keller in the Mandalay Bay Hotel and Casino, Las Vegas.

199

Truffled Onion Velouté Shooters

STEVEN WOLF, ONE OF MY FORMER CHEFS IN LAS VEGAS, developed this ivory-colored, deeply flavored soup. We serve it at Fleur as a shooter. The sweet onion flavor makes a delicious backdrop for the truffle flavor. The soup would make an elegant passed hors d'oeuvre or appetizer for a very special party, perhaps Christmas or New Year's Eve. Make sure to read the ingredients label of any truffle oil you plan to buy and choose one that says it is made from oil and truffles, nothing more. Or less.

Makes 8 to 10 demitasse portions

- 3 tablespoons unsalted butter or extra-virgin olive oil
- 2 pounds yellow onions, thinly sliced (about 10 cups)
- 2 cloves garlic, sliced
- 1 ounce black Périgord truffle, finely chopped by hand
- 2 cups low-salt chicken or vegetable broth
- 1 bouquet garni (page 65)
  Sea salt and freshly ground white pepper
- ½ cup heavy cream
- 1 tablespoon black truffle oil
- 8 to 10 small sprigs fresh chervil (optional)

Melt the butter in a large heavy sauté pan over low heat. Add the onions and garlic, stir well, cover, and cook for about 10 minutes to allow the onions to soften. Uncover and continue to cook, stirring frequently, until the onions are very soft but not browned, about 20 minutes. Stir in three-quarters of the truffle (reserve the rest for garnish) for the last few minutes of cooking so the flavor can bloom.

Add the chicken broth, bouquet garni, ½ teaspoon salt, and ¼ teaspoon pepper. Bring to a gentle simmer and cook, uncovered, for 20 minutes. The liquids will begin to reduce and the soup will thicken. Add the cream and continue to cook very slowly to meld the flavors, another 10 minutes. Let cool slightly.

Transfer the soup to a blender, add the truffle oil, and blend until very smooth. Pour the soup through a fine-mesh sieve into a clean saucepan and reheat gently over low heat. The soup should be fairly thick but still easily pourable. Taste and adjust the seasoning with salt and pepper. Ladle the soup into small shooter glasses or demitasse cups, sprinkle with the remaining black truffle, add a small chervil sprig, and serve immediately.

Notes

♣ A velouté, a classic sauce in the French repertoire, is based on stock and thickened with a roux. This soup, however, comes to its velvety thickness simply by cooking. For the best result, take your time and make sure your onions do not brown.

Chantal and me in the Presidio on a Sunday morning. This route above the bay is one of our favorites.

Roast Chicken on Fire with Preserved Lemon

♣ Even if you don't have a vertical roaster, you can make this dish. You can jury-rig a vertical roaster by using the beer can chicken technique: Pour off between a quarter and half of the beer or empty the can and refill it with chicken broth. Put the flavorings inside the chicken and sit it on the can. Put the chicken in an ovenproof skillet, which acts the part of the catch pan of the vertical roaster. And if you want to flame your rosemary, buy it in advance to give it a chance to dry out.

CHANTAL OFTEN ROASTS A CHICKEN on our Staub vertical roaster. Staub now is so popular among cooks and chefs. It's hard to remember that it was once a small Alsace business turning out pots and pans that everyone had and no one thought anything about. But Francis Staub, son of the founder, was a young, totally eccentric, brilliant guy whose vision and drive turned his small family business into a global brand. The presentation here is a showstopper.

Serves 3 to 4

1 organic or pasture-raised chicken (about 4 pounds)
   Sea salt and freshly ground black pepper
2 preserved lemons (page 283)
6 cloves garlic, peeled
3 tablespoons unsalted butter, at room temperature
2 teaspoons chopped fresh thyme
2 sprigs fresh thyme
1 bay leaf
2 tablespoons extra-virgin olive oil, divided
2 carrots, cut into ½-inch dice
1 medium yellow onion, cut into ½-inch dice
1 stalk celery, cut into ½-inch dice
1 cup low-salt chicken broth
1 small bundle long-stemmed dried rosemary (optional)

Preheat the oven to 375°F and place the rack in the lowest position. To prepare the chicken, remove the wings and save for another use. Loosen the skin over the breast and season the cavity with salt and pepper.

Rinse both preserved lemons under cold water. Discard the pulp from both. Chop the peel of one of them finely and then place it in a bowl. Set the peel of the second lemon aside. Finely chop 1 clove of the garlic and add it to the bowl with the chopped lemon peel. Crush the remaining 5 cloves of garlic.

Add the butter and chopped thyme to the bowl with the chopped lemon peel and mash them together well. Rub the chicken breast under the skin with the butter mixture. Stuff the lemon peel from the remaining preserved lemon into the chicken's cavity with the thyme sprigs, the bay leaf, and the remaining crushed garlic. Rub the outside of the chicken with 1 tablespoon of the olive oil and season with salt and pepper. Sit the chicken on the vertical roaster with the neck facing up.

Place the carrots, onion, and celery in a bowl and toss with the remaining tablespoon of oil and salt and pepper to taste. Arrange them in the bottom of the vertical roaster all around the chicken. Place in the oven and roast for 45 to 50 minutes. Baste the chicken with the pan drippings every 10 minutes.

When the chicken is ready, place it, still on the vertical roaster, on top of the stove. Spoon off the fat. Turn the heat to medium-high under the roaster and add the broth. It will come to a boil right away and dissolve the browned bits on the bottom of the pan. Stand the dried rosemary bundle up in the neck side of the chicken, carefully set it alight with a match, and march the flaming chicken immediately to the table. Have a platter at the table so you can lift the bird off the roaster and carve it. Or, once you've caused a sensation with the flaming bird, return it to the kitchen and carve it there.

One Thing Leads to Another
HEALTHY COOKING, DR. DEAN ORNISH, AND THE WHITE HOUSE

Probably because of the press notices I'd received for my vegetarian menus and lighter style of French cuisine, Dr. Dean Ornish (from left: Michael Lomonaco, Dr. Dean Ornish, Jean-Marc Fullsack, and me during our second visit to the White House), the noted cardiologist, asked me to develop recipes for his heart program. It used diet as a tool to treat heart disease without surgery. I accepted, and then he gave me the parameters: no salt, no sugar, no butter, very little fat, no meat, no fish or shellfish. I thought, If you take all that away from me, I can't cook! But once I started really getting involved, the limits opened doors, and great ideas starting popping.

In 1993 I suggested to Chantal that we just disappear and spend a couple of great days by ourselves at L'Auberge du Soleil (the Napa Valley resort owned by Claude Rouas, brother of my partner, Maurice Rouas). We thought no one knew where we were.

On the first or second night we were eating dinner in the dining room, having the best time, when the maître d' interrupted and said to me, "You have a telephone call." (There were no cell phones then. You had to get up from the table and go to the telephone booth in the front of the restaurant.) At first I thought it was a joke because no one knew where we were, but the maître d' insisted that I had to take the call. When I came back to the table, Chantal asked who it was. "The White House," I

said. She burst out laughing. "No," I insisted, "it's not a joke. Next Tuesday, I have to be in DC at the White House." The next morning, right away it started: the faxes to the White House confirming details. Our vacation was over.

Hillary Clinton was interested in healthy cooking for her family and had gotten in touch with Dr. Ornish because of his book *Eat More, Weigh Less*. She wanted to introduce some of his healthy cooking ideas to the staff. Some of my recipes were in the book. And perhaps because the White House chef at that time, Pierre Chambrin, was French, they thought it would be a good idea to include another French chef—but one who had changed his cooking to a lighter, healthier style. Never before had an outside chef been invited into the White House to cook. In this chapter I've included some of the recipes that demonstrate the principles of creating flavor with great technique and with unexpected combinations of ingredients. For instance, Chicken Breasts Stuffed with Wild Mushrooms and Spinach (page 206) gets a surprising touch of walnut oil in its light sauce of reduced broth.

I went twice, each time demonstrating the healthy recipes for the staff in the morning and cooking a private dinner for the family that evening. On my second visit, I was told the president would like to see me in the Oval Office the next day. As I sat in the little anteroom, my heart was thumping. Just like in the movies, the president entered his office from the garden outside, and I saw his shadow passing. Then the door opened. I walked in, first seeing the huge symbol in the middle of the rug, and then the desk, and then President Clinton standing there. He shook my hand, and it felt exactly like a customer at the restaurant saying "Thank you so much. I had a great time."

Later in San Francisco, we hosted chefs from Camp David, Air Force One, and the White House in the kitchen at Fleur de Lys. They had been trained by the Army and had little experience in high-end restaurants. They experienced firsthand what we were doing, that the style was not a special diet but a new, lighter, healthier way to cook.

Raw Asparagus, Radish, and Shiitake Mushroom Salad

Notes

♣ Hazelnut oil would make a good addition to the dressing. If you substitute 2 table-spoons toasted hazelnut oil for an equal amount of olive oil, the nut fla-vor comes through nicely. If you love nut oil, replace the olive oil entirely.

THIS IS A DISH I DID for *Top Chef Masters* as part of the alfresco buffet at the SLS Hotel in Beverly Hills. I will never forget how bright and hot it was up there. This is a different combination of ingredients, including one we don't usually think of eating raw—asparagus. Doing so can be a nice surprise. Make this salad in the spring with fresh, young asparagus. Its flavor is delicate and the texture is very crisp. Slice the spears on a sharp diagonal to make pretty, pale oblongs.

Serves 6

1 pound medium asparagus

⅓ cup plus 2 tablespoons extra-virgin olive oil

½ pound shiitake mushrooms, stemmed and sliced about ¼ inch thick

Sea salt and freshly ground pepper

4 medium radishes, halved lengthwise and sliced thinly crosswise

2 tablespoons freshly squeezed lemon juice

2 teaspoons Dijon mustard

1 bunch watercress, coarse stems discarded, washed well, and spun dry

A small block of Parmesan cheese

With a vegetable peeler, trim the asparagus stalks of their skin until just the pale green flesh shows. Start peel-ing just below the tip. Then trim off the bottom 1 to 1½ inches of the asparagus stalks by lining several stalks up next to each other and cutting through the stems at a sharp diagonal. Using that first cut as a guide, continue to slice the stalks on a sharp diagonal so the slices are about ⅓ inch thick and about 1 inch long. Leave the tips whole. Trans-fer the prepared asparagus to a large mixing bowl.

Place a large sauté pan over medium-high heat. Add the 2 tablespoons of olive oil, and then add the mushrooms, making sure not to crowd the pan. Don't touch the mushrooms for the first minute, until they have a chance to brown, then stir and cook them until tender, about 5 minutes. Season them with salt and pepper. Add the mushrooms and the radishes to the asparagus.

In a small bowl, whisk together the lemon juice, mustard, and salt and pep-per to taste. While whisking, add the remaining ⅓ cup olive oil in a stream and whisk until the dressing has formed an emulsion.

To preserve the salad's color, dress it just before serving. In a large bowl, toss some of the dressing with the watercress. Spread the watercress on a serving platter. Drizzle more dressing over the asparagus and mushrooms, toss well, and arrange over the water-cress. With a vegetable peeler, shave curls of Parmesan over the salad and serve immediately.

Figs and Blackberries in Citrus Broth

THIS IS A VERSION OF THE DISH I CREATED IN 1995 for Molly O'Neill, then a regular food writer with the *New York Times*. At Le Prieuré in the Loire Valley, we had enormous bushes of wild blackberries. If one of my apprentices had not done something correctly, I borrowed a trick from M. Daniel at L'Auberge de L'Ill. The apprentice would be sent to pick blackberries instead of taking an afternoon break just the way we sometimes had to clean the fish pond at L'Auberge. For a few weeks in San Francisco, you can find both ripe black figs and blackberries at farmers' markets. Here they are steeped in citrus juice with a little spicy bite of fresh ginger and the fresh coolness of mint.

Serves 4

1½	cups freshly squeezed orange juice
1	cup freshly squeezed grapefruit juice
3	tablespoons freshly squeezed lemon juice (preferably Meyer lemon juice)
½	teaspoon grated peeled fresh ginger
2	tablespoons honey
1	tablespoon light rum
16	ripe black figs, pricked a few times with a fork
1	cup fresh blackberries or blueberries
1	banana, peeled and cut diagonally into ¼-inch-thick slices
8	fresh mint sprig tips

Place the orange, grapefruit, and lemon juice in a medium nonreactive saucepan with the ginger, honey, and rum. Bring to a boil over medium-high heat and then reduce the heat to a gentle simmer. Gently lower the figs, berries, and banana into the juice. Cover, remove from the heat, set aside until cool, and then refrigerate until cold.

Remove the figs from the liquid, halve them, and return them to the pan. Divide the fruit and juices among 4 bowls, add 2 mint sprig tips to each, and serve very cold.

Notes

♣ There is certainly nothing wrong with floating a scoop of vanilla ice cream or crème fraîche in a bowlful of the fruit or, to maintain your good intentions, a spoonful of nonfat Greek-style yogurt. Use the broth to glaze ice cream and yogurt as well or to blend into smoothies.

Chicken Breasts Stuffed with
Wild Mushrooms and Spinach

THIS IS ONE OF THE FULL-FLAVOR-LOW-FAT DISHES I created for Dr. Dean Ornish's healthy foods program for cardiac patients. Because of my participation in that program, I was invited with Dr. Ornish to share my light interpretations of French dishes with the staff of the Clinton White House. Back then, in 1993, putting vegetables in the center of the plate and trimming fat, butter, and cream from French recipes was still very new. This is a slightly more elaborate version of the recipe the *New York Times* printed as part of its coverage of the visit. You can serve the rolls warm, room temperature, or cold, making them a great dish for hot summer evenings, picnics, potlucks, and as sandwich fillings.

Serves 4

2   tablespoons ruby port
4   cups low-salt chicken broth
1   bouquet garni (page 65)
    Sea salt and freshly ground black pepper
2   teaspoons cornstarch (optional)
2   teaspoons extra-virgin olive oil
1   medium shallot, very finely chopped
1   clove garlic, very finely chopped
2   bunches young spinach (about 1 pound), stems removed
    About 5 ounces wild mushrooms (such as black chanterelles, shiitake, morels, or truffles), coarsely chopped
1½ teaspoons finely chopped fresh thyme or oregano
4   skinless, boneless chicken breasts, without tenders (about 6 ounces each)
    About ½ teaspoon Spanish sweet paprika (optional)
1   teaspoon toasted hazelnut oil
1   small ripe tomato, peeled, seeded, and cut into ¼-inch dice
1   tablespoon finely chopped fresh flat-leaf parsley

Begin by making the sauce. Place the port in a medium saucepan over medium heat. Boil until reduced by half and add the chicken broth and bouquet garni. Bring to a boil and cook over high heat until reduced to about ¾ cup. Discard the bouquet garni. Adjust the seasoning with salt and pepper.

If the reduced broth is not of a light sauce consistency, you can thicken it with a little cornstarch. In a small, lidded jar, mix the cornstarch with twice as much cold water. Shake well and whisk a little of the mixture into the simmering sauce and watch for signs of thickening. Continue adding cornstarch, shaking well before each addition, until your sauce is as thick as you would like it. Keep the sauce warm.

Heat 1 teaspoon of the olive oil in a large nonstick skillet over medium heat and add the shallot. Stir and cook until the shallot is tender, about 3 minutes. Add the garlic and cook until fragrant, about 30 seconds. Add the spinach, season with salt and pepper, and toss and cook the leaves until they have wilted and the pan is dry, about 4 minutes. Transfer it to a plate to cool. Use your hands to squeeze out as much liquid as you can and coarsely chop the spinach. Put it in a bowl and set aside.

Heat the remaining teaspoon of oil in the same skillet over medium-high heat. Scatter the mushrooms loosely in the pan and cook without moving them until they have browned on one side, about 1 minute. Stir and cook until the mushrooms are browned and cooked through and the pan is dry, about 5 minutes. Add the thyme for the last minute of cooking. Season with salt and pepper and add to the bowl with the spinach. Toss together well.

Lay the chicken breasts on a work surface, cover them with a heavy-duty plastic bag, and pound them with a meat mallet or with the bottom of a heavy pan until flattened to an even thickness of about 1/3 inch. Season with salt, pepper, and a pinch of paprika. Pat an equal amount of spinach on top of each breast, leaving a border all around.

Moisten the work surface and lay a 12-inch length of plastic wrap on top. Arrange a chicken breast in the center of the wrap. Roll the breast around the filling into a firm roll and wrap it tightly in the plastic wrap. Tie the ends securely. Lay a second piece of wrap on the work surface, this time with the short end parallel to the table edge, and roll the chicken breast up tightly in the wrap so it is watertight. Repeat with the remaining 3 chicken breasts. Refrigerate until ready to cook. You can shape the rolls as long as a day ahead. Let them sit at room

temperature for 30 minutes before cooking or give them an extra couple of minutes of poaching time.

Meanwhile, fill a 6-quart pot half full with water and bring to a boil over high heat. Lower the heat so the water just simmers and gently lower the chicken rolls into the water. If you are not sure that your rolls are watertight, seal them in a heavy-duty plastic bag. Weigh them down with a plate, if necessary, to keep them submerged. Poach for about 16 minutes, transfer the rolls to a cutting board, and let them rest for 2 minutes. With a sharp knife, trim off one end of each roll. Hold onto the tie at the opposite end and pull while using the flat of the blade to push the roll out of the wrap.

Pour any chicken juices into the sauce and whisk in the hazelnut oil, tomato, and parsley. Slice each breast diagonally into slices about 1/2 inch thick. Fan them out on warm dinner plates, spoon the sauce around them, and serve immediately.

♣ All the flavor in the sauce comes from the broth, which is cooked until very reduced. So be sure to make your own or buy no-salt-added, high-quality broth, such as those sold these days by butcher shops.

♣ This is another dish in which having restaurant-sized plastic wrap makes it easier to wrap the rolls watertight.

The HK Burger

CUSTOMERS AT BURGER BAR FREQUENTLY ASK what my favorite burger is. I love the naturally lean buffalo burger and its fantastic meaty flavor. Being French, I'm not a ketchup-and-mustard man for toppings. I like a red wine sauce with my burger, and I top it with sautéed spinach and sweet caramelized onions offset by the pungent tang of blue cheese. My favorite bun is the ciabatta bun. It's the closest to my favorite bread, baguette, and with just enough crunch and substance to absorb all the burger's juices. The flavors really work together, and the combination is one of our most popular signature burgers.

Serves 4

Caramelized Onions

- 2 tablespoons extra-virgin olive oil
- 2 pounds yellow onions, very finely sliced (about 10 cups)
- 1 tablespoon brown sugar
- 1 tablespoon finely chopped fresh thyme
- 1 bay leaf
  Sea salt and freshly ground black pepper

Sautéed Spinach

- 1 tablespoon extra-virgin olive oil
- 1 clove garlic, very finely chopped
- 1 pound fresh baby spinach
  Pinch of freshly grated nutmeg
  Sea salt and freshly ground black pepper

Buffalo Burgers

- 2 pounds coarsely ground buffalo
- 2 tablespoons extra-virgin olive oil
  Sea salt and freshly ground black pepper
- 4 ciabatta buns
- 6 ounces crumbled blue cheese
  About ½ cup Red Wine–Shallot Sauce (page 211)
- 4 leaves butter lettuce
- 4 slices ripe tomato

To make the caramelized onions: In a large skillet, heat 2 tablespoons of the oil over medium-high heat. Add the onions, sugar, thyme, bay leaf, a large pinch of salt, and ¼ cup water. Stir well, cover, and cook over medium heat until the onions have softened, about 5 minutes. Uncover and cook slowly over low heat, until the onions have thoroughly melted and turned golden brown, about 45 minutes. Season with salt and pepper. Remove the onions from the heat and keep warm until needed. You can make the onions well ahead and even freeze them.

To make the sautéed spinach: In another large skillet, heat the oil over medium heat. Add the garlic and cook briefly just until fragrant. Add the spinach and stir and toss the leaves just until the spinach wilts and softens and remains brightly colored, about 1 minute. Add the nutmeg and season to taste with salt and pepper. Keep warm until needed.

To make the buffalo burgers: Shape the meat into 4 evenly sized patties about 1 inch thick. Handle the meat lightly to keep the texture light and juicy. The burgers can be shaped and refrigerated, covered, for several hours or overnight.

When ready to cook, preheat the broiler. Heat the olive oil in a large skillet over medium-high heat. Generously season the burgers on both sides with salt and pepper. Add the patties and cook on the first side until brown, about 3 minutes. Turn and continue to cook, basting with any fat in the pan, until brown on the second side, another 3 to 4 minutes for medium-rare meat. Transfer them to an ovenproof platter and keep warm.

While the burgers cook, toast the buns briefly in the broiler. Arrange a lettuce leaf and tomato slice on each bun bottom. Top with a burger and then divide the spinach, caramelized onions, and blue cheese among them. Place the burgers briefly under the boiler to melt the cheese. To serve, slide the burgers onto warm plates, tilt the bun top against the burger, and serve the sauce on the side.

Red Wine–Shallot Sauce

Makes about 1 cup

This is a fantastic, versatile sauce based on red wine reduction sauces I learned during my apprenticeship. We serve it at Fleur de Lys as well as at Burger Bar. I really encourage you to try it. Make more than you need and keep it on hand to add wonderful flavor to all sorts of meats and chicken as well as a dip for French fries.

- 1 tablespoon extra-virgin olive oil
- 1 large shallot, very finely chopped
- 1 clove garlic, very finely chopped
- ½ cup dry red wine
- 1½ cups low-salt chicken or beef broth
- 1 teaspoon finely chopped fresh thyme
- ½ teaspoon finely chopped fresh rosemary
- 1 tablespoon ruby port
- 1½ teaspoons cornstarch
  Sea salt and freshly ground black pepper
- 1 tablespoon unsalted butter

In a medium saucepan, heat the oil over medium heat. Add the shallot and stir and cook until the shallot is very tender and translucent, about 5 minutes. Add the garlic and cook until fragrant, another 30 seconds. Add the wine, bring to a boil, and cook until about 2 tablespoons of liquid remains. Add the broth, thyme, and rosemary, return the liquid to a boil, and simmer gently to let the flavors meld, about 5 minutes.

Place the port and cornstarch in a small jar, shake well, and dribble into the sauce while whisking and watching for signs of thickening. Simmer gently for another 7 minutes. Season with salt and pepper. If made ahead, let cool, cover, and refrigerate or freeze. When ready to serve, heat the sauce over low heat and swirl in the butter.

Far left: Stacked mini fry baskets at Burger Bar. *Below:* Burger Bar fries, *from left clockwise:* sweet potato skinny fries, deep-fried pickles, fried onion rings, deep-fried zucchini.

Triple-Threat Beer Burger

LAURENT PILLARD, OUR CORPORATE CHEF, uses our special-event dinners at Fleur and Burger Bar as an opportunity to be creative and a little out there. For a souvenir of our beer dinners, we wanted to show that burgers don't just go with beer—beer can be an important ingredient, too. Laurent starts with a Black Angus burger and tops it with shredded short ribs braised with pale malt (an ingredient in beer making), caramelized onions cooked with beer, our grainy homemade mustard made with beer, and bacon first poached in blond beer and then grilled. Finally, the assembled burger is served with beer-battered onion rings.

Serves 4

Braise

- 4 pounds meaty, bone-in beef short ribs
  Sea salt and freshly ground black pepper
- 2 tablespoons unsalted butter
- 2 tablespoons extra-virgin olive oil
- 1 large carrot, peeled and thinly sliced
- 1 medium yellow onion, halved and thinly sliced
- 2 stalks celery, thinly sliced
- 3 cloves garlic, peeled
- 1 cup red wine vinegar
- 2 tablespoons barley malt syrup
- 2½ cups dark beer
- 3 cups low-salt chicken broth
- 3 cups low-salt beef broth
- 1 bouquet garni (page 65)

Mustard

- ¼ cup whole yellow mustard seeds
- 2 tablespoons whole brown mustard seeds
- ¾ cup wheat beer
- 2 tablespoons white wine vinegar
  Pinch of sea salt
- 1¼ cups Dijon mustard

Burgers

- 2 large yellow onions, finely sliced (about 5 cups)
- 4 tablespoons extra-virgin olive oil, divided
  Sea salt and freshly ground black pepper
- 1 teaspoon finely chopped fresh thyme (optional)
- 1 bay leaf (optional)

- 1 cup plus ½ cup blond beer
- 4 thick slices apple-smoked bacon, halved crosswise
- 6 ounces braised, shredded beef short ribs
- 2 pounds coarsely ground high-quality beef chuck, such as Black Angus
- 4 whole-wheat buns
- 4 large leaves butter lettuce
- 1 large ripe tomato, very thinly sliced

To braise the short ribs: Season the meat well on all sides with salt and pepper. Heat 1 tablespoon each of the butter and the olive oil in a large heavy Dutch oven over medium-high heat. Add the meat and brown it well on both sides, about 3 minutes per side. Transfer the meat to a platter and set aside. You may need to cook the meat in batches, using the rest of the butter and oil.

Add the carrot, onion, celery, garlic, and a pinch of salt to the pan and sauté over medium heat until lightly browned, about 10 minutes. Add the vinegar to the pan and stir and scrape all over the bottom and sides of the pan. Let boil until reduced by about half. Return the meat to the pan with the barley malt syrup, dark beer, chicken broth, beef broth, and bouquet garni. Add enough water, if needed, to just cover the meat. Cover the pan and bring the liquid to a boil. Reduce the heat and cook at a very gentle simmer, covered loosely, until the meat is tender, about 3 hours. Turn the meat every hour so that it cooks evenly. To test for doneness, pierce the meat with a sharp

Notes

♣ This recipe makes far more short ribs than you will need for the burgers. But if you take the time to make them, you will get two or more meals from your efforts. Use to top polenta or pasta. The meat freezes well; wrap it in individual portions in plastic wrap and then again in aluminum foil. Label and freeze it for up to 3 months.

♣ You can find barley malt syrup in specialty and health food shops.

paring knife. When the knife enters easily (it's the same as testing a boiled potato), the meat is done.

Transfer the meat to a bowl to cool. Strain the cooking liquid into a clean saucepan and discard the solids. You should have about 4 cups. Spoon off the fat that rises to the surface. Bring the liquid to a boil and reduce by about half. Taste and adjust the seasoning. Shred the meat, discarding the fat and bones. Pour about ½ cup of the reduced cooking liquid over the meat and toss until well coated. Transfer 6 ounces of the meat to a small bowl, add another few tablespoons of the reduced braising liquid, cover, and refrigerate until ready to make the burgers. Freeze the remaining meat and sauce separately for another use.

To make the mustard: Combine the yellow and brown mustard seeds in a medium saucepan with the wheat beer, vinegar, and salt. Bring to a boil over high heat and immediately pour the mixture into a bowl. Cover and set aside at room temperature overnight.

Drain the seeds through a fine sieve. Discard the liquid and put the seeds in a bowl. Add the Dijon mustard and mix well. Pack into jars and refrigerate for at least 1 day before use and for as long as 1 month.

For the burgers: Begin by caramelizing the onions. Heat 2 tablespoons of the olive oil in a large skillet over medium heat. Add the onions and a good pinch each of salt and pepper, the thyme, and the bay leaf. Stir well, cover, and cook for several minutes, until the onions have softened. Uncover and cook, stirring occasionally to prevent scorching, until the onions have melted and turned golden brown, about 45 minutes. Regulate the heat as needed so the onions do not brown around the edges. When done, add 1 cup of

To Hubert Keller With Best Wishes,

the blond beer and bring to a boil while stirring and scraping all around the pan. Simmer until the pan is nearly dry. Scrape the onions into a container and keep warm until needed. The onions may be completed a day or more ahead of time and refrigerated until needed, or frozen.

In a small saucepan, bring the remaining ½ cup of blond beer and the bacon to a simmer over medium heat. Poach the bacon gently for 2 minutes to render the fat. Drain the bacon and then cook it in a medium skillet over medium heat until very crisp. Set aside and keep warm.

In another small saucepan (or in the microwave), heat the short ribs over low heat until very warm. Set aside.

Divide the ground beef into 4 evenly sized thick patties. Season them well on both sides with salt and pepper. Heat the remaining 2 tablespoons of olive oil in a large skillet or grill pan over medium-high heat until very hot. Place the burgers in the skillet and cook, turning once or twice and basting with the fat in the pan, about 7 minutes for medium-rare meat. Let rest for several minutes. While the burgers rest, toast the buns.

To build the burgers: Spread the bun bottoms with mustard. Arrange the lettuce and tomato on top and add a generous spoonful of caramelized onions. Set the burgers on the onions, divide the shredded beef among the patties, and arrange 2 pieces of bacon on each. Cover with the bun tops and serve immediately.

Oysters with Margarita Sorbet and Orange Segments

AT FLEUR, WE'VE DESIGNED EVERY DISH and its presentation to create an effect. For these oysters we use a narrow glass container and line up three underwater lights in the bottom. We drop in three pieces of dry ice and fill the container with the colored glass "stones." On top goes some seaweed, then the oysters. Finally, we pour boiling water into the container. When it hits the dry ice, the whole thing starts smoking. That's when it goes directly to the guest. The delicate, fresh oysters make an unusual and exciting pairing with the sorbet. And then the presentation takes the dish to another level and makes it something to write home about.

Makes 2 dozen

24	fresh oysters on the half shell, preferably Kusshi oysters
	About 3 cups rock salt (optional)
½	cup (3½ ounces) sugar
¾	cup freshly squeezed lime juice
	Freshly grated zest of ½ lime
1	tablespoon (½ ounce) good-quality orange liqueur, such as Cointreau
2	tablespoons (1 ounce) tequila
	Pinch of sea salt
2	large handfuls fresh seaweed (optional)
1	seedless orange

To save yourself time, or if you are not practiced at shucking oysters, ask the fishmonger to do this for you. Just be sure to let the counterman know you plan to serve them on the half shell. He or she will then open the oysters and pack them up correctly. If you shuck the oysters ahead of time, you can refrigerate them on a bed of rock salt. It has the advantage of not melting. But you could also use crushed ice and replace it with fresh cracked ice at serving time. The food processor is a noisy but effective way to make crushed ice.

Line a sheet pan with parchment paper and then spread a layer of rock salt or crushed ice over it. Shuck the oysters, discard the top shells (or put them in your compost), and settle the bottom shells with the oysters into the salt so they balance securely. You do not want to lose the oyster liquor. Refrigerate until ready to serve, up to several hours.

To prepare the margarita sorbet: Place 2 cups of water and the sugar in a small saucepan. Bring to a boil over high heat, remove from the heat, and stir in the lime juice and zest, liqueur, tequila, and sea salt. Let cool, cover, and chill well. Pour into an ice-cream maker and freeze according to the manufacturer's instructions. Transfer the sorbet to a bowl, cover, and freeze. Makes about 3 cups. The sorbet can be completed up to a day ahead of time.

With a small sharp knife, pare away the skin and pith from the orange. Working over a bowl to catch the juices, cut the segments free: Hold the fruit in one hand and cut down between the segments and the membranes. Cut the segments crosswise into tiny, thin triangles. Reserve the juice for another use.

When ready to serve, cover a serving platter or large, deep plate with crushed ice. Spread the seaweed over the ice and arrange the oysters on top. Using a teaspoon, spoon a little sorbet onto each oyster along with a piece of orange. Serve immediately, before the sorbet melts.

Notes

♣ Kusshi oysters are small, meaty oysters with a deep bottom shell. Kumamoto oysters would be a good substitute.

♣ You could also serve the oysters as shooters. Put small martini or shot glasses in the freezer to chill with your bottle of tequila. Put a spoonful of the sorbet in each glass and top first with an oyster and then with an orange triangle. Serve as is or add a teaspoon of the frozen tequila immediately before serving.

Mini Tuna Tacos with Avocado-Lime Cream

THE MINI TUNA TACOS ARE ONE OF OUR BEST SELLERS at Fleur. Our focus at the restaurant is cuisines from around the world. These tacos combine ideas from Japanese sashimi and Mexican tacos. Unlike most fish tacos, the fish in these is not cooked. Instead we start with sushi-grade tuna. And unlike most sashimi, these are not served with soy, wasabi, or rice. We add texture with crisp taco shells and shredded cabbage and richness with the avocado-lime cream.

Serves 4

- 1 small red onion, very thinly sliced
   Juice of 1 lime
   About 1 pound sushi-grade raw tuna in 1 large piece
- 12 purchased mini crisp taco shells, about 3 inches in diameter
   About 4 cups finely shredded green cabbage
- 2 jalapeño peppers, cut into very thin rounds
- 1 handful cilantro microgreen, or about 2 tablespoons chopped fresh cilantro

Avocado-Lime Cream

Makes 2 cups

- 1 ripe avocado, such as Hass, peeled and pitted
- 1 cup sour cream
- 2 tablespoons freshly squeezed lime juice, plus more if needed
   Sea salt and freshly ground white pepper

Place the red onions in a small bowl and squeeze the lime juice over them. Toss them well and let sit for at least 15 minutes and as long as overnight. They will turn bright pink.

To make the avocado-lime cream: Place the avocado, sour cream, lime juice, and a pinch each of salt and pepper in a food processor and process until smooth. Taste and adjust the seasoning with salt, pepper, and more lime juice if needed. Scrape the cream into a squeeze bottle and refrigerate until needed.

To finish the tacos: Cut the tuna into 12 finger-shaped pieces. They should be as long as your taco shells and about 1/2 inch wide and 1/4 inch thick. Keep very cold.

When ready to serve, squeeze a generous line of avocado-lime cream into the bottom of each taco shell and arrange 3 of them on each plate. Line the shells with the cabbage and top with a finger of tuna. Top with red onion and a dollop of avocado-lime cream on the fish, and prop a jalapeño slice in the cream. Tuck a tuft of cilantro in each taco and serve. Pass more of the avocado-lime cream at the table.

Nampol Meesa's Deep-Fried Chicken Wings

NAMPOL MEESA (WE CALLED HIM PAUL, AND HE DOES TOO) started cooking with us at the beginning of our adventure in Las Vegas. Paul is Thai and was for a time the chef of Fleur, our tapas-style restaurant. He created these very popular spicy wings for the opening menu. They are sweet, spicy, and salty, and they leave your lips tingling. Paul insists that their flavor depends on Golden Mountain Seasoning Sauce, a Thai soy sauce. You can find it in shops specializing in Asian ingredients and online. Serve the wings with pickled carrots or daikon.

Makes 2 dozen wings

¼ cup oyster sauce

¼ cup Golden Mountain Seasoning Sauce

1½ tablespoons unseasoned rice vinegar

1 tablespoon honey

1 tablespoon fish sauce

½ teaspoon freshly ground white pepper

½ teaspoon chili flakes

½ teaspoon garlic powder

¼ to ½ teaspoon cayenne

8 to 10 cups vegetable oil, for deep-frying

24 chicken wing pieces (drumettes or second joints or both), about 4 pounds

1 tablespoon finely chopped garlic

4 scallions, white and pale green parts, very thinly sliced

Preheat the oven to 200° to 250°F. In a large mixing bowl, combine the oyster sauce, seasoning sauce, vinegar, honey, fish sauce, white pepper, chili flakes, garlic powder, and cayenne. Whisk until smooth and set aside.

Frying time depends on the size of your wings. At Fleur the wings are small and we serve 6 to a portion, but the ones we serve at Burger Bar are larger. When we tested these, the wings we bought were very large and needed to fry twice as long as the small ones.

In a large deep pot, heat the oil to 360°F. Pat the chicken wings dry with paper towels. Working in batches, fry the wings until golden brown and crisp, 5 to 6 minutes, stirring them as needed. When done, remove them with long-handled tongs, quickly blot off the excess oil with paper towels, place them in the bowl with the sauce, and toss to coat well with the sauce. Keep warm in the oven, tossing occasionally, until all the wings are cooked. Add the garlic to the bowl and toss everything together well. Arrange the wings on a warm serving dish and sprinkle with the scallions. Serve them immediately.

Notes

♣ If your wings are large and you like lots of sauce, double the recipe.

♣ If you do not want to fry at all, marinate the wings in the sauce for at least 2 hours and then grill slowly until done, finishing over higher heat until crusty. Brush the wings with the sauce several times while they cook to glaze them.

♣ Use leftover sauce to marinate chicken, tuna, or swordfish before grilling.

No Rules

WITH JACQUES MAXIMIN AT LE CHANTECLER AT HÔTEL LE NEGRESCO, NICE, CÔTE D'AZUR

Working with Jacques Maximin as his *chef de partie* for fish, *poissonier*, was another great experience, totally different from anything I had known before. The menus at L'Auberge de L'Ill and Moulin de Mougins were set. My job was to execute them exactly the way Chef Haeberlin or M. Vergé wanted. You would not walk into M. Vergé's kitchen and think: *I'll just change this a little bit.* No, it was his cuisine; that was what he was known for, and it was why you were there—to learn from him, not to change things.

But at Le Chantecler we did not know what we would cook from one day to the next. Jacques would go to the market early and then come back with all these fresh ingredients. He would sit in his little office, pulling his hair, and writing, writing. About 10 a.m. out he would come. He'd grab Joachim Splichal, his saucier, and say, "Okay, here's what we're doing for lunch." Then he would come to me, his poissonier, and instruct me. And then he would do the same with the chef garde-manger. After lunch, he went back in his office and started on the dinner menu. At first I thought: *This is crazy. I can't stay here. It's a zoo, too disorganized.* But then I saw it beginning to work. I saw how we talked together, firing ideas off each other. For the first time, a chef asked me what I thought. And he listened.

Maximin kept coming up with new stuff, crazy stuff. He made up dishes; he didn't read about them in a book. Some worked brilliantly, and everyone would come to eat that dish. I remember asparagus ice cream and injecting the tails of live lobsters with syringes full of truffle juice just before we roasted them. What he did with French cuisine did not exist before. We thought: *Wow, his mind is working. He is thinking in a new, innovative way.* It was very exciting. This was the beginning of *la nouvelle cuisine*, creating a lighter, more modern approach to classic French cooking. And it was also part of another movement linked to *la nouvelle*

cuisine and one that is so important today: *le retour du marché*, cooking with whatever is available in the market, the freshest of the fresh and locally produced ingredients.

I had never before experienced cooking *à la vapeur*. Just like sous-vide is today, steam cooking was then the latest, greatest thing. We created our steamer with a big copper pot and copper colander enclosed in aluminum foil. Steaming was the basis of two of our groundbreaking fish dishes. Before Maximin, in kitchens from Paul Haeberlin to Paul Bocuse and Roger Vergé, fish was either braised, sautéed, roasted, or poached. And then served with a rich sauce, perhaps a lobster or crayfish sauce, or the sorrel cream sauce that became so famous and a classic pairing with salmon in the 1970s.

For Maximin's *saumon gros sel*, we started with a rich vegetable stock. It became the base of a little butter sauce. We took the freshest piece of salmon and steamed it just until it was still translucent in the center. We filmed the plate with a thin coat of sauce, topped it with the salmon, and surrounded it with baby leeks, carrots, hearts of celery, and pearl onions. And then we gently warmed the most fragrant extra-virgin olive oil, folded in a few diced tomatoes, a chiffonade of basil cut at the very last moment, and a little fennel seed to scatter over the dish. As a final touch, we sprinkled the fish with fleur de sel. It was my first experience with fleur de sel. Now times have changed, and when I describe the dish you might think it was nothing special. But back then everyone talked about it; everyone came to try it. It was totally new. Another example of how Maximin lightened dishes is the feuilleté in Chapter Two, Feuilleté of Crayfish, Scallops, Summer Vegetables, and Basil in Hollandaise Sauce (page 85). Maximin replaced the traditional béchamel with a frothy, light hollandaise. Today it doesn't sound so radical, but then it was.

Smoked-to-Order Glazed Baby Back Ribs

Notes

♣ A rack of baby
back ribs weighs
1 to 1½ pounds.
Count on cooking
1 whole rack for
every 2 people. You
can also use the
more readily avail-
able St. Louis–style
ribs or spareribs.
These are perhaps
a little less meaty.
Butchers usually
cut thick loin chops
off the ribs and cut
closer to the ribs
(thus "spare ribs")
to make a bigger
chop. Braise the
spareribs a little
longer than baby
back ribs, closer to
3 hours than 2. And,
if you want to make
smaller ribs—for
instance, for a
cocktail party—ask
the butcher to halve
the slab lengthwise.
Then you'll have 16
small ribs per slab.

THE PRESENTATION OF OUR BABY BACK RIBS at Fleur in Las Vegas goes back to the fine-dining tradition of presenting dishes to the diner covered with a silver dome. This helped keep the dishes hot on the long trip from the subterranean kitchens to the dining room. At Fleur the ribs are smoked *à la minute*. They come to the table covered with a glass dome full of swirling smoke that flavors the ribs as they travel from the kitchen to the guest. The waiter lifts the dome, the smoke drifts away, and there is a pile of glossy ribs with a light cherry-wood smoked flavor.

Serves 4

2 slabs pork baby back ribs (about 1½ pounds each)
  Sea salt and freshly ground black pepper
1 large carrot, peeled and coarsely chopped
2 stalks celery, coarsely chopped
1 medium yellow onion (about 6 ounces), coarsely chopped
1 head garlic, cloves separated and peeled
¼ cup (1¾ ounces) dark brown sugar, preferably dark muscovado sugar
¼ cup Grade B maple syrup
2 tablespoons very finely chopped chipotle chili in adobo sauce
1 or 2 sticks cinnamon (about 3 inches long)
1 tablespoon ground cumin
1 tablespoon ground coriander
½ bunch fresh thyme
1 bay leaf
2 to 4 cups low-salt beef, chicken, or vegetable stock, or water
1 to 2 tablespoons apple cider vinegar
  About ½ cup wood chips, preferably cherry wood, soaked for at least 30 minutes

Preheat the oven to 250°F. Pull off the silver skin from the slabs of ribs. Season with salt and pepper and place them in a roasting pan large enough to hold them in a single layer with the carrot, celery, onion, garlic, sugar, maple syrup, chipotle pepper, cinnamon, cumin, coriander, thyme, and bay leaf. Add enough stock to come one-fourth of the way up the sides of the pan and bring to a simmer on top of the stove. Cover tightly with aluminum foil and braise in the oven until the meat is ready to fall off the bones, 2 to 3 hours.

Transfer the slabs to a cutting board, cut them into ribs, and then transfer them to a bowl. Strain the sauce into a bowl, let the fat rise to the top, and then spoon it off. Return the sauce to a large ovenproof skillet and bring to a boil over high heat. Boil until the sauce is syrupy, about 20 minutes. Stir regularly, being careful not to scorch the sauce. Taste and adjust the balance of flavors with the vinegar and salt and pepper.

Preheat the broiler and move the rack 5 inches below the heat. Transfer the ribs to the skillet with the sauce and turn them until well and evenly coated. Place over medium heat and toss well until the ribs are very hot and the sauce has reduced even more and glazed the ribs all over. Put the pan under the broiler and watch carefully. Turn and toss the ribs until they get crusty and brown, about 5 minutes. You can serve the ribs immediately or smoke them.

To smoke the ribs, you need a cast-iron frying pan and several heatproof mixing bowls that fit the pan as well as over the dinner plate or platter you plan to use. If the bowls have rims, they will be easier to grab and move. Take a cast-iron frying pan and pile the soaked wood chips in the center. Place the pan over high heat until it's

very hot and the chips begin to char and smoke. Pass a pastry torch over the wood until the chips are fully alight and smoking. Take a mixing bowl that fits inside the pan (or closely over it) and clamp it over the pan to trap the smoke. Leave it in place for a minute in order to fill with smoke.

Meanwhile, arrange the ribs on individual warm dinner plates. To lift up the bowl and capture the smoke inside, slide a spatula under the edge and steady it with a hot pad on top. Or use tongs to grab the bowl's rim. Keeping the bowl level, quickly place it over a portion of ribs. Repeat for all of the portions. Let sit for a few minutes for the smoke to infuse the ribs. Or do all the ribs at once: Arrange them on a large round platter and use a wok to heat the wood chips. Capture the smoke under the wok lid and cover the platter with the lid. Wait a few minutes, then set the platter in the middle of the table and uncover in front of your guests. The effect will be startling, and it will taste really good. If you prefer a stronger smoke flavor, place a cake rack in the wok over the smoking wood chips. Make sure your plate holding the ribs is heatproof and does not touch the edges of the wok. Put the ribs in the wok, cover, and let smoke.

♣ This is an indoor, individual method of smoking. You can, of course, smoke the ribs outdoors in a smoker or on the barbecue. Use this smoking method only with a fire extinguisher close at hand.

221

"More and more, restaurants are about theater, about surprising and delighting our guests. This beautiful dessert combines pineapple, cilantro, and lemon in a complex layering of flavors and textures."

Pineapple Carpaccio with Lemon Sorbet, Cilantro Granité, Pineapple Chips, and Crystallized Cilantro

THIS DESSERT COMES FROM THE GREAT FRENCH PASTRY CHEF and friend Pierre Hermé. He is from a tiny town close to Ribeauvillé. The interesting combination of pineapple, cilantro, and black pepper caught my imagination. We made it first for a New Year's Eve menu at Fleur de Lys and serve a version at Fleur, too. It does have a lot of separate elements, but they can all be completed ahead of time. Just at serving time, the pineapple sweetness is offset with a sprinkling of cracked black pepper and the color by a sprinkling of pomegranate seeds. When pomegranates are not in season, sprinkle the plates with edible flowers.

Serves 6

Pineapple Chips, Carpaccio, and Crystallized Cilantro

- 1 fresh pineapple, peeled but not cored
- ½ cup (3½ ounces) plus ½ cup (3½ ounces) sugar
- 1 large egg white
- 24 to 30 large fresh cilantro leaves

Cilantro Granité

Makes 2 cups

- ½ cup (3½ ounces) sugar
- ¼ cup lemon juice
- ½ cup orange juice
     Leaves from 15 cilantro sprigs
- 3 fresh basil leaves
- 3 medium (about 4 inches long) young spinach leaves
- ½ cup ice cubes (about 4 cubes)
- ¾ cup ice water

Lemon Sorbet

Makes about 2 cups

- 1 cup (7 ounces) sugar
     Freshly grated zest of ½ lemon
- 1 cup freshly squeezed lemon juice

Ingredients for Assembly

     Cracked black pepper
     Seeds from ½ pomegranate (optional)

Notes

♣ Making the pineapple chips is a several-day process developed by Fleur de Lys's pastry chef Gilberto Villarreal. The long waits both allow the sugar to work on the fruit, preserving it, and allow him the freedom to take the next step when he has time. Each step takes just a few minutes. Gilberto uses the same method for all our chips, including apple, pear, beet, rhubarb, turnips, and butternut squash—"nearly anything that does not dissolve into the syrup," says Gilberto. We use the meat slicer to achieve paper-thin slices, and good chips do need to be as thin as possible.

For the pineapple chips and carpaccio: Slice the pineapple into very thin rounds with a mandoline or meat slicer. If the slices tear, they will still be tasty chips. You can also slice as thinly as possible with a knife, but these will take longer to crisp up. Set aside a fourth of the slices for the chips and reserve the remaining slices, the carpaccio, in a covered container, refrigerated, for assembly.

Place ½ cup of the sugar and 1 cup water in a medium saucepan and bring to a boil over high heat, stirring until the sugar has dissolved. Remove from the heat and immediately immerse the slices in the syrup. Cover, cool, and refrigerate the slices for at least 2 hours or as long as overnight.

Drain the pineapple slices on a rack for 10 minutes. Arrange them on a baking sheet lined with a nonstick baking mat or parchment paper sprayed lightly and evenly with oil. Especially if you plan to shape the completed chips decoratively, perhaps curving them or rolling them into "cigarettes," arrange only a few slices per sheet. Then later you will be able to deal with them all before they cool too much to be flexible. Cover with a second sheet of oiled parchment paper and set aside at room temperature for 24 hours.

Preheat the oven to 150° to 200°F. Bake until crisp and lightly colored, about 2 hours. Increase the temperature to 350°F. Bake the chips for 1 minute. If you plan to bend or shape them, immediately remove them from the baking mat or parchment paper while they are warm and flexible. Store the chips in an airtight container to keep dry for up to 2 days, or freeze.

To crystallize the cilantro: Scatter the remaining ½ cup sugar on a plate or in a pie pan. Whip the egg white in a large bowl just until it is broken up and a little frothy. With a small brush, paint the cilantro leaves on both sides with the egg white and then dip them in the sugar. Lay the coated leaves on a rack and let them dry for at least 3 hours and as long as overnight.

To make the granité: Place the sugar and lemon juice in a small saucepan. Bring to a boil over medium-high heat, stirring until the sugar has dissolved. Remove the pan from the heat and let cool.

Place the orange juice, cilantro, basil, and spinach in a blender with the ice cubes and blend until the mixture is smooth and bright green. Strain through a fine-mesh strainer into a medium bowl.

Stir in the cooled lemon syrup and the ice water. Pour the mixture into a large glass baking dish so the mixture is no deeper than about 1 inch and place it in the freezer. Once the mixture begins to freeze, use a fork to stir and scrape the mixture about every 30 minutes until frozen solid so it forms a granular texture.

To make the lemon sorbet: Place 2 cups water and the sugar in a small saucepan and bring to a boil, stirring until the sugar has dissolved. Remove from the heat and stir in the lemon zest. Let the mixture cool to room temperature and stir in the lemon juice. Chill it until very cold. Freeze the lemon sorbet mixture in an ice-cream maker according to the manufacturer's instructions. Transfer to a container, cover, and store in the freezer.

To assemble the dessert: Transfer the sorbet to the refrigerator for about 30 minutes to allow it to soften enough to scoop easily. Arrange the reserved pineapple carpaccio on 6 large plates, curling the slices and placing them on two sides, leaving the center empty. Place a generous spoon of the cilantro granité in the center of the plates and top with another spoonful of lemon sorbet. Gently and decoratively arrange the crystallized cilantro and pineapple chips on and around the desserts. Sprinkle the plates with the cracked pepper and pomegranate seeds and serve immediately.

♣ Gilberto's chips are perfect, of course, but there is a quicker process that yields very good chips that are not quite up to his standard: Cut the pineapple into paper-thin rounds, lay them on oiled parchment paper on a baking sheet, brush them with simple syrup (1 cup sugar and 1 cup water brought just to a boil, then cooled), and bake at 250°F for 45 minutes to 1 hour, until crisp. The timing will depend on the thickness of the slices.

Caramel Latte Milkshakes

VANILLA ICE CREAM IS MY FAVORITE, but I love a great coffee ice cream, too. Growing up, when my dad pulled the warm *babas au rhum* out of their poaching syrup, my brother and I would rush for a bowl. In would go a baba and then ice cream on top. I always chose coffee on my baba. When we created the original milkshake menu for Burger Bar, I wanted to feature one made with coffee ice cream. Our experiments took off from there, playing with the idea of frozen coffee drinks. The addition of the cookie is my salute to America and milk and cookies. The caramel latte milkshake is now one of our best sellers.

Serves 4

Whipped Cream Topping

- 1 cup heavy cream
- 1 tablespoon powdered sugar
- 2 teaspoons vanilla extract

Shakes

- 1½ cups whole milk, very cold
- 5 cups premium coffee ice cream
- ½ cup caramel sauce (page 170) or honey-caramel sauce (page 131)
- 6 graham crackers (about 2-inches square)
- ½ cup (4 ounces) tequila-and-coffee-flavored liqueur (optional)

Toppings

- 4 tablespoons caramel sauce (page 170) or honey-caramel sauce (page 131), divided
- 4 tablespoons chocolate sauce (page 174, optional)
- 2 tablespoons butterscotch morsels
- 4 graham crackers (2-inch squares)
   Coffee beans or chocolate-covered coffee beans

To make the whipped cream topping: In a large bowl, whip the cream with the powdered sugar until firm. Whisk in the vanilla and refrigerate until needed. When ready to garnish the shakes, transfer the cream to a pastry bag fitted with a large star tip.

To make the shakes: Place the milk, ice cream, caramel sauce, graham crackers, and tequila in a blender and blend until smooth. Refrigerate to keep cold while you assemble the toppings.

To assemble the shakes: Lightly drizzle the inside of 4 chilled tall glasses with half of the caramel and all the chocolate sauce. Fill the glasses with the shake mixture. Pipe a high cap of whipped cream on top of each glass and sprinkle the morsels over the cream. Drizzle with the remaining half of caramel, tuck a cracker into the cream, and top with the coffee beans. Serve with a long-handled spoon and a fat straw.

Pink Monkey Milkshakes

Notes

♣ Make more strawberry puree than you need and add a splash of framboise to it. Keep the puree in a small piping bottle in the fridge as an adult topping for ice cream.

LISA BURNEY, THE GENERAL MANAGER of Burger Bar Las Vegas, came up with this milkshake that became a Burger Bar signature. This milkshake is a cross between a shake and a smoothie. For a lighter version on a hot summer day, use strawberry sorbet.

Serves 4

Whipped Cream Topping

1 cup heavy cream
1 tablespoon powdered sugar
2 teaspoons vanilla extract

Shakes

1½ cups whole milk, very cold
5 cups premium strawberry ice cream
3 medium bananas, peeled and sliced (¾ pound total when peeled)
¾ to 1 cup quartered ripe strawberries
½ cup balsamic vinegar, boiled until reduced to 2 tablespoons
1 teaspoon freshly ground black pepper or cubeb pepper
½ cup framboise (optional)

Toppings

½ cup very ripe strawberries (frozen and defrosted are fine) plus 4 large ripe strawberries, each cut lengthwise into 4 to 6 small wedges
1½ teaspoons plus 1½ teaspoons sugar
1 tablespoon balsamic vinegar, boiled until reduced to about 1 teaspoon
  Pinch of freshly ground black pepper or cubeb pepper
4 (½-inch-thick) banana slices
4 small fresh mint sprig tips

To make the whipped cream topping: In a large bowl, whip the cream with the powdered sugar until firm. Whisk in the vanilla and refrigerate until needed. When ready to garnish the shakes, transfer the cream to a pastry bag fitted with a large star tip.

To make the shakes: Blend the milk, ice cream, bananas, strawberries, balsamic reduction, pepper, and framboise in a blender until smooth, and refrigerate.

To make the toppings: In a small food processor, puree the ½ cup berries with 1½ teaspoons of the sugar, or to taste, until very smooth. Add the balsamic reduction and pepper and pulse in. Taste for balance and adjust as needed. You want a sauce you can drizzle. Scrape it into a small piping bottle.

Place the bananas on a small baking sheet and sprinkle generously with the remaining 1½ teaspoons of sugar. With a pastry torch, or under the broiler, caramelize the sugar.

To assemble the shakes: Drizzle half of the strawberry puree around the inside of 4 chilled tall glasses. Fill the glasses with the shake mixture. Pipe a high cap of whipped cream on top of each glass and tuck in the caramelized bananas, the strawberries, and the mint sprigs. Drizzle the remaining strawberry puree over the top of each glass and serve with a long-handled spoon and a fat straw.

Strawberry-Rhubarb Variation

Make a seasonal milkshake in the late spring and early summer when strawberries and rhubarb are in season. Simmer or bake equal amounts of strawberries and rhubarb together with brown sugar and a split vanilla bean until very tender. Puree it and add 1 cup of the puree to the shake instead of the fresh berries and omit the balsamic reduction. Use more of the puree as the sauce to drizzle over the top.

Pumpkin Pie Milkshakes

DURING THANKSGIVING WEEK 2009, I was invited to appear on *Live with Regis and Kelly* to give some ideas for using up holiday leftovers. When they handed me part of a pumpkin pie, I was inspired to make a milkshake. Everything went into the blender—the filling and the dough. After all, I thought, some ice creams include cookie dough. And to my surprise, everyone loved it. That's when I decided to add it to the Burger Bar menu. I like chocolate with pumpkin. If you do too, add some chocolate sauce (page 174) to the garnishes. You might want to serve the shake in small glasses alongside a pie or cake, such as a pumpkin-spice or apple cake, for a holiday dessert.

Serves 4

Whipped Cream Topping

- 1 cup heavy cream
- 1 tablespoon powdered sugar
- 2 teaspoons vanilla extract

Shakes

- 1½ cups whole milk, very cold
- 5 cups premium coffee, vanilla, or pumpkin ice cream
- ¾ cup canned pumpkin
- ⅓ cup caramel sauce (page 170)
- 4 graham crackers (2-inch squares)
- 1½ teaspoons ground cinnamon
- ½ cup spiced rum (optional)

Toppings

- 2 tablespoons pumpkin seeds
- 4 tablespoons caramel sauce (page 170), divided
- 4 tablespoons marshmallow topping (page 230)
- 4 graham crackers (2-inch squares) or chocolate wafers or chocolate sandwich cookies
- 4 small cinnamon sticks
- 1 teaspoon ground cinnamon

To make the whipped cream topping: In a large bowl, whip the cream with the powdered sugar until firm. Whisk in the vanilla and refrigerate until needed. When ready to garnish the shakes, transfer the cream to a pastry bag fitted with a large star tip.

To make the shakes. Place the milk, ice cream, pumpkin, caramel sauce, graham crackers, cinnamon, and rum in a blender and blend until smooth. Refrigerate to keep cold while you assemble the toppings.

To assemble the shakes: Toast the pumpkin seeds for the topping in a small dry skillet over medium-low heat until lightly browned and fragrant, about 5 minutes. Set them aside to cool. Pipe half of the caramel sauce and all of the marshmallow down the inside of 4 chilled tall glasses. Fill the glasses with the shake mixture. Pipe a high cap of whipped cream on top of each glass. Tuck a graham cracker or cookie and a cinnamon stick into the cream, and drizzle with the remaining half of the caramel. Dust with cinnamon and sprinkle with the pumpkin seeds. Serve with a long-handled spoon and a fat straw.

Nutella Milkshakes

Notes

♣ Keep your milkshake toppings in small piping bottles so you can decoratively drizzle the inside of the glasses.

THIS IS ONE OF THE MOST POPULAR MILKSHAKES at Burger Bar. The combination of chocolate and hazelnut is very popular in Europe. Chantal and her family grew up on it and still enjoy it. It is one of those classic combos frequently used in cake fillings, pastry, stuffed crêpes, and ice cream that really work.

Serves 4

Whipped Cream Topping

- 1 cup heavy cream
- 2 tablespoons and 1½ teaspoons Dutch-process cocoa powder
- 1 tablespoon powdered sugar
- 1½ teaspoons vanilla extract

Shakes

- 30 hazelnuts (about ½ ounce)
- 1½ cups whole milk, very cold
- 5 cups premium chocolate ice cream
- ½ cup Nutella, at room temperature
- ½ cup chocolate liqueur (optional)

Toppings

- 4 tablespoons Chocolate Sauce (page 174), divided
- 2 tablespoons marshmallow topping
- 2 tablespoons mini chocolate chips
- 20 mini marshmallows
- 2 large ripe strawberries, halved lengthwise
- 4 fresh mint sprig tips

To make the whipped cream topping: In a large bowl, whip the cream with the cocoa powder and powdered sugar until firm. Whisk in the vanilla and refrigerate until needed. When ready to garnish the shakes, transfer the cream to a pastry bag fitted with a large star tip.

To make the shakes: Toast the hazelnuts in a small dry skillet over medium to medium-low heat until fragrant and lightly browned, about 8 minutes. Be sure to stir so they toast evenly. Wrap the nuts in a kitchen towel and let cool for a minute or two, then rub them

briskly against each other inside the towel to loosen the skins. Chop the nuts coarsely. Set a third of the nuts aside to use as a topping and put the remainder in a blender with the milk, ice cream, Nutella, and chocolate liqueur and blend until smooth. Refrigerate to keep cold while you assemble the toppings.

To assemble the shakes: Lightly drizzle the inside of 4 chilled tall glasses with half of the chocolate sauce and all of the marshmallow. Fill the glasses with the shake mixture. Pipe a high cap of chocolate whipped cream on top of each glass and sprinkle the mini chocolate chips over the cream. Sprinkle with the remaining chopped hazelnuts. Lightly drizzle the remaining half of the chocolate sauce over all the shakes and dot each with 5 mini marshmallows, a strawberry half, and a mint sprig. Serve them with a long-handled spoon and a fat straw.

Marshmallow Topping for Milkshakes

Vanilla extract will tint the marshmallow a light brown. To avoid that, use vanilla powder, or scrape the seeds of half a vanilla bean into the sugar syrup and you'll have a speckled marshmallow.

- 1 teaspoon gelatin
- 1 cup sugar (7 ounces)
- 2 tablespoons light corn syrup or glucose
- 1½ teaspoons vanilla powder, or ½ vanilla bean

Place ¼ cup of water in the bowl of a stand mixer, sprinkle the gelatin over the water, and let soften. Meanwhile, place the sugar, another ¼ cup of water, and the corn syrup in a small saucepan and bring to a boil over high heat, stirring just until the sugar dissolves. Boil until it reaches the soft-ball stage, 235° to 250°F. With the mixer on high, very slowly add the syrup to the gelatin and whip until the mixture is white, thick, and cool, about 5 minutes. Add the vanilla powder and whip until evenly mixed.

Pour the marshmallow topping into a microwave-safe squeeze bottle and use immediately, or store in the refrigerator where it will become stiff. To warm so it becomes soft and runny again, microwave briefly on high just until the mixture softens; it will melt quickly, so watch it carefully. To make a chocolate marshmallow topping, melt 2 ounces of dark chocolate and whip it into the finished marshmallow.

"We were the first in Las Vegas to make frozen drinks and desserts with liquid nitrogen."

Affogato

AT FLEUR THE *AFFOGATO* SERVICE makes a spectacular show. The waiter brings a special bowl filled with the ice-cream base and a thermos of nitrogen to the table along with shots of Irish cream liqueur and espresso. The nitrogen is poured into the bowl while the waiter whisks gently. But almost all the guest sees is a cloud of smoke as the nitrogen flows into and out of the bowl and over the table. In a few minutes, the crème anglaise base has become a very cold, smooth, airy ice cream with an exceptional texture. Nitrogen makes a great show, but it is harmless once it gets to the table.

Serves 4

½ cup heavy cream

1½ teaspoons sugar

1 pint premium vanilla ice cream

1 cup Irish cream liqueur

4 shots hot, fresh espresso

Dutch-process cocoa powder, for dusting (optional)

Dark chocolate shavings, for dusting (optional)

In a medium bowl, whip the cream with the sugar until it holds soft mounds. Stop here if you will spoon the cream onto the dessert. If you want to pipe it, continue to whip the cream just until it's firm. Set it aside until needed.

Place 2 generous scoops of ice cream in 4 large coffee cups or heatproof glasses. Pour 1½ to 2 ounces of Irish cream liqueur into each cup and then add a shot of espresso. Top with the whipped cream, dust with cocoa powder and chocolate shavings, and serve immediately.

Love & Partnership

"When we have an unscheduled day at home together, we look forward to it for weeks."

A RARE SUNDAY AT HOME IN LAS VEGAS

HUBERT: We have very, very few unscheduled days. When we do have one, we talk about it together for weeks ahead of time. I can't wait until we can lock ourselves up together.

CHANTAL: I can sit with a book sometimes and relax. Not Hubert. Once we rented a house in the south of France. There were fruit trees, peaches and apricots, dropping their fruit. Next thing I knew Hubert and my mom were making jam.

HUBERT: That's why I love the Las Vegas house so much. I can work for a while and then go outside. If I sit down, I am planning what to move or plant or trim. During my runs through the neighborhood, I see what the gardeners are up to, how they train the trees. Then I go to the store, buy what I need, and do the same. But that's not

238

From left: I'm cutting prosciutto with my vintage Berkel meat slicer with Debra and Mark Dommen. A detail of Chantal's centerpiece. Chantal and me preparing the brioche for breakfast.

Pages 236 and 237: Chantal and me enjoying cocktails at home in Las Vegas.

work for me; instead, it restores me. We usually don't go to bed until sometime between midnight and 2 a.m. So on our day off, we sleep in. After a workout, we have breakfast about 11 a.m. or noon.

CHANTAL: Sometimes Hubert will go out for a loaf of the ciabatta bread that I like. The bakery is just a ten-minute drive. They also have great brioche filled with pastry cream (page 126).

HUBERT: And the best panettone—one with a bittersweet chocolate filling and one with a vanilla cream.

CHANTAL: While Hubert is gone, I will make the coffee and orange juice and get out some of my compote (page 245) or jam. The weather is always spectacular here, and the house has a great

From left: A French antique copper bucket. Chantal's colorful table setting for an outdoor lunch party. Cooking lobsters on the grill. Shirlene Miyake prepares to tuck into a lobster.

outdoor dining space, so we take everything outdoors.

HUBERT: The weather and being outdoors are maybe the most important reasons we are here. It reminds us both of the time we used to live in the south of France.

CHANTAL: Sometimes we'll have a soft-boiled egg (page 242) the way I had them growing up—with sugar instead of salt and thin, finger-shaped brioche toasts to dip into the egg. In the winter, we might watch a movie before we get up.

HUBERT: When the sun goes down, Chantal makes us one of her cocktails (page 261) before dinner. The table is always beautifully decorated and has a theme. She might pick some fresh flowers or greens from the garden and arranges them on the table with some of her large collection of linens and napkin rings. We have huge candles all over the place. There are oversize candle lanterns outdoors and candles of all sizes indoors, too.

CHANTAL: I think it's important to set a pretty table, to make an occasion out of every meal together. I am always adding to my tabletop collection and love candles. So I light them all even when it's just the two of us.

HUBERT: I've found a supplier in Las Vegas who makes mini-bretzel (page 126) buns, and I will bring home a half dozen. I flash them on the barbecue for two or three minutes, and then we dip them into honey mustard and have them with our cocktails. Afterwards, I'll go choose a good bottle of wine, open it, and pour Chantal and me a glass. Then we enjoy it as we cook. We are always eating late.

CHANTAL: We love to cook outside in Las Vegas. It's something we've discovered since we bought the house here.

HUBERT: It keeps the house cool and keeps the mess of cooking outdoors, too. I love to use cast-iron pans on the barbecue. Often, I'll use the barbecue just as a heat source—I crank up the heat, preheat the pan until it's really hot, and then I can give scallops a nice sear. Or I might give steaks a dry rub and sear them in the pan. Then the rub doesn't fall into the fire.

CHANTAL: I leave the outdoor cooking to Chef. But when I'm in the kitchen, I love dishes that include everything in one pot, like our friend Frenchy's paella (page 278).

Soft-Boiled Sweet Eggs with Brioche Mouillettes

IN CHANTAL'S HOME, her mom soft-boiled eggs and put them in little egg cups, an appealing way to serve them, especially for kids who can be fussy. And Chantal liked to sprinkle hers with a little sugar instead of salt or pepper. When they are teamed with brioche toasts spread with honey-butter for dipping into the egg, I am not sure there is a child who could resist. At least not in our house, where Chantal and I will sometimes have these for breakfast. Egg cups that hold a single egg upright used to be in nearly every household. Look for some in houseware stores.

Serves 2 to 4 (1 or 2 eggs per person)

- 4 large eggs
- 2 tablespoons unsalted butter, at room temperature
- 1 tablespoon and 1 teaspoon honey
- 4 (³⁄₈-inch-thick) slices brioche (page 126)

  Sugar or truffle salt or sea salt and freshly ground black pepper, for seasoning

Preheat the oven to 375°F. Line a small sheet pan with a nonstick baking mat or parchment paper. Remove the eggs from the refrigerator.

In a small bowl, mash together the butter and honey. Spread the brioche with the honey-butter and refrigerate for 10 minutes until the butter firms up. Cut the bread into "fingers" of an equal size, about 2½ inches long and ³⁄₈ inch wide. Arrange them on the prepared baking sheet and place them in the oven until lightly toasted, about 10 minutes.

While the *mouillettes* toast, cook the eggs. Bring a covered 1½-quart saucepan of water to a boil. Turn off the heat. Put the eggs in a slotted spoon and very slowly lower them into the water. They will fizz slightly as the air forces itself out through the shell, but they will not crack if you go slowly. Immediately cover the pot and set the timer for 8 minutes. Remove the eggs and place them in the egg cups on saucers and arrange the hot brioche *mouillettes* next to them. Provide a knife or an egg topper so each person can trim off the top of the eggs as well as a small spoon for scooping the egg. Sprinkle the egg with the seasoning of your choice: sugar, salt and pepper, or truffle salt.

Chantal's mom, Pierrina Martin (*right*), is a great jam maker and Chantal loves to make jam, too.

Spiced Apple and Orange Compote

WHEN WE WERE GROWING UP, everyone made jam at home. Chantal remembers her mother's jars of jam cooling upside down on the kitchen counter. She used whatever fruit was in season and stored the jars in the cellar, where they stayed cool and dark. Chantal makes jam and compotes occasionally at home, and we have them for breakfast on the weekend or warm over ice cream or yogurt.

Makes about 7 (8-ounce) jars

- 1½ pounds Valencia oranges, well scrubbed
- 2 pounds tart apples, peeled
- 3 cups sugar
- Juice of 1 lemon
- 1 teaspoon ground cinnamon or 1 cinnamon stick
- ½ teaspoon ground ginger
- ½ teaspoon ground cardamom
- ¼ teaspoon ground coriander
- ¼ teaspoon ground allspice
- ¼ teaspoon freshly grated nutmeg
- ⅛ teaspoon ground cloves

Quarter the oranges lengthwise, remove and discard any seeds, and slice the quarters crosswise as thinly as you can. Put them into a deep heavy saucepan. Quarter the apples, core them, and then slice the quarters crosswise into 3 or 4 thick slices. You want the chunks large so they don't break down during cooking. Add the apples to the oranges with the sugar, lemon juice, cinnamon, ginger, cardamom, coriander, allspice, nutmeg, and cloves. Add 2 cups water to the pan to prevent burning as you bring the fruit to a boil over high heat. Simmer, uncovered, until the orange peels are tender, about 40 minutes. Especially toward the end of cooking, make sure to stir well to prevent scorching.

Let the compote cool and pour it into jars, cover, and refrigerate. They will keep for several weeks. Or let the compote cool slightly and then pour it, while still warm, over ice cream.

Notes

♣ A compote is a chunky mixture, and this one is low-sugar, compared to a jam, so it is best to keep it refrigerated. Chantal keeps her compotes in a container in the fridge and puts some into jars when she plans to give them away.

♣ Chantal always returns from Alsace with a suitcase stuffed with favorite ingredients, including a supply of the spice blend used in *Pain d'Épices* (page 298), which she used in her compote. American pumpkin-pie spices would work, too, if you don't want to measure individual spices.

Living the Mobile Life on the Côte d'Azur

HUBERT: Chantal and I drove back to Alsace between leaving Moulin de Mougins and going to Le Chantecler on the Côte d'Azur. We passed a field full of caravans, trailers to live in. I thought it would be pretty funny and unique to live in one of those. And it would allow us to be free, to move when and where we wanted. Chantal immediately agreed.

CHANTAL: Hubert's brother installed a radio for us. We had a little shower, a nice big bedroom, kitchenette, dining room, even a TV.

HUBERT: We were able to buy the big caravan because I had a big military Land Rover, the model with the lights on top and the double roof to let the air circulate when in the desert. I had bought it with dreams of traveling. We hung the trailer off the back of the car and headed south. We had no idea where we would park the trailer, but we found a beautiful campground, empty because it was the off-season. It was an exceptional spot, and I think the owner let us lease a space because I told him about my job at Le Negresco. That is where we found our first cat. She was just a little cat who showed up and we started feeding her. Soon we had two cats.

CHANTAL: It was such a pretty spot, and we had it all to ourselves. The owner had a big house above the park, and this was really his private property. He only rented spaces in the summer for a little extra money. It was as if we had a great little house surrounded by a beautiful garden. We just slept in the trailer and lived outdoors. On days off, everyone from the restaurant would come over. Hubert's parents came twice to vacation with us while we were there.

HUBERT: When we moved to Le Prieuré in the Loire Valley, we arrived with the trailer, the cats, the whole thing. In the beginning, for the first month or two, we stayed in the trailer and did not move into the house, La Pistol-

lerie, which the hotel owner M. Traversac had provided for us. We felt cozy in the trailer. Eventually we did move into La Pistollerie and lived there for over a year. Then one day I got a call from Roger Vergé asking me to open his restaurant in Brazil. When I told Chantal about the call, she had no hesitation about leaving. She is always ready for a new adventure.

CHANTAL: Brazil? I was ready to go that very day.

HUBERT: By then we had been together for about five years and never talked about marriage.

CHANTAL: Our parents didn't like it that we weren't married. And in France at that time, couples didn't usually live together without marriage, but it wasn't important to either of us. We were very independent.

HUBERT: But, in order for Chantal to come with me and be able to stay in Brazil during the length of my contract, we had to be married. So I said, "Let's get married. Then, whatever happens, we are together."

CHANTAL: We went to city hall and arranged the date and time. As soon as we got back to the car, we remembered that we wanted to have dinner at Charles Barrier, a three-star in Tours.

HUBERT: We'd planned to marry on our day off, but Charles Barrier was not open that day. So we rushed back into city hall and changed the date because the dinner was the most important part of the wedding day.

CHANTAL: It was a really fun day. In the morning we sat at our house, La Pistollerie, and had coffee and croissants. And champagne. Then we went to city hall. I still have the dress I wore. Then the official asked for the wedding rings.

HUBERT: We hadn't planned on rings. We thought they were for church weddings and this wedding was just for the paperwork for Brazil.

CHANTAL: François Tournet, the dining room manager at Le Prieuré, and his wife, Pascale, lent us their rings. Afterward, we went back home and had more champagne.

HUBERT: Dinner at Charles Barrier was small, just six of us: Chantal and me, plus Philippe Doumerc, the general manager of Le Prieuré, François and Pascale, and our friend Michel Veron who came for the event. He was in the

Army and got a two-day pass to attend. Later he came with me to Brazil as my sous chef.

CHANTAL: We have no pictures of our wedding. Zero. François took pictures all day on his brand-new camera. But, because he was unfamiliar with it, he accidentally opened the back and exposed all the film. Before we went to Brazil, we went back to Alsace and got married again, a church wedding this time with all the families.

HUBERT: My grandmothers, especially Grand-ma Keller, would not have survived without a church wedding. We married in this chapel at the Monastery at Dusenbach.

247

"The house in Las Vegas has great outdoor spaces, so we eat outside as much as possible. It reminds us of when we lived in the south of France."

La Tourte de la Vallée de Munster/Alsatian Pork Pie

THIS DELICIOUS MEAT PIE comes from Munster, close to Chantal's home village. Her family had it often, but it was not something we ate. Instead my dad made a *pâté chaud*. Both are meat pies, but the filling for the *tourte* is finely chopped by hand and the meat for a *pâté chaud* is cut more coarsely. In Alsace, you will find versions made with beef or mixed meats as well as this pork version. Serve it warm or at room temperature for an informal lunch or supper, or take it along on a picnic. You can chop the meat yourself—buy pork shoulder, trim away large pieces of fat, and then chop the meat coarsely—but for ease I suggest buying coarsely ground meat with a loose, fluffy texture.

Serves 8 to 10

4 slices stale bread or brioche (about 4 ounces)
6 tablespoons whole milk
1 tablespoon unsalted butter
1 medium yellow onion, thinly sliced
3 cloves garlic, very finely chopped
1¾ pounds coarsely ground pork
¼ teaspoon ground coriander
    Pinch of freshly grated nutmeg
¼ cup finely chopped fresh flat-leaf parsley
1 teaspoon finely chopped fresh thyme
2 large eggs
    Sea salt and freshly ground black pepper
2 sheets puff pastry (11 by 15 inches)

Preheat the oven to 400°F. In a large bowl, soak the bread in the milk until very soft. Meanwhile, heat the butter in a medium skillet over medium heat. Add the onion and garlic and cook until the onion has softened, 5 to 8 minutes. Do not let it brown.

Scrape the onion and garlic into the bowl with the bread and milk mixture, the pork, coriander, nutmeg, parsley, thyme, and 1 of the eggs. Separate the second egg, reserve the yolk in a small bowl, and add the white to the pork. Season generously with salt and pepper and knead the stuffing mixture thoroughly until evenly combined.

To check the seasoning, pinch off a small amount (about a tablespoon-ful) of the pork mixture and cook it in a small pan over medium heat until done, about 3 minutes. Taste for seasoning and adjust the rest of the pork mixture as needed with salt and pepper.

On a lightly floured work surface, roll out 1 sheet of pastry until ⅛ inch thick and trim into a 15-inch circle. Gently fit the pastry into a large pie pan 10 or 11 inches in diameter. Leave a generous 1-inch pastry border hanging over the edge. Heap the uncooked pork mixture into the pan, mounding it in the center.

Add ½ teaspoon of cold water to the reserved egg yolk and beat with a fork until smooth. Brush the exposed pastry edge with the egg wash. Roll out the second sheet of pastry as you did the first. Fit the pastry onto the top of the pie and trim the edges to match the bottom pastry. Press the edges together to seal, then roll them up and crimp the edges together to seal well. Brush the top with the egg wash and cut a small central hole, a chimney, through the pastry to allow the steam to escape. If desired, with the back of a knife make some decorative lines through the glaze onto the pastry.

Bake until the filling is cooked through—160°F and the juices run clear—and the pastry is a rich golden brown, about 40 minutes. You will be able to see the juices bubbling around the chimney. Allow the *tourte* to rest for 10 minutes before cutting and serving.

Notes

♣ You can use either puff pastry or pie pastry (page 257) to enclose the pork stuffing. When Chantal makes this at home, she buys puff pastry. In fact, the first time she made it at home she discovered that she had bought frozen puff pastry shells, not sheets. Her solution: "I went to my favorite cook-book and made the puff pastry from scratch, all the turns, everything." You, however, might want to just buy a package of frozen puff pastry sheets.

♣ The *tourte* is baked in a special earthenware mold, a big round with a ½-inch rim. The pastry is wrapped around the filling in such a way that you don't see a seam. If you use a regular pie dish, you can't easily seal the pas-try in the traditional way. But your *tourte* will still be beautiful and delicious.

Thinly Sliced Salmon with Caviar and Mustard-Seed Sauce

CHANTAL AND I LOVE SALMON, and this is a great dish, because when you eat it, it really comes together nicely. I made it on *Top Chef Masters* in a college dorm room, and we serve it at Fleur de Lys, too. But if I could make it in a dorm with a toaster oven, I am sure you can make it at home. The salmon is so thinly sliced that it is *mi-cuit* (half-cooked) to prevent overcooking. The caviar is definitely optional but does make a more elegant dish.

Serves 4

- 8 slices baguette, cut on the diagonal about 6 inches long
  Extra-virgin olive oil for drizzling
  Sea salt and freshly ground white pepper
- ¼ cup mayonnaise
- 1 tablespoon coarse-grain Dijon mustard
- 1 tablespoon thinly sliced fresh chives
  Freshly squeezed lemon juice
- ½ pound salmon fillet with the skin on, pin bones removed
- 4 lemon wedges
- 2 tablespoons caviar—such as white fish roe, salmon roe, or sturgeon caviar (optional)
- 4 sprigs fresh flat-leaf parsley (optional)
- 4 cherry tomatoes, halved (optional)
- ¼ English cucumber, thinly sliced (optional)
- 4 or 8 baby radishes (optional)

Preheat the oven to 400°F. Drizzle or brush the baguette slices with olive oil, sprinkle lightly with salt, place them on a baking sheet, and toast in the oven until brown and crunchy, about 10 minutes, turning them over and rotating the pan to ensure even browning. Increase the heat to 450°F and set the croutons aside until needed. In a small bowl, whisk together the mayonnaise, mustard, chives, a squeeze of lemon juice, and salt and pepper to taste. Set aside until needed.

With a very sharp thin-bladed knife held at a 30-degree angle, cut the fillet crosswise into 4 thin slices, separating them from the skin. The slices should be a little thicker than smoked salmon, about 3/16 inch thick.

Wipe a sheet pan pretty generously with water. Dip your hand in a bowl of water and smear it around the pan. Sprinkle it with salt and pepper. Line a second sheet pan with plastic wrap. Lay the salmon slices on the wet, seasoned pan and drizzle the fish with just a little more water to keep it moist. Roast just until the fish is opaque, 1 to 2 minutes. Remove it from the oven and let it sit for just a minute. With a thin-bladed spatula, transfer the fish to the second sheet pan, cover with more plastic wrap, and refrigerate. The fish can be cooked up to 5 or 6 hours ahead of time.

When ready to serve, smear a thin layer of the mustard sauce on each plate, making a circle a little larger than the slice of salmon. Place the salmon on top; there should be a border of sauce about 1½ inches all around the fish. Serve with 2 croutons and a lemon wedge on the side of the plate and spoon a little mound of caviar in the center of the salmon slices. Arrange the parsley, tomatoes, cucumber, and radishes around the salmon and serve.

Notes

♣ The vegetables—the tomatoes, cucumber, radishes—are just to add crunch and color to the plate. Especially if you are not serving caviar, it would make a pretty dish to cut radishes into a thin julienne and scatter them over the fish with perhaps microgreens or celery leaves. It's up to you.

251

Let's Go Dancing

HUBERT: The first time I met Chantal was on a weeknight. I didn't want to go out. But Christian Bouvarel, who was then a *commis* at L'Auberge de L'Ill, had a girlfriend he wanted to see. Christian and I were close friends. I was still an apprentice and had almost no money, but I had a car that my dad had bought for me when I turned eighteen. And Christian had a little salary but no car. He twisted my arm until I agreed to drive. That's the night we went to Munster and I met Chantal. (Later, he and I worked together again, when I was putting together the production recipes for Epcot Center and worked in Paul Bocuse's kitchen. By then Christian was the sous chef there.)

CHANTAL: Actually, Hubert met my father before he met me. They shared a room in the hospital. My father had had some surgery and Hubert was in for appendicitis. My father told me Hubert worked at L'Auberge de L'Ill. And when I saw him in his hospital bed, he looked really tall and so skinny. I never spoke with him, though. The night we met, we didn't recognize each other, but as we talked, I figured out that he was the one in the hospital with my father.

HUBERT: Then we started dating. It was 1973.

CHANTAL: I was living at home, and Hubert and I would go out every Saturday after he finished service, about 11 p.m. My parents would think I was crazy to go out at eleven, so I would go out earlier with friends and tell

Hubert where to meet me. I sometimes wonder how we managed it without cell phones.

HUBERT: Smoke signals.

CHANTAL: Early on while we were dating, I asked Hubert over for lunch while my parents were gone on vacation. I've always loved to eat, but when I was living at home I didn't like to cook. My mom always complained, "What will you do when you are married one day and do not cook?" When I met Hubert, I came home and announced that she no longer had to worry; I had met a chef.

HUBERT: That lunch would be the first time Chantal cooked for me.

CHANTAL: It was summertime. I remember really well that we had melon and ham. That was safe because it didn't involve cooking. And roasted chicken with some vegetables.

HUBERT: Diced carrots, celery, petits pois, haricots verts, all cut the same size, cooked, and then bound with a little mayonnaise—and you have a *macédoine de legumes*, a classic.

CHANTAL: I had no idea how long to cook the chicken and wanted to make sure it was done. I put it on the rotisserie at 8 a.m. and did not take it off until noon. It was a little dry, but we ate it. A couple of months later, Hubert explained to me in detail how to properly cook a chicken.

HUBERT: And since then, Chantal has followed my advice.

252

Braised Brussels Sprouts with Bacon

BRUSSELS SPROUTS ARE ONE VEGETABLE Chantal really likes. This old-fashioned style of cooking results in very tender sprouts with nothing crisp about them. But some vegetables taste their best when cooked all the way through like this. Rosemary may be an unusual herb to use with sprouts, but Chantal and I cook with it often at home because we have a bush in the backyard. Try to choose sprouts of equal size so that they cook evenly. Sure, you can cut them in half, but then they can fall apart during cooking.

Serves 4

This twisted, asymmetrical stone arch is the only one of its kind in all of Alsace, and the only one I've ever seen anywhere.

3 slices bacon (3 ounces), cut crosswise into ½-inch-wide strips

1 small yellow onion, chopped

1 clove garlic, very finely chopped

1½ pounds medium-size brussels sprouts, stems trimmed

1 sprig fresh rosemary

2 cups vegetable broth or chicken broth
   Sea salt and freshly ground black pepper

In a large saucepan over medium heat, cook the bacon until crisp, about 8 minutes. Add the onion and garlic and cook until soft, 5 to 8 minutes. Add the sprouts to the pan with the rosemary, broth, and salt and pepper to taste. Cover, bring to a boil, and simmer until the sprouts are tender, 12 to 15 minutes. If more than ¼ inch of cooking liquid remains, uncover and boil off any surplus. Discard the rosemary, taste and adjust the seasoning, and serve immediately.

Les Choux Farcis à l'Alsacienne / Braised Stuffed Cabbage Leaves

THIS IS A VERY HOMEY DISH you find in nearly every household in Alsace. It is one of Chantal's favorite dishes from her home. "My mom would make it on Sundays," she says. "I remember her cooking the cabbage leaves and draping them over an upside-down colander to drain. She cut the ribs out of the leaves, stuffed them, rolled them, and put them in a pan with some butter and a chicken consommé. All morning my father hovered in front of the oven, opening the door, taking a spoon, and basting the rolls with the consommé. It was a favorite dish of his and mine. If there were any leftovers, we would reheat them and have them for lunch the next day. When I think about it like this, I can almost smell it cooking." If your butcher carries loose, uncooked sausage meat, choose that. Or buy links and remove the casing. Use your favorite sausage, spicy or sweet. Ground veal can be difficult to find and is more expensive than most other ground meats. You can substitute ground pork with great success.

Serves 4

¾ pound ground veal
½ pound pork sausage meat
¼ pound bacon, finely chopped
1 cup finely chopped shallots
3 tablespoons finely chopped fresh flat-leaf parsley
2 cloves garlic, minced
½ cup dried breadcrumbs, such as *panko*
2 large eggs, lightly beaten
Pinch of freshly grated nutmeg
Sea salt and freshly ground black pepper
1 large savoy or green cabbage (about 4 pounds)
1 tablespoon unsalted butter, plus more for buttering the baking dish
1 large yellow onion (8 to 10 ounces), finely chopped
1 medium carrot, finely sliced
½ cup aromatic white wine such as Tokay or Riesling
1½ cups low-salt vegetable, chicken, or beef broth
2 sprigs fresh thyme
1 bay leaf

In a large bowl, combine the veal, sausage, bacon, shallots, parsley, garlic, breadcrumbs, eggs, and nutmeg. Season the mixture with 1 teaspoon of salt and ½ teaspoon pepper. Knead together with your hands until evenly combined. Fry a little nut of the meat mixture in a small skillet until cooked through and taste for seasoning. Adjust the seasoning in the remaining meat mixture, cover, and refrigerate.

Bring a large pot of water to a boil and add a tablespoon of salt. Prepare an ice-water bath. Core the cabbage with a small, sharp knife. Discard the outermost leaves. Carefully separate at least 8 large leaves (plus several more leaves to use for patching), making sure to keep them whole. Plunge the leaves into the boiling water and cook until limp and flexible, about 6 minutes. Immediately drain the leaves and submerge in the ice-water bath to stop the cooking. Spread the leaves on kitchen towels or paper towels to dry. Cut the rib from the center of each leaf, but do not cut the leaf all the way in half.

Generously butter a 9-inch square baking pan. Divide the stuffing into 8 equal portions. Line the inside of a wide, round coffee cup or small bowl with a 12-inch square of plastic wrap. Fit a large cabbage leaf inside the cup, placing the outside of the leaf against the wrap and overlapping the edges where the rib was removed. If you need to use 2 leaves, overlap them. Trim the leaves, if necessary, to make them more manageable.

Spoon one portion of the filling into the leaf and fold it over the stuffing, making sure that the filling is completely enclosed. Use the extra leaves for patching wherever you need them. Twist the corners of the plastic wrap firmly together. As you twist, the leaf will form itself into a tight ball around the stuffing. Unwrap the stuffed leaf and place it seam side down in the prepared baking pan, and repeat with the remaining leaves and filling. The cabbage rolls should fit snugly in a single layer. Place the baking pan on a sheet pan to make it easier to get in and out of the oven without spilling.

Preheat the oven to 350°F. Melt the 1 tablespoon of butter in a medium skillet over medium heat. Add the onion and carrot, cover, and cook until the vegetables are soft but not browned, about 8 minutes. Uncover and add the wine, broth, thyme, and bay leaf. Season lightly with salt and pepper. Bring the broth to a boil and pour it over the stuffed cabbage leaves. Cover the pan tightly with a lid or with parchment paper and a layer of heavy-duty aluminum foil and bake until the cabbage is very tender and the stuffing registers 160°F on an instant-read thermometer, about 35 minutes. When done, serve directly from the baking pan in soup plates, spooning the braising liquid around the rolls.

Pâte Brisée / Pie Pastry

WHEN WE WERE KIDS, my brother and I helped my dad in the pastry shop. If he said, "Now add another two scoops of flour," we felt we were really participating. It wasn't until I got to L'Auberge de L'Ill that I learned to make pie pastry. Our guests expected a choice of two or three seasonal pies. This recipe is the simple ratio I learned. All these years later, I can still remember it without thinking. It may be simple and easy to remember, but it also is a great recipe and really works.

Makes enough for a 2-crust pie

- 3 cups and 3 tablespoons (1 pound) unbleached all-purpose flour, plus more for dusting the work surface
- ½ teaspoon sea salt
- 1 cup (2 sticks or ½ pound) unsalted butter, chilled and cut into small bits
- ½ cup ice water
  Softened or melted butter, for brushing on the baking mold

Place the flour and salt in a food processor and pulse to combine. Add the butter and pulse quickly until the mixture resembles sand. Add the ice water and pulse again just until the dough forms numerous small lumps. Do not let it form a ball or the dough will have been overworked.

Scrape the dough onto a work surface. With your hands, gather and knead the mass together into a ball and divide it in half. Shape each into a flat disk, wrap them well in plastic wrap, and refrigerate for at least 1½ hours and for as long as 24 hours. The dough can be frozen for up to a month.

To roll out the pastry, place the disk on a floured work surface and roll gently, easing the dough into a circle. After each back-and-forth roll of the rolling pin, give the pastry a quarter turn or so, flouring underneath and on top as needed. Flip the pastry occasionally and continue to roll until the pastry is between ⅛ and 1/16 inch thick and a 15- to 16-inch circle.

Butter the pie pan or tart mold and then fit the dough into it. Lift the dough up and ease it down, gently pushing it into the sides and bottom so there are no gaps. The most important thing is to leave no air pockets between the pan and the dough, but be careful not to stretch the dough. The pastry should hang over the edge by 1½ inches all around the rim.

Fold an inch of the pastry overhang into the pan, doubling its thickness, and then roll your rolling pin over the rim to cut off excess pastry. Lift the folded pastry from the inside and pinch it nicely onto the rim. Where you have pinched and the pastry is thin, that is where the heat will penetrate first and secure the pastry onto the rim. With a fork, prick the pastry all over.

Chill the pastry for at least 1 hour before filling or baking. Or wrap the mold well in a double layer of plastic wrap and freeze for up to a month. If blind baking, do not defrost your crust first. Just bake for a few minutes longer than usual.

When ready to bake, preheat the oven to 375°F. To blind bake the crust, line the mold with aluminum foil, shiny side down. Fill the pan to the top with dried beans or pie weights and bake until the pastry has firmed, about 20 minutes. Remove the weights and foil and return the pan to the oven to bake until pale gold, about another 5 minutes.

To fully bake the pie shell, continue to bake until the pastry is well browned, about 35 minutes total.

Notes

♣ For a single crust, cut the recipe in half.

♣ If the dough is overworked, the gluten will have formed and no amount of relaxing will fix it. Overworked dough will be harder to roll out and will slump during baking.

♣ I make my dough in a food processor now. When I learned at L'Auberge de L'Ill, we used the electric mixer fitted with the paddle attachment. But the degree to which the butter and flour would be mixed together—until the texture resembled sand (*sablé*, we called it)—is the same. Once you get the hang of it, I think the food processor makes the best dough. It's so fast and not messy.

Whenever we are in Ribeauvillé we shop for antique molds to add to our collection.

Allumettes aux Fromages / Cheese Straws

Notes

♣ Sprinkling the pastry with cheese is just the beginning. Let your imagination loose. You can dust the pastry strips with poppy seeds, toasted cumin seeds, sesame seeds, and even some mustard seeds, finely chopped herbs, and chili flakes. Serve the cheese straws with thinly sliced prosciutto or other cured meats, such as duck breast. To make a simple, very easy cookie, dust the pastry very generously with granulated cinnamon-sugar and bake.

WHILE PREPARING FOR AN EPISODE OF MY COOKING SHOW for public television, *Secrets of a Chef*, every recipe has to be prepared at least three times. This means lots of leftovers. All my training has taught me not to waste. After filming the Beef Wellington (page 314) episode, I had lots of extra puff pastry pieces. For some reason, I remembered cheese straws. My dad used to make them for restaurants, and I hadn't eaten them for so long. While Chantal set the dinner table, I searched the refrigerator to see what cheeses we might have and then made them. It was fun, and we ate nearly the whole basketful with cocktails.

Makes about 50

1 sheet puff pastry (11 by 15 inches)
   Unbleached all-purpose flour, for dusting the work surface
2 egg yolks
   Sea salt
1½ cups coarsely grated Mimolette or Gruyère cheese
¼ cup freshly grated Parmesan cheese

Preheat the oven to 375°F. Lay the pastry out on a lightly floured work surface and roll it into a very thin (less than ⅛ inch) rectangle. Prick the pastry all over. In a small bowl, whisk the egg yolks with a teaspoon of water until smooth. Brush the pastry all over with the egg yolk glaze. Season lightly with salt, sprinkle the cheese evenly over the pastry, and press lightly to help the cheese adhere. Using a sharp knife or a pizza wheel, cut the pastry into strips ½ or ¾ inch wide and 4 to 5 inches long.

Line 2 baking sheets with parchment paper. Pick up each pastry strip and twist the ends in opposite directions, with the same motion as wringing out a towel, to put two or more twists in each piece. Arrange them on the prepared baking sheets and bake until brown and crisp, about 15 minutes. Let them cool for a few minutes, arrange in a basket, and serve.

After rolling out the pastry, sprinkle it generously with cheese.

Using a sharp knife, cut the pastry into strips ½ or ¾ inch wide and about 4 to 5 inches long.

Give each strip one or two twists, transfer to the baking sheet, and gently press the ends down.

Bake the *allumettes* in a hot oven until they are crispy and golden brown.

Chantal's Pitcher of Cosmopolitans

CHANTAL LEARNED TO MAKE COCKTAILS after the fire (see page 154) at Fleur de Lys; it was only then that we actually spent any time at home. Now she makes her cocktails in a large glass pitcher and keeps it in the freezer. Even when guests surprise us by dropping by the house, Chantal can pour a festive drink right away. She always measures, using the same ratio of ingredients whether she is mixing up four or twenty cocktails. In the heat of Las Vegas, a drink warms up in no time at all. By keeping the mixture in the freezer, the oranges freeze hard but the alcohol does not. When you pour the drink, the alcohol tastes as if it has little icicles in it and the orange slices act like ice cubes. This is a great way to serve cold drinks so they don't get diluted from melting ice. Make sure each cocktail contains at least two orange wedges; it's fun to fish them out of your glass and eat them once you've finished your drink. Chantal says, "I prefer to use pomegranate juice instead of cranberry juice in my cosmos, for the flavor and also for the color."

Notes

♣ If you don't make the cocktail ahead of time, shake it with ice in a cocktail shaker until cold, and then strain into a chilled martini glass.

Makes about 6 cocktails

1 seedless orange
1 cup pomegranate juice
1 cup vodka
¼ cup Grand Marnier
¼ cup gin
¼ cup freshly squeezed orange juice
Juice of 1 juicy lime

Trim off the flower and stem end of the orange and then cut it lengthwise into wedges, each about ½ inch thick. Place the orange pieces in a 1- or 1½-quart pitcher with the pomegranate juice, vodka, Grand Marnier, gin, orange juice, and lime juice. Stir well and store in the freezer.

To serve, stir the cocktail well with a long-handled spoon and pour into chilled martini glasses. Add several orange wedges to each glass.

Alsatian Plum Tart with Cinnamon-Sugar

ALSACE IS FAMOUS FOR *quetsch*—a small, sweet, oval plum. During their season, in late summer, we make lots of jam and tarts. The plums have a velvety blue-black skin and golden flesh. The riper they are, the stronger their spice aroma. Here in America, look for small plums with a good sweet/tart balance such as Santa Rosa plums. Another good plum to use is a French plum or a prune plum. When the fruit is in season, assemble several tarts, but do not bake them. Wrap them well in plastic wrap and aluminum foil and freeze them. Then just preheat the oven, unwrap the tart, and put it, still frozen, in the oven.

Serves 8

Generous ½ cup cookie crumbs—such as dried ladyfingers, Anise Cookies (page 301), or amaretti

1 (10-inch) tart shell (page 257), baked until pale gold

2 to 2½ pounds ripe small plums, such as prune plums

¼ cup sugar

Cinnamon-Sugar

¼ cup sugar

4 teaspoons ground cinnamon

Preheat the oven to 375°F. Sprinkle the cookie crumbs over the bottom of the tart shell. To prepare the plums, cut them in half but try not to cut all the way through the skin along one side, so the fruit opens like a book. Remove and discard the pits. With the tip of a sharp knife, make a vertical notch from the center of each half through the end. When stood on end, the notched fruit will look similar to a pair of ears sticking straight up. Stand the fruit up on the unnotched end in the tart shell and the cut surface toward the center of the tart, making concentric circles until the tart shell is full. Pack the fruit close together and have the inner circles lean into and overlap the outer rows. Sprinkle the fruit with the ¼ cup of sugar.

Bake until the plums are very soft and caramelized around their edges and the juices are bubbling, 1 to 1½ hours. If the edges threaten to brown too much, protect them with aluminum foil. Let cool on a rack.

While the tart bakes, in a small bowl, toss the ¼ cup sugar with the cinnamon. Generously sprinkle the cinnamon-sugar all over the tart while it is still warm. The pie should have a strong cinnamon flavor, but you may have some left over. Serve warm with sweetened whipped cream or vanilla ice cream.

Tied with Ribbon

LETTERS AND POSTCARDS WHILE CRUISING WITH PAQUEBOT MERMOZ

CHANTAL: I was living on my own in a small apartment in Colmar, and Hubert was working as a chef on the French cruise ship *Mermoz*, which was on its way across the Atlantic. On New Year's Day I went out with my friend Jacqueline and she asked if I had heard the news.

HUBERT: In the middle of the night the ship hit a coral reef at full speed in the middle of the ocean off Guatemala.

CHANTAL: A few days before my birthday in mid-January, I got a note from Hubert saying he would be back in time for my birthday. But he wasn't.

HUBERT: We put an SOS out and a huge Norwegian cruise ship heard us and came to help. We transferred all the passengers from the *Mermoz* onto the Norwegian ship. But the staff remained on board. For two weeks tugboats tried to pull us off. To help the ship float higher in the water, we unloaded water and wine and whatever we could onto an old tanker that came to our aid crewed by a young American couple.

CHANTAL: A couple of years ago, the daughter of the couple on the tanker came into Fleur de Lys for dinner.

HUBERT: A storm finally came and shifted the boat. It went for repairs to Jacksonville, Florida, and my friends and I had several free weeks before we needed to rejoin the ship. We rented a car and made a road trip. I mapped our route and sent it to Chantal. It was during that trip that I decided I would come back to the States one day to work.

CHANTAL: On Valentine's Day, I was at home in the evening when the doorbell started ringing. I wasn't expecting anyone, and when I opened the door, I didn't recognize the man standing there. He had very long hair, a huge beard, and very tan skin. I closed the door immediately.

HUBERT: I was completely tan. While we waited for the ship to unlock from the reef we would lie on the deck chairs reserved for passengers in normal times. We couldn't swim because of sharks and barracuda. But it was so hot, we really needed to cool off. So we'd hose each other down with the fire hoses.

CHANTAL: Then I recognized Hubert's voice and it turned out to be the best Valentine's ever.

Les Cannelés de Bordeaux

IN THE LATE 1980s, Chantal and I vacationed in Bordeaux. The first night it was fairly late and we couldn't find anyplace to eat. We drove by this one place where the parking lot was full. So we thought, Let's stop here. When we walked in, the maître d' said the restaurant was completely booked. But the owner had noticed and stopped us as we were walking out and said, "Oh, *les amoureux* [the lovers], I will find you a table. Sit down, *les amoureux*, and have dinner with us." After dinner, we started talking restaurants with the owner and mentioned that we had one in America. He said, "But we have two Americans with us tonight." He introduced us to each other. They were from the Bay Area and became customers at Fleur de Lys. At the end of dinner, usually every guest gets one or two of the delicious cookies of the region, *cannelés de Bordeaux*, with coffee. But for us, the owner put a whole platter on our table. We decided the cookies were so good that we had to get a recipe and make them for Fleur de Lys. It took Gilberto Villarreal, our pastry chef, many tries to get everything just right so the fluted cookies (*cannelé* means "fluted") tasted like the ones Chantal and I remember.

Makes about 4 dozen small cookies

1½	cups (one 12-ounce can) evaporated milk
3	tablespoons unsalted butter, at room temperature
1	vanilla bean, split lengthwise
1	cup (7 ounces) sugar
2	large eggs
½	cup, (2½ ounces) unbleached all-purpose flour
2	tablespoons (1 ounce) dark rum

Place the milk and butter in a medium saucepan and scrape the seeds from the vanilla bean into the milk. Drop in the pod. Bring just to a boil over medium-high heat, remove from the heat, and set aside.

Place the sugar and eggs in the bowl of a stand mixer fitted with the whisk attachment. Turn the machine on high and whip until the eggs are very thick and pale colored, about 6 minutes. When lifted, the mixture will form a ribbon as it falls back into the bowl.

Sift the flour over the egg mixture and fold together with a large rubber spatula until evenly incorporated. While stirring with the spatula, very slowly pour the hot milk through a sieve into the egg mixture. Stir in the rum. Cover and refrigerate the batter for at least 24 hours and up to 2 days. The batter is not very thick; it's more like a crêpe batter.

Preheat the oven to 250°F. If you have convection, use it. If not, bake the cookies in the middle of the oven, one sheet at a time if necessary. Generously butter metal mini brioche pans or mini muffin pans and set them on a baking sheet. Stir the batter just to mix it and fill each mold with 1 tablespoon batter. The molds should be about half to three-fourths full. Bake until the cookies are slightly puffed, golden brown on top, and dark brown around the edges, 45 to 60 minutes. Rotate the pans halfway through baking. Let the cookies cool in their molds a few minutes and then turn them out and let them cool on a rack for about an hour before serving.

Notes

♣ When we make these at Fleur de Lys, we bake them in mini brioche molds; the fluted shape gives them lots of crust and adds to the sweet, crispy, chewy pleasure. Bake the cookies the day you plan to serve them, but the batter is made the day ahead, so these can work well for entertaining.

♣ These cannelés were photographed at La Boulange bakery in San Francisco.

Tomato, Caper, and Anchovy Crostini

CHANTAL AND I CREATED THESE WARM, COLORFUL, AND SAVORY crostini when we were recipe testing at home on a Monday night. It was in December, and we had a bowl full of mandarins. So we added some to the crostini. We had friends over and demolished the whole platterful since we didn't serve anything else as a canapé and it was a while before we got the Chicken Demi-Deuil (page 164) going. That's one of the things about recipe testing—friends love to be part of it, but they often have to wait for their dinner.

Serves 6 to 8

1 fresh baguette
   Extra-virgin olive oil, for brushing
   Sea salt and freshly ground black pepper
1 or 2 cloves garlic, halved
1 pint cherry tomatoes, preferably a mix of colors, halved
1 mandarin, peeled and segmented (optional)
1 tablespoon nonpareil capers, drained
½ teaspoon very finely chopped fresh rosemary
1 (2-ounce) tin anchovies in olive oil or a small jar of pickled anchovies or boquerónes in brine, or more
   Small parsley snips

Preheat the oven to 400°F. Slice the baguette ¼ inch thick on a sharp diagonal so the slices are about 3½ inches long. Brush the slices on both sides with oil, arrange on a baking sheet, season lightly on one side with salt and pepper, and toast until lightly browned, turning once, about 10 minutes. If you are proceeding directly with the recipe, leave the oven on and rub one side of each crouton with the garlic. If making the croutons ahead, transfer them to a rack to cool and rub them with the garlic. You can make these up to a day ahead of time and store them in a tightly sealed tin.

Our friend Shirlene Miyake.

Arrange several cherry tomato halves on each crouton, making sure they are different colors. Cut the mandarin segments crosswise into little triangles and scatter a few of these on each crouton. Then sprinkle with a few capers, some rosemary, and very lightly with salt and pepper. Halve or quarter the anchovy fillets so they fit nicely on the croutons and then arrange one piece over each crouton. If you love anchovies, add more. Return the crostini to the hot oven for just 1 to 2 minutes, until warmed through. Transfer to a platter, add a tiny parsley snip to each, and serve immediately.

Grilled Lobster
with Lemon-Caper Butter and Herb Salad

THIS IS THE KIND OF SIMPLE FOOD Chantal and I do when we are together. We love to grill lobsters outdoors and serve them with a little flavored butter. To make it, I mix the lobster tomalley (that is where the flavor is) into the butter with a few other flavorings, such as shallots, capers, and mustard. I make enough so that I can wrap some up and freeze it for another time. The nice little mixed herb salad is so refreshing. Serve a crusty baguette or ciabatta along with the lobsters and salad.

Serves 2

2   fresh, lively whole lobsters (about 1¼ pounds each)
    Extra-virgin olive oil, for brushing

Lemon-Caper Butter

3   tablespoons unsalted butter, at room temperature
    Tomalley from lobsters (optional)
1½ teaspoons Dijon mustard
1   teaspoon nonpareil capers, drained
1   small shallot, very finely chopped
    Freshly grated zest of ¼ lemon
    Sea salt and freshly ground black pepper

Herb Salad

1½ teaspoons freshly squeezed lemon juice
1½ tablespoons extra-virgin olive oil
    Sea salt and freshly ground black pepper
    Handful of fresh basil leaves
    Handful of fresh flat-leaf parsley leaves
    Handful of fresh chervil leaves
    Handful of fresh cilantro leaves
½   small bunch fresh chives, cut into 1-inch lengths
    Leaves from 1 good sprig fresh tarragon

HOW TO OPEN A LOBSTER

Lay the lobster belly down on a cutting board. Insert the tip of a heavy, sharp knife right between and just behind the eyes.

Cut down and then straight back down the length of the tail. Make a second cut through the head.

Clean the tomalley out of the body. Remove and discard the intestinal tube. Crack the claws but leave them attached to the body.

Notes

♣ The lobster is poached for a few minutes, but it will not be cooked enough to hold, even in the refrigerator. So be prepared to poach and then grill the lobsters directly.

To cook and clean the lobsters: Bring a large pot of water to a boil and prepare a large ice-water bath. Drop the lobsters into the pot headfirst. Quickly cover the pot and cook for just 2 minutes. Pull the lobsters out of the pot and plunge them into the ice bath to stop the cooking.

To cut the lobsters: Set the lobster belly down on the counter. Insert a sharp, heavy knife right between and just below the eyes and then cut straight down to the tail through the back, cutting the lobster in half lengthwise. Then, beginning from the same point

and cutting toward the mouth, cut through the rest of the head. Remove and discard the intestine tube that runs down the center of the tail. Scrape the greenish-looking tomalley into a bowl and reserve. Crack the claws by hitting them hard with the back of a knife just below the knuckle of the two pincers. Set the lobsters aside while you build a medium-hot fire in the grill. The biggest mistake people make when grilling shellfish is to crank up the heat to the maximum. That's when the shells burn and the flesh easily overcooks.

To make the butter: Add the softened butter to the tomalley with the mustard, capers, shallot, lemon zest, and a pinch each of salt and pepper. Mash together with a fork until evenly blended. Set aside until needed. Do not chill it, since you want it to remain very soft and spreadable.

To make the salad: Measure the lemon juice and oil into a medium bowl. Add a good pinch each of salt and pepper. Stir together with a fork or whisk. Pile the basil, parsley, chervil, cilantro, chives, and tarragon on top of the dressing and set aside. Toss the salad only just before serving.

When the fire is ready, brush the flesh side of the lobsters with olive oil. Place them flesh side down on the grill. Sear them lightly, no more than 2 minutes. Turn them flesh side up and shell down. Smear the butter over the lobsters, cover the grill, and cook just until tender, about another 4 minutes at the most.

While the lobsters cook, toss the salad and taste for seasoning. Arrange 2 lobster halves on each of 2 large plates and arrange a handful of herb salad on top of each. Serve immediately, making sure to have nutcrackers on the table for the claws.

Grilled Squab Glazed with "Secret" Sauce

Notes

♣ When we made this dish at home, Chantal began by making apricot jam. It may seem a long way round, but we ate the rest of it for breakfast the next day. And the quality of the jam comes through in the sauce. So make a jam in the summer when great apricots are in season. You can cook a pound or more of fruit with sugar to taste and a little lemon juice, puree, and freeze. Otherwise, you can use dried apricots soaked until plump or purchased apricot jam. You could also substitute plums for the apricots.

SQUAB IS CHANTAL'S FAVORITE MEAT. Whenever we cook squab—and we don't cook it often enough—I am reminded of the time Paul Bocuse came to Fleur de Lys to do a special champagne dinner. Besides being one of the greatest chefs, he is also a great showman and did things others wouldn't dare to do. Once, I remember at an event in Paris, many great chefs (Paul Bocuse and Roger Vergé among them) were each to cook a signature dish. But M. Bocuse arrived with a cotton-candy machine and created great clouds of the spun-sugar candy for the guests. It was a smash hit. For his world tour with Mumm, the champagne house, he created a number of recipes. One of them was squab with a "secret" sauce. He made it with barbecue sauce and ketchup. In France at that time, it was avant-garde because barbecue sauce was practically unknown there. I worried it would not go over too well—a Frenchman serving barbecue? But people loved the combination of the squab and the sauce.

Serves 2

Brine

- 1 cup apple cider
- ½ cup kosher salt
- ½ cup (6¼ ounces by weight) honey
- 1 small yellow onion, halved
- 1 whole clove
- 1 medium carrot, quartered
- 1 stalk celery, cut into 2-inch lengths
- 4 cloves garlic, peeled
- 2 generous sprigs fresh thyme
- 1 bay leaf
- 1 tablespoon cracked black pepper
- ½ teaspoon cracked allspice berries (optional)

Squab

- 2 whole squab
- 8 cups low-salt beef broth
- 1 bouquet garni (page 65)
- 1 medium yellow onion, coarsely chopped
- 1 large carrot, peeled and coarsely chopped
- 1 stalk celery, coarsely chopped
- 1 large fresh, ripe apricot or 1 whole dried apricot or 2 tablespoons apricot jam
    About 1 teaspoon sugar
    Squeeze of fresh lemon juice
- 2 tablespoons barbecue sauce or A.1. steak sauce
- 2 tablespoons ketchup
- 1 tablespoon apple cider vinegar

- 2 teaspoons finely chopped peeled fresh ginger
- 1 teaspoon freshly grated orange zest
- ½ teaspoon chili flakes, or more or less for seasoning
    Sea salt and freshly ground black pepper
- 1 teaspoon cornstarch
- 8 large leaves savoy cabbage
- 1½ teaspoons extra-virgin olive oil, plus more for brushing
    About 10 very thin rounds of chorizo (optional)

To make the brine: In a nonreactive stockpot, combine 4 cups water with the apple cider, salt, and honey. Stick the onion with the clove and add it to the pot with the carrot, celery, garlic, thyme, bay leaf, cracked black pepper, and allspice berries. Cover, bring to a boil over high heat, and simmer gently for 20 minutes. Remove from the heat and let cool completely.

To prepare the squab: Trim off the necks and wing tips and reserve them. Immerse the squab in the cooled brine, making sure they are submerged. Weight them down with a plate if needed. Refrigerate for 1 hour. Remove the squab from the brine, discard the brine, and rinse the squab under cold running water. Set it aside.

Meanwhile, in a large pot, bring the beef broth, reserved squab necks and wing tips, bouquet garni, onion, carrot, and celery to a boil over high heat. Reduce the heat to a gentle simmer and cook, uncovered, for 20 to 30 minutes. Lower the squab into the broth. Weight them down with a plate so they are completely submerged. If not, add more beef broth. Poach the birds slowly, uncovered, for 15 minutes. Remove the pot from the fire and let it sit for 10 minutes. Transfer the squab to a plate and keep them covered with plastic wrap to prevent them from drying out. Strain the broth into a bowl and discard the solids. Refrigerate the broth to allow the fat to come to the surface.

To make the glaze and sauce: Pit and chop the apricot; you should have about ½ cup. Place it in a small saucepan with the sugar and lemon juice and cook over low heat, stirring well to prevent scorching, until the apricot is thoroughly soft, about 7 minutes. You should have about ¼ cup cooked apricot. If you are using a dried apricot, chop it and soak it in about 2 tablespoons of hot water until soft.

In a food processor, combine the cooked apricot with the barbecue sauce, ketchup, vinegar, ginger, orange zest, and chili flakes. Mix together well and set the glaze aside.

To finish the sauce: Dip out 1 cup of the broth and transfer it to a small saucepan. Bring the broth to a boil over high heat and cook until reduced to about ¼ cup. Stir half the glaze into the reduced broth, taste, and season with salt and pepper. If the sauce needs thickening—you want it to have the texture of heavy cream—in a small, lidded jar, mix the cornstarch with twice as much cold water. Shake well and drizzle into the simmering sauce little by little while whisking and watching for signs of thickening. Keep the sauce warm.

While the squab poach, prepare the cabbage. Bring a large pot of water to a boil and add a handful of salt. Prepare an ice-water bath. Cook the cabbage leaves until tender, 6 to 8 minutes. Transfer the leaves to the ice water to cool. Drain well, cut the ribs from the leaves with a sharp knife, and then cut each into strips 1 to 1½ inches wide. Set them aside.

Build a medium-hot fire in the barbecue or preheat the broiler and arrange the rack about 5 inches below the heat. Uncover the squab and use scissors to cut along both sides of the backbones to remove them. Flip the birds over and press them firmly under the flat of your hand to snap the breastbone and flatten them. Brush them with the olive oil. Arrange the squab skin side up and bone side down on the grill, close the lid, and grill for 4 minutes. Brush the birds with the glaze, flip them over to skin side down, reclose the grill, and cook until well marked and the glaze has caramelized, another 3 to 4 minutes. Brush the bone side lightly with the glaze, flip them again, and let the glaze caramelize, about 2 minutes. If broiling, follow the same process and timing, but start the birds bone side up on the broiler pan. Brush any remaining glaze on the birds and remove them from the heat. Keep them warm.

While the squab are grilling, place a large skillet over medium heat and add the 1½ teaspoons of olive oil and the chorizo. Cook until crispy, add the reserved cabbage, and toss well until heated through. Season to taste with salt and pepper.

To serve: Divide the cabbage between 2 warm dinner plates. Top with a squab and drizzle the sauce all around. Serve immediately.

Notes

♣ You end up with a dividend when you make the squab—the flavorful broth. You need only a cup of it for the sauce. But I'd advise you to at least double the sauce recipe and freeze the extra. We use the sauce as a drizzle for grilled vegetables (page 277), chicken breasts, and burgers. And we were inspired to have the remaining broth, cold and carefully defatted, for lunch the next day. I don't remember when I last drank a cold consommé, but it is a classic soup, and in the hot Las Vegas weather it was just what we wanted.

Harissa

WHEN I GREW UP THE SPICY LAMB SAUSAGES merguez served with harissa were popular at local fairs. I remember it being the hottest thing I had ever put in my mouth. Harissa is a traditional companion to couscous. But its rich, complex flavor adapts itself to many other uses in the kitchen. Try it with roasted winter squash or soup and cheese dishes, such as cheese sandwiches or cheese melted over roasted potatoes.

Makes about 1 cup

4 ounces dried hot chilies, such as a mix of New Mexican, árbol, and ancho
3 tablespoons cumin seeds
3 tablespoons coriander seeds
2 tablespoons caraway seeds
5 to 6 cloves garlic, peeled
2 tablespoons dried mint
   Sea salt
3 tablespoons extra-virgin olive oil, plus more to cover

Place the chilies in a bowl and cover with boiling water. Let them soak until soft, about 30 minutes.

Meanwhile, toast the cumin, coriander, and caraway seeds in a medium skillet over medium-low heat. Stir the seeds and shake the pan regularly until the seeds are fragrant, about 5 minutes. Immediately pour the seeds onto a plate to cool. Grind them to a powder in a spice mill.

Drain the chilies and place them in a food processor or blender with the toasted spices, garlic, mint, a pinch of salt, and the olive oil. Process until you have a thick paste.

Scrape the harissa into a clean jar, pour in a little olive oil to cover, screw on a lid, and refrigerate for about a week.

From left: **Laurent Pillard, me, Grant MacPherson, Mark Dommen.**

Grilled Vegetable Platter with Three Flavors

USUALLY WHEN WE GRILL VEGETABLES, I keep it very simple—just brushing the vegetables with olive oil and sometimes adding minced garlic and herbs. I think it was on my birthday in June, I brought home some porcini mushrooms and grilled those. Whenever we grill vegetables, we grill too many and use them the next day in salads. Serve the vegetables straight off the grill or add one or more sauces. Add a cheese or two and a baguette and you have a delicious, easy dinner party ready to go.

Serves 2 to 4

¼ cup extra-virgin olive oil, plus more for brushing

1 teaspoon very finely chopped garlic

1 teaspoon very finely chopped fresh thyme or rosemary

10 to 12 large fresh basil leaves

2 small heads garlic, halved crosswise

2 small firm zucchini (about 1 inch in diameter), halved lengthwise

1 medium globe eggplant, cut lengthwise into ½-inch-thick slices

2 Roma tomatoes, halved lengthwise

1 large red onion, cut into ½-inch-thick rounds

1 large sweet red bell pepper, quartered, seeded, and deveined

2 to 4 portobello mushrooms (about 2 inches in diameter), gills removed

Sea salt and freshly ground black pepper

1 loaf crusty bread, such as baguette or ciabatta, cut into ½-inch-thick slices

Harissa, for serving

Chimichurri, for serving (page 282)

Preserved Lemon Vinaigrette, for serving (page 283)

Build a medium-hot fire. In a small bowl, stir together the ¼ cup of olive oil with the garlic and thyme. Set the mixture aside. Stack 5 of the basil leaves, roll them up, and cut them crosswise into a fine chiffonade. Repeat with the remaining leaves and set them aside in a small bowl. Brush all the vegetables all over with olive oil and season well with salt and pepper. Place them diagonally across the grill and cook just until they are nicely marked: Cook for about 1 minute, then rotate them about 90 degrees for another minute to create a crosshatch pattern. Cook the mushrooms gill side up, brushing them while on the grill with the garlic-oil mixture. The juices will collect in the cup and the garlic will be protected from burning. Once the vegetables are browned on both sides, move them to a cooler part of the grill, brush them with the garlic-oil mixture, if desired, cover, and cook them until tender. The garlic heads will need the longest time, about 30 minutes. Check frequently and transfer the vegetables to a platter as they are done. Brush the bread on both sides with more oil and grill until lightly browned.

When all the vegetables and bread have grilled, sprinkle the basil over the vegetables and serve with the sauces and the remaining garlic-oil mixture at the table.

♣ A good trick for keeping the onion slices together is to thread one or two skewers through the slices.

♣ Other sauces to try are the Aioli with Miso (page 89) and the Rouille (page 89).

Notes

DJ Frenchy Le Freak's Paella

ONE OF MY GOOD FRIENDS, DJ Frenchy Le Freak, makes the best paella. He's very serious about it and makes it just the way he learned from his mother. So that I could learn how to make it, I asked him to bring his paella equipment to our house and told him I would gather the ingredients. Paella needs to be cooked and served right away. If you have all the ingredients set out ahead of time, you can build the dish in front of your guests and make it part of your evening together. Chantal and I love Frenchy's paella so much that I included it in the third season of *Secrets of a Chef*. You can find paella rice, Spanish chorizo, piquillo peppers, and saffron in specialty food shops and online.

♣ Because it is such a great party dish, I always make paella for a crowd, but you can cut the recipe in half for smaller gatherings. You need a very large pan for this amount of ingredients, but you can also use 2 (14- to 16-inch) paella pans or deep, wide skillets or 2 large Dutch ovens.

♣ You can't reheat paella. Unfortunately, in many restaurants, what you get is reheated paella. Once you've had paella freshly cooked, you understand what an amazing dish it is.

Serves 10 to 12

6 tablespoons extra-virgin olive oil, divided

2 small chickens (about 5 pounds total), each cut into serving pieces

12 extra-large shrimp (16-20 count), heads on, tails peeled, and shells reserved

2 large yellow onions (8 to 10 ounces each), thinly sliced

9 cloves garlic, finely chopped, plus 1 whole clove garlic

2 bay leaves

4 sprigs fresh thyme

6 cups low-salt chicken broth

  Sea salt and freshly ground black pepper

6 large squid, about 6 inches long, cleaned

1 slab pork baby back ribs (about 1¾ pounds), cut into individual ribs

1 (14½-ounce) can diced tomatoes

1½ teaspoons saffron (threads or ground)

3 cups Bomba Spanish paella rice (or long-grain white rice)

4 ounces chorizo, cut into ¼-inch-thick rounds

3 pints fresh clams in their shell

1 cup sweet green peas

4 roasted piquillo peppers, or roasted sweet red bell peppers

1 quart fresh mussels (optional)

1 heirloom tomato

1 baguette, cut diagonally into about 10 to 12 (½-inch-thick) slices and toasted

10 to 12 very thin slices Serrano ham

Heat 2 tablespoons of the olive oil in a large saucepan over medium-high heat. Add any chicken bones or trimmings and the shrimp shells. Sear the pieces until lightly browned, about 5 minutes. Pour off all but about 1 tablespoon of the fat and return the pan to the heat. Add one-fourth of the onions, along with one-third of the chopped garlic, the bay leaves, and the thyme. Stir and scrape the bottom of the pan to loosen all the browned bits and cook until the onions have softened, 5 to 8 minutes.

Add the chicken broth, ½ teaspoon salt, and ¼ teaspoon pepper. Bring the mixture to a simmer, reduce the heat to low, and cook, uncovered for about 5 minutes. Skim off any foam that rises to the surface. Continue to simmer gently for at least 20 to 25 minutes and up to 1 hour. Strain the stock through a fine-mesh strainer and reserve. Discard the solids. If using immediately, skim off the fat. Otherwise, let cool, cover, refrigerate, and lift off the fat once it has solidified.

Cut the tentacles off of the squid bodies and then slice the bodies into 1-inch rings. Heat another 2 tablespoons of the oil in a very large paella pan over medium-high heat. Add the squid rings and tentacles, season with ½ teaspoon salt and ¼ teaspoon pepper, and stir and cook just until the squid turns opaque, about 2 minutes. With a slotted spoon, transfer the squid to a bowl and set it aside.

Add another 1 tablespoon of the oil to the pan and return it to medium-high heat.

Add the remaining onions and garlic and cook until the onions have turned translucent and begun to brown lightly, about 5 minutes. With a slotted spoon, transfer them to a separate bowl and set them aside.

Season the chicken pieces and pork ribs with about 1 teaspoon salt and ½ teaspoon pepper. Add the remaining 1 tablespoon of oil to the pan and return it to medium-high heat. Add the chicken and pork and sear on all sides until golden brown, about 8 minutes. Cook in batches if necessary.

Tilt the pan and spoon off and discard the fat. Add the tomatoes and stir and scrape to get up all the browned bits from the bottom of the pan. Add the squid, onions and garlic, chicken and pork ribs, and reserved stock. Stir in the saffron, cover the pan with a tight-fitting lid or aluminum foil, and let it cook over medium-low heat for 20 minutes.

Stir in the rice and chorizo, re-cover, and cook for 15 more minutes. Uncover and taste the rice to judge how tender it is. When it has just a few minutes to go, add the clams, shrimp, peas, piquillo peppers, and mussels. Push and stir all the ingredients into the rice and liquid so they cook evenly. Re-cover and cook just until the shrimp are cooked, the clams and mussels have opened, and the rice is thoroughly tender, another 3 to 4 minutes.

While the paella cooks, cut the heirloom tomato in half and rub it over both sides of the baguette slices. Then rub the slices with the remaining whole clove garlic. Top each slice of baguette with a slice of ham and serve one to each person with the paella.

DJing is one of my passions. Frenchy Le Freak (above), the great DJ who often appears in San Francisco at Ruby Skye, gave me my first gig on Bastille Day—the French Independence Day—several years ago. It's sort of mushroomed since then.

Grilled Potatoes

SINCE CHANTAL AND I ALMOST ALWAYS COOK OUTDOORS in Las Vegas, I've learned quickly how to cook potatoes on the grill. I like them to get really crusty, and this can be a challenge if the olive oil drips and the flames flare up. My secret is to blanch them first and cook them in my cast-iron pan on the grill. I guess they are actually grilled and sautéed potatoes, but with the barbecue lid closed they absorb the distinctive smoky flavor. And then we dig in.

Serves 4

1¼ to 1½ pounds mixed baby potatoes
　　Sea salt and freshly ground black pepper
¼ cup extra-virgin olive oil
1 bay leaf
4 to 6 garlic cloves, unpeeled
2 to 3 good sprigs fresh thyme
　　Leaves from 1 sprig fresh rosemary
　　Freshly grated zest of 1 lemon (optional)

Place the potatoes and 1 teaspoon salt in a large saucepan, cover with water, and bring to a boil over high heat. Simmer until the potatoes are about three-fourths cooked, about 5 minutes—the tip of a sharp knife will meet some resistance, but timing will depend on the size of the potatoes. Be careful not to overcook.

Meanwhile, prepare an ice-water bath. When the potatoes are done, drain and immediately plunge them into the ice water to cool. Drain when the potatoes are chilled, and gently pat dry.

Toss the potatoes in a bowl with the olive oil, bay leaf, garlic, thyme, rosemary, and salt and pepper until well coated. You can prepare the potatoes an hour ahead of time to this point.

Preheat the grill to high and put a cast-iron skillet on the grill to preheat. Transfer the potatoes to the skillet, lower the heat to medium, close the grill lid, and cook, tossing occasionally, until crusty and brown, about 20 minutes. Roll the potatoes with the lemon zest in the last few minutes of cooking. Serve them immediately.

Chimichurri

Notes

♣ You can make the sauce in a food processor, but the blender gives a smoother sauce and, because of the extra air beaten into the sauce, the blender turns it a brilliant green. The same is true of beet puree, which turns Valentine pink in the blender and re-mains deep red in the food processor.

♣ At Fleur we make our chimichurri with parsley, but every cook tends to make the sauce his or her own, and I hope you will, too. Some additions might be a little onion, more garlic, more hot sauce, Spanish paprika with its smoky fla-vor, some oregano, or cilantro.

THIS IS ARGENTINE KETCHUP. Because chimichurri is so popular, we knew when we developed the menu for Fleur with its "tastes from around the world" theme that we should include it. But then we had to make an exciting dish. We serve a bowl of the bright-green sauce with thinly sliced raw skirt steak. And a very hot rock. Guests use the stone to cook their meat and then douse it with the sauce. Serve the chimichurri with omelets, chicken, fish, pasta, baked potatoes, grilled vegetables, even the parsnip blinis (page 304).

Makes about 1½ cups

2 bunches fresh flat-leaf parsley
¾ cup extra-virgin olive oil, plus more as needed
1 tablespoon champagne vinegar
About ¼ teaspoon hot sauce
1½ teaspoons freshly squeezed lemon juice
2 cloves garlic
Sea salt and freshly ground black pepper

Remove and discard any large, tough stems from the parsley. Place the pars-ley, olive oil, vinegar, hot sauce, lemon juice, garlic, and a good pinch each of salt and pepper in a blender or food processor and blend on high speed until pureed. Scrape down the sides of the container as needed. If the sauce is too thick and not pourable, pulse in a little more oil. Taste and adjust the seasonings with salt, pepper, hot sauce, and lemon juice as needed to make a bright-green sauce with a smart, snappy flavor.

Preserved Lemons

BECAUSE WE HAVE A MEYER LEMON tree in our San Francisco backyard, Chantal will sometimes make preserved lemons. She makes them in small batches, giving away all but one jar. This way, the lemons get used up and not forgotten in the back of the refrigerator. When she roasts a chicken on our vertical roaster, she stuffs the cavity with several of the lemons.

Makes a 1-quart jar (8 to 10 lemons)

- 8 to 10 organic lemons, well scrubbed
  About ½ cup kosher salt
- 1 (1-quart) jar, sterilized, with lid
- 2 small cinnamon sticks
- 2 bay leaves
- 15 whole coriander seeds
  About ½ cup freshly squeezed lemon juice

Cut the lemons lengthwise into quarters. Generously sprinkle the lemons with the salt. Pack the lemons into the jar, squishing them down so that the juice is released. Add the cinnamon sticks, bay leaves, and coriander seeds as you pack in the lemons. If the lemons do not release enough juice to cover them, add more until the fruit is well covered. Add any remaining salt to the jar and close tightly. Shake and let sit at room temperature for a couple of days. Turn the jar upside down occasionally. Refrigerate the lemons for at least 3 weeks, again turning upside down occasionally, until the rinds soften.

To use them, remove the lemons from the jar and rinse thoroughly under running water to remove the salt. Discard the pulp and use the peel. The lemons keep, refrigerated, for several months.

Preserved Lemon Vinaigrette

TO HELP USE THE PRESERVED LEMONS, I made this thick vinaigrette. We like it on just about everything—green salads, hot and cold grilled chicken and salmon, burgers, fries of all kinds, and vegetables, whether steamed, roasted, baked, or grilled (page 277). If you don't make your own preserved lemons, you can buy jarred preserved lemons in specialty food shops. I use the whole lemon, including the flesh for my vinaigrette, but Chantal does not. You can choose either way.

Makes about 2¼ cups

- 1 whole preserved lemon
- 1 large shallot, peeled and halved
- 1 clove garlic, peeled (optional)
- 2 teaspoons Dijon mustard
- ½ cup champagne vinegar
  Freshly ground white pepper
- 1½ cups extra-virgin olive oil

Rinse the lemon to remove salt, pat dry, halve it, and discard the pulp. Place the lemon peel, shallot, and garlic in a food processor with the mustard, vinegar, and a good pinch of pepper.

Pulse until the ingredients are well chopped. Scrape down the sides of the work bowl. With the machine running, add the oil drop by drop until an emulsion forms. Then slowly drizzle in the rest of the oil. Taste for acidity and seasoning. Transfer the vinaigrette to a clean lidded jar and refrigerate for about 3 days. The dressing will eventually separate and needs to be whisked before use.

Notes

♣ The type and size of your preserved lemons will naturally affect the balance of your dressing. Taste and adjust the flavors to your palate.

283

Strawberries with White Wine, Mint, and Lime Sorbet

Notes

♣ Make this only when strawberries are in season. The flavor depends on having very aromatic fruit with the best flavor possible. Remove the stems only after washing so the berries don't get waterlogged.

♣ The amount of sugar you need depends on the sweetness of your berries as well as the quality of the wine you choose. Try an Alsatian Riesling or gewürztraminer.

WE DO THIS TYPE OF LIGHT, WINE-BASED DESSERT in Alsace, and Chantal first made it for me on my birthday. We were in Las Vegas and it was hot. She had found the recipe in Simone Morgenthaler's *Mon Alsace Gourmande*. Chantal likes this dish because it takes almost no effort, looks pretty, and tastes refreshing. I've added a fresh, tart sorbet, not sweet at all. Serve the dessert with a cookie such as the Anise Cookies (page 301) or madeleines to dip into the fruit juices.

Serves 6 to 8

Lime Sorbet

1 cup (7 ounces) sugar
Freshly grated zest of 2 limes
1 cup freshly squeezed lime juice (about 10 limes), chilled

Strawberries

About 1¼ cups (8¾ ounces) sugar
2 cups dry white wine
2 pounds ripe fresh strawberries
20 fresh mint leaves
Freshly squeezed juice of 1 lemon (optional)

To make the sorbet: Prepare an ice-water bath. In a large saucepan, bring 2 cups water and the sugar to a boil over high heat, stirring until the sugar has completely dissolved. Pour the sugar syrup into a bowl and place it in the ice-water bath. Whisk occasionally until chilled. Or make the syrup a day ahead and refrigerate. Add the lime zest and juice to the sugar syrup. Pour the sorbet mixture into the container of an ice-cream maker and freeze according to the manufacturer's directions. Scrape the sorbet into a container and freeze for at least 2 hours or until needed. Remove the sorbet from the freezer about 20 minutes ahead of time to let it soften a bit before serving.

To prepare the strawberries: Place the sugar and wine in a large bowl and whisk until the sugar dissolves. Hull the strawberries and cut them in half or into quarters if very large. Add them to the bowl with 10 of the mint leaves and a good squeeze of lemon juice. Toss them well and taste for sweetness. Add more sugar or a little lemon juice to balance the flavors. Let the berries marinate for at least 30 minutes and for as long as 4 hours.

When ready to serve, pick out the mint leaves and replace them with the remaining 10 fresh mint leaves. Put a scoop of sorbet into each dessert bowl. Spoon berries and their juices around and over the sorbet. Serve immediately.

CHAPTER

7

Holiday Traditions

"Maybe Alsatians celebrate so extravagantly over the holidays because of the long, dark winters."

WIHNACHTE CHEZ CHANTAL AND HUBERT

WIHNACHTE MEANS "HOLY NIGHT" in the Alsace dialect. The holidays are such a big deal in Alsace that Chantal and I always make a big deal of them at home, too. Maybe Alsatians celebrate so extravagantly because of the long, dark winters. Or maybe it is because our holiday traditions date back to the sixteenth century. One of the earliest records of Christmas trees is from Sélestat, a tiny town just a few kilometers from Ribeauvillé. Just as Ribeauvillé has its Medieval Christmas fair, Sélestat holds a fair to celebrate the Christmas tree. A huge forest of trees is created in the town for the children to wander through. It was not until the 1700s that Marie Leszczyńska, wife of Henri XV, introduced Christmas trees to the court, setting them up in the palace at Versailles. The trees were decorated with paper flowers, dried roses, cookies, and dried apples.

From left: Home-
made head cheese
by Lili Baltenweck
with foie gras buns
made by Rémy
Schaal. Ribeauvillé
under snow. Me, Lili
Baltenweck, Dany
Haas, and his wife,
Michele, at our holi-
day party in Alsace.

Pages 286 and 287:
During the holiday
fair in Ribeauvillé.
Do you see the castle
outlined against the
sky in the back-
ground?

Everyone at home makes the most of the holidays. We shop the
Christmas street fairs while drinking *Vin Chaud* (page 302) and
eating *Pain d'Épices* (page 298) baked in the shape of St. Nicholas. The breads have an antique image of St. Nicholas pasted
on them with sugar glaze. Children and adults alike peel off
the picture, eat the bread, and hang the souvenir on their tree
at home. And we buy or bake all the traditional holiday treats:
Petits Bonhommes (page 292), brioche baked in the shape of
boys with raisin eyes and buttons; the *pain d'épices* shaped or
cut into squares and sometimes baked as loaves; the Christmas
Star (page 296) baked in traditional, old-fashioned star-shaped
molds; and Anise Cookies (page 301). *Kugelhopf* (page 24) and
stollen are always included as well. The treats are set out in

From left: **Dusk during the December holiday fair. I was so excited when Ribeauvillé's mayor took me up into the town's bell tower and let me pull the rope to ring the bell. For my first cookbook, my mom and dad sent me the recipe for *Schnetzwecka*, a traditional Christmas bread. Chantal and me admiring Christmas window displays.**

every household as buffets and offered to visitors—adults and children—throughout the day.

I have not included a recipe here for stollen, which I think is more German than Alsatian in origin. It is basically a brioche dough with dried fruit, nuts, candied orange zest, and marzipan folded in. You can easily make a similar bread by using the brioche dough on page 126 and kneading in a half pound or so of fruits and nuts.

Early in December Chantal begins decorating our house—lining the front steps with poinsettias and hanging red bows all over. We set up a tree, and every year it has a new look. Usually Chantal chooses a color theme and then goes from there. When it was white, the tree was covered in white feathers. When it was blue, the lights and balls were blue and there were little mirrors to create reflections. Like everyone else, we have an ornament collection. Many are gifts from friends and Fleur de Lys guests who often choose ornaments in the shapes of fleurs-de-lys, burgers, and boxes of fries. By the week before Christmas, Chantal has set the table. She will have collected all sorts of decorations to fill out her ideas. For a red-and-white-themed year she set up a tray of champagne flutes and put a candy cane in each one to act as a stirrer for her champagne cocktails. And she bought solid chocolate Santas in dark and white chocolate. These were the place cards—she glued the name of each guest underneath the Santas. Finding your seat became a game of hide-and-seek.

Every year, for many years, the same group of friends has gathered at our house for Christmas dinner. Everyone brings a dish (when we first moved to San Francisco and lived in a small apartment, guests had to bring their own chairs) to round out the menu. And Chantal and I do the appetizers and the *plat principal*, which is usually from Fleur de Lys. (The restaurant has a new, special menu each Christmas Eve and closes Christmas Day.) It could be roasted lamb chops (page 74), venison (page 167), *baeckeoffe* / laundry day stew made with lots of black truffles (page 30), or Beef Wellington (page 314). To begin, we always have oysters and smoked salmon, which are traditional for the holidays in Alsace, too. If we were in Alsace, we would have foie gras as well. It is made throughout the region and comes to market especially for the holidays.

291

Petits Bonhommes

ONE OF THE MANY TREATS my brother and I looked forward to during the Christmas holidays was having a freshly baked *petit bonhomme* for breakfast or for an afternoon snack. The breads seemed to have a best friend, too: hot chocolate. Still today shop windows display the *petits bonhommes* in sizes ranging from seven or eight inches to several feet high. Some families buy a large bread to put in the middle of the holiday breakfast table. My father made his *petits bonhommes* from brioche but tells me they can also be made from the *kugelhopf* dough (page 24).

Makes about 10 individual petits bonhommes

1 recipe Brioche Bretzel dough (page 126), through first rise

2 egg yolks

Raisins, nuts, dragées, or other such decorations

½ cup (2 ounces) powdered sugar (optional)

Punch the dough down and turn it out onto a lightly floured work surface. Cut the dough into 10 evenly sized pieces (about 3 ounces each) and roll each into a ball. Cover with a kitchen towel and let them rest for about 15 minutes.

Line 2 baking sheets with nonstick baking mats or parchment paper. Preheat the oven to 400°F.

To shape the petits bonhommes: Make sure your figures are very distinct; otherwise the shape will be lost in the oven as the breads rise. Use very little to no flour on the work surface. You need the dough to stick slightly to the countertop. Roll each ball into a log

about 6 inches long. To form the head, about 1 to 1½ inches in from one end, press down with the edge of your hand. Roll your hand back and forth. A neck will form and the head above it. Taper the body so it's wider at the shoulders and narrower toward the feet. Pat the body down to flatten it. With a sharp knife or with sharp scissors, make a single cut to form the legs and pull them apart. (Dipping the blades in water helps them cut more cleanly.) Make 2 diagonal cuts beginning at about the waist and angling in and up to below the shoulders. Pull the arms out. After that you can play, perhaps making a hat or muffler from scraps. Transfer the breads to the baking sheets, cover with kitchen towels, and let them rise for about 30 minutes.

In a small bowl, whisk the egg yolks with 1 teaspoon of water. With a pastry brush, brush the breads with the egg wash. Press the raisins or other decorations firmly into the breads to make eyes, noses, buttons, and other details as your imagination prompts. Bake the breads for about 20 minutes or until dark golden brown. Let them cool on a rack.

You can leave the breads glossy from the egg-yolk glaze or give them a sugar glaze. In a small bowl, mix the powdered sugar with just enough water to make a brushable paste, about 1 tablespoon. Brush the glaze all over the breads while they are still warm. Serve them the same day you bake them.

292

A Christmas Menu

Appetizers
(served in the living room)
Oysters on the Half Shell with Citrus,
Toasted Coriander, and Olive Oil
(page 305)

Parsnip Blinis with Caviar (page 304)

At the Table
Peruvian Prawn and Sea Scallop Ceviche
(page 308)

Truffled Onion Velouté Shooters
(page 201)

Classic Salmon "Soufflé" Paul Haeberlin
(page 90)

Beef Wellington (page 314)

Olive Bread

Turnip Confit Enhanced with Orange, Ginger,
and Rosemary (page 197)

Braised Brussels Sprouts with Bacon (page 253)

Assortment of Cheeses
Brie, Mimolette, Brillat-Savarin, Époisses,
Garrotxa (a Spanish goat cheese),
Roaring Forties Blue, and Tomme de Savoie

Pistachio and Fig Bread

Bûche de Noël de Henri (page 321)

Holiday Petits Fours and Eaux-de-Vie

Despite Chantal's feelings about Époisses—the only cheese she likes is Parmesan, and the strong-smelling cheeses like Époisses make her feel nauseous—it was the one cheese from our menu's selection that we completely devoured. Rémy Schaal, who was my father's apprentice and later bought Pâtisserie Keller when my brother, Francis, retired, made the amazingly detailed and delicious *bûche de Noël* above for our holiday party in 2011. It's interesting that the *bûche de Noël* comes from another, older holiday tradition. In the very old days, a tree trunk burned in the hearth in every house. The logs were blessed by the priest and, as long as they burned throughout midnight mass, guaranteed good harvests in the following year. Even the ashes were saved for their powers against disease.

The Alsatian cookbook writer and food authority Simone Morgenthaler tells a charming story in her cookbook *Mon Alsace Gourmande* (la Nuée bleue, 2009). She writes that on Wihnachte everything is possible, that during the twelve strokes of midnight anything can happen and often does: The fruit trees flower and the bees are as busy as they are in spring, and for a moment, the wine sitting in casks referments in order to participate in the magic of Christmas.

Dark Hot Chocolate
with Chocolate Whipped Cream

AS MUCH AS YOU HEAR ABOUT FRENCH PEOPLE and their love of dark chocolate, we do not drink much hot chocolate. But during the holidays, it is a traditional treat for children served with a *Petit Bonhomme* (page 292). I remember the promise of hot chocolate and *petits bonhommes* being used to attract us kids to Thursday's catechism class. During the rest of the year, we got café au lait. Some years ago on one visit to Paris, Chantal and I went to La Maison du Chocolat, famous for their hot chocolate. I think Chantal might have had two chocolate éclairs and a hot chocolate.

Serves 4

Chocolate Whipped Cream

- 1   cup heavy cream
- 2   tablespoons Dutch-process cocoa powder
- 1   tablespoon sugar
- 1   teaspoon vanilla extract

Hot Chocolate

- 2   cups whole milk
- 1   cup heavy cream
- 2   tablespoons sugar
- ½   teaspoon ground cinnamon, plus more for dusting
- 5   ounces bittersweet chocolate (at least 60% cacao), chopped
- 4   small, thin cinnamon sticks (optional)
- 4   dark chocolate cigarettes (optional)

To make the chocolate whipped cream: In a medium bowl or the bowl of a stand mixer, whip the cream with the cocoa powder, sugar, and vanilla until the mixture forms soft mounds. If you plan to spoon it on top of the hot chocolate, stop whipping now. If you would like to pipe the cream onto the chocolate, continue to whip until the cream is stiff but still smooth, not grainy. The cream can be whipped ahead of time, covered, and then refrigerated for up to several hours.

To make the hot chocolate: In a saucepan over medium heat, bring the milk, cream, sugar, and cinnamon just to a boil. Remove the pan from the heat, add the chocolate, and let the mixture sit for a minute to allow the chocolate to melt. Stir until smooth. Pour into large, warm cups, spoon or pipe a generous cap of whipped cream on top, tuck a cinnamon stick and chocolate cigar into each cup, and dust lightly with cinnamon. Serve the hot chocolate immediately.

Notes

♣ Pour the hot chocolate into a vacuum bottle to keep it warm. And if you want to add a little extra zip, add a shot or two of espresso or a chocolate or coffee liqueur.

♣ You can make the whipped cream ahead of time and keep it, covered and refrigerated, for up to a day. It also makes a nice little icing for cupcakes or a filling and icing for génoise. Once you have covered the cake with a thin layer of whipped cream, warm the spatula and run it over the cream to get a smooth surface. Then you can pipe rosettes or decorate the cake however you wish.

Christmas Star

♣ Once we'd tasted
this cake, we liked it
so well that Gilberto
Villarreal, the Fleur
de Lys pastry chef,
adapted it to use
as a birthday cake
choice at the res-
taurant. He added
strawberry jam to
the buttercream
and teamed the
cake with tuiles
(page 167) made
with cracked black
pepper. Bake the
cake in two 9-inch
rounds and plan to
split each layer in
half to make a spec-
tacular four-layer
cake.

ONE OF MY ANTIQUE BAKING MOLDS FROM ALSACE is an earthenware star-shaped mold. My dad tells me that during the holidays *kugelhopf* dough would be baked in these molds for the Christmas star. But even when I was young, that tradition had been almost forgotten. For this book, I wanted to revive the Christmas star and use my mold. This old recipe is based on a classic almond cake with buttercream filling. For Chantal, it has the unmistakable taste of the Christmas season at home in Alsace.

Serves 12

Cake

Unsalted butter for the pan

Generous ½ cup (3 ounces) unbleached all-purpose flour, plus flour for the pan

Sea salt

4 large eggs, separated

3 whole large eggs

1 cup (7 ounces) sugar

2½ cups (8 ounces) ground almonds

Freshly grated zest of 1 orange (optional)

1 teaspoon almond extract or vanilla extract, or ½ teaspoon of each

7 tablespoons (2 ounces) cornstarch

2 teaspoons powdered sugar

Buttercream

3 large eggs, lightly beaten

1 cup plus 2 tablespoons (8 ounces) sugar

½ teaspoon sea salt

1½ cups and 2 tablespoons (3 sticks plus 2 tablespoons or 13 ounces) unsalted butter, at room temperature

2 tablespoons (1 ounce) kirsch

Glaze and Decorations

2 cups (8 ounces) powdered sugar

2 tablespoons (1 ounce) kirsch

Candied decorations (such as silver dragées, sugar stars, nonpareils, or pearl or coarse sparkling white sugar)

To make the cake: Preheat the oven to 350°F. Generously butter and flour a 10-inch springform pan. In a large bowl, beat the 4 egg yolks with the 3 whole eggs and the sugar on high speed until white and very thick. When the beaters are lifted, the mixture will fall back into the bowl in a thick ribbon, about 6 minutes. With a large rubber spatula, gently fold in the almonds, orange zest, and almond extract. Sift the cornstarch and ½ cup flour over the batter and fold in.

Moving quickly, in another large bowl whip the remaining 4 egg whites with a pinch of salt on medium-low speed until foamy. Increase the speed to medium and add the powdered sugar by spoonfuls, whipping until the whites hold soft peaks. Scoop about one-third of the beaten whites into the batter and fold in to lighten the batter. Then delicately fold in the remaining whites, being careful to deflate the batter as little as possible.

Pour and scrape the batter into the prepared pan. Bake until a cake tester inserted in the center comes out clean, about 30 minutes. Remove from the oven and let it sit on a rack 3 to 4 minutes. Then unmold and continue to cool the cake on the rack to room temperature.

Meanwhile, prepare the buttercream filling: Prepare an ice-water bath. Place the eggs, sugar, and salt in a small saucepan over low heat and whisk continuously until the mixture is hot, about 140°F. Do not let the eggs curdle. Remove from the heat, pour into a bowl, and set over the ice water to cool to room temperature. Stir occasionally.

In a large mixing bowl, beat the butter with the whisk attachment of a stand mixer until light and creamy. Beat in the egg-sugar mixture and the kirsch on medium to medium-high speed until smooth and light. Cover and refrigerate until needed. Let it soften to room temperature before using.

To assemble the cake: Cover a cardboard circle the size of the cake with aluminum foil. When the cake has thoroughly cooled, cut it into 3 horizontal layers. Arrange the bottom layer on the cardboard circle. Spread half the buttercream over the cake. Repeat with the second layer and the remaining buttercream. Top with the third layer, making sure the cut side is down.

To make the glaze: Measure the sugar into a large bowl and mix in the kirsch and enough water, 2 to 3 tablespoons, to make an easily pourable glaze. Spread the glaze over the top of the cake, letting it run and drip down the sides in a decorative pattern. Immediately add the cake decorations so they stick in the glaze. Transfer the finished cake to a platter.

Alcohol-Free Variation

Use almond extract and orange zest in the buttercream instead of the kirsch, or perhaps melted dark chocolate. For the glaze, instead of the kirsch use 2 tablespoons freshly squeezed orange juice and 1 teaspoon freshly squeezed lemon juice, plus water as needed.

♣ This is a really good recipe for buttercream. It stands easily in soft swirls and peaks. You can flavor the buttercream any way you like—with strawberry jam or other strongly flavored jam, sour cherry syrup, melted dark chocolate, espresso, matcha (powdered green tea), or toasted almonds. You could also divide the buttercream filling in half and flavor each half with something different.

SECRETS OF A CHEF, SEASON 3

Above left: **Me with Lili and Yves Baltenweck and their home-cured hams and bacon.** *Left:* **At work filming my PBS cooking show,** *Secrets of a Chef.*

Pain d'Épices / Christmas Spice Bread

Notes

♣ We make *pain d'épices* in Alsace in winter when it is cold, so it's easy to find a cool place to store the dough before baking. But if you do not have a cool place or you are worried about the dough, refrigerate it. But then do age it for at least eight days.

BOTH CHANTAL AND I REMEMBER boxes and boxes of *pain d'épices* as part of our families' holiday preparations. Chantal's mom started her dough right after St. Nicholas Day. The honey dough was flavored with warm spices and kirsch and aged for eight days before she baked it. She sugar-glazed her breads, packed them into decorative tins, and stored them in the attic. Every holiday visitor would get one. This is Chantal's mother's recipe. It has a very appetizing aroma unlike anything else I could name. The bread bakes up just slightly puffy, with a medium dense and slightly dry texture. As it ages, it gets both darker and moister. It's become a popular addition to Fleur de Lys's petits fours tray, and it would be equally good accompanying a cheese plate. The recipe can be halved (but you might regret it). I hope *pain d'épices* will become part of your holiday traditions.

Makes about 10 pounds of dough—enough to fill 4 (9 by 12-inch) baking pans or 2 (11 by 17-inch) pans; about 240 (1-inch) cookies

3⅓ cups (40 ounces by weight) honey

2½ cups and 1 tablespoon (18 ounces) sugar

5¼ cups (21 ounces) sliced blanched almonds

¾ cup (3½ ounces) coarsely chopped candied orange rind

¾ cup (3½ ounces) coarsely chopped candied lemon rind

Freshly grated zest of 4 lemons

½ cup (¾ ounces or 50 grams) ground cinnamon

1 tablespoon ground anise seeds

1 tablespoon ground cardamom

1 tablespoon ground ginger

½ teaspoon ground cloves

½ teaspoon freshly grated nutmeg

½ teaspoon sea salt

½ teaspoon freshly ground black pepper

18 tablespoons (9 ounces) unsalted butter, at room temperature

8⅔ cups (44 ounces) unbleached all-purpose flour

1 tablespoon (11 grams) baking powder

⅞ cup (7 ounces) kirsch

Freshly squeezed juice of 2 lemons

Glaze

1 cup (4 ounces) powdered sugar

Freshly squeezed juice of 1 lemon

Heat the honey and sugar in a large saucepan over low heat, stirring occasionally, until the sugar has dissolved and the mixture is warm. Add the almonds, candied orange and lemon rind, lemon zest, cinnamon, anise, cardamom, ginger, cloves, nutmeg, salt, pepper, and butter. Mix well with a sturdy wooden spoon until blended.

Place the flour and baking powder in a very large bowl and whisk to mix evenly. Scrape the honey mixture into the bowl with the kirsch and lemon juice. Mix until all the ingredients are evenly blended. Cover and set aside at cool room temperature for at least 4 days and up to 8 days to allow the flavors to develop.

Preheat the oven to 350°F. Line 4 (9 by 12-inch) pans with parchment paper. Divide the dough into 4 equal portions and pat 1 portion into each pan. To smooth out the tops, cover with parchment paper or wax paper and roll with a short rolling pin or a Bordeaux-style wine bottle. Bake until the bread has puffed slightly and turned a medium brown, about 25 minutes.

Meanwhile, in a medium bowl, stir the powdered sugar with the lemon juice until you have a smooth lemony glaze. As soon as the breads come out of the oven, brush them all over with the glaze. Continue to cool in the pans for about 20 minutes and then cut the breads into small squares. The bread will keep for several weeks stored in tightly sealed tins.

Anise Cookies

In Alsace this traditional cookie appears in pastry shops at Christmastime. The squat mushroom-shaped cookie features two distinct textures. This is achieved in a simple but surprising way. You make the batter, pipe the cookies, dust them with sugar, and then leave them on the counter to dry overnight. When they bake the next day, the top puffs above a crispy base layer. The cookies keep very well, staying crisp in an airtight container for up to two weeks. And they taste best when slightly dry, so make them at least several days ahead of time. This also makes them a great cookie for holiday parties, gifts, and cookie swaps.

Makes about 90 (1½-inch) cookies

    Butter or oil spray, for greasing the
    baking sheets
3½ cups (17½ ounces) unbleached
    all-purpose flour
 1 tablespoon (½ ounce) baking powder
    Pinch of sea salt
 6 large eggs
 2 cups (14 ounces) superfine sugar
    plus about 2 cups (14 ounces)
    for dusting
 2 tablespoons and 1 teaspoon (1 ounce)
    anise seeds

Very lightly and evenly grease 2 or 3 baking sheets. To do this most easily, spray the sheets with cooking spray and then wipe them down with paper towels. Sift the flour, baking powder, and salt together onto a sheet of parchment paper and set it aside.

In the bowl of a stand mixer, beat the eggs and 2 cups of the sugar on high speed until tripled in volume and very thick, about 8 minutes. When the whisk is lifted, the batter will form a thick ribbon as it falls back into the bowl. Lower the speed to stir and carefully tap the dry ingredients into the eggs. As soon as all the flour has been added to the eggs, stop the machine. With a large rubber spatula, fold the anise seeds into the batter. Let the dough rest for 5 minutes.

Scrape about one-third of the dough into a pastry bag fitted with a large round tip and pipe out 1½- to 2-inch rounds onto a prepared baking sheet. Space the cookies about ½ inch apart.

Keep the tip close to the baking sheet to avoid a central dimple. (Don't worry—the sugar coating will hide small dimples.) You can fit about 30 cookies on each baking sheet. Generously dust the cookies on one baking sheet with the remaining 2 cups of sugar and then quickly lift the sheet on end and pour the excess sugar over the cookies on the second baking sheet. Give the first baking sheet a couple of sharp taps to loosen as much sugar as possible. Repeat the process until all the cookies are dusted with sugar.

Leave the cookies uncovered on a work surface overnight. When ready to bake, preheat the oven to 400°F. Bake the cookies until they are puffed and very lightly browned on top, 5 to 8 minutes. Rotate the pans, top to bottom and front to back, halfway through the baking time. Immediately run a metal spatula under the cookies to remove them from the baking sheets and transfer them to a rack to cool completely. Store them in an airtight container for up to 2 weeks.

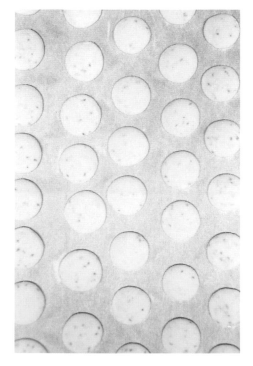

♣ Once the batter has been made, the flour begins to absorb the liquid and the batter will thicken. The trick is to wait just long enough for the batter to stiffen a little, but not too much. If the batter is too thin, the cookies spread and don't rise; if too thick, the batter becomes too hard to pipe.

Vin Chaud / Hot Spiced Wine

Notes

♣ When I was young, I never saw a *vin chaud* made with white wine, but there is no reason not to make the recipe with an Alsatian white, perhaps a pinot gris, pinot blanc, or a gewürztraminer.

OVER THE HOLIDAYS IN ALSACE, *vin chaud* is sold everywhere on the street. During the Christmas fairs when you buy your first *vin chaud*, it comes in a ceramic mug. Then, as you continue shopping, you simply buy refills. It's served extremely hot and goes really well with the Christmas Star (page 296) and *Pain d'Épices* (page 298). We don't drink coffee or hot chocolate on the street, just this wine—even we kids would have a sip or two to warm us up. To go with it we'd buy *marrons chaud* (roasted chestnuts) from a street vendor who roasted the nuts over charcoal until the shells cracked. Then he'd pile the hot nuts in a paper cone and we held it to warm our hands. To make *vin chaud*, choose a wine that's not too tannic, such as a pinot noir or a lighter-style cabernet.

Serves 4

1   orange
1   lemon
1¼ cups (8¾ ounces) sugar
1   cinnamon stick
2   star anise
2   slices peeled fresh ginger
2   crushed cardamom pods
2   cloves
    Pinch of freshly grated nutmeg
1   (750-milliliter) bottle dry red wine

Using a vegetable peeler, remove the zest in strips from half of the orange and half of the lemon. Cut the remaining orange and lemon halves into thin slices.

Place the orange and lemon zest and slices, the sugar, 1 cup water, and the cinnamon stick, star anise, ginger, cardamom pods, cloves, and nutmeg in a nonreactive saucepan and bring to a boil over high heat. Simmer for 5 minutes to infuse the syrup with the flavorings. Add the wine and simmer for another 3 to 5 minutes. Strain the flavorings out and serve the wine in cups or mugs with slices of orange and lemon in each. Serve the wine very hot.

Below from left: Hot roasted chestnuts bought from a vendor at the street fair. Ribeauvillé mayor Jean-Louis Christ, Chantal, and me drinking *vin chaud* from our commemorative cups.

Parsnip Blinis with Caviar

THESE LITTLE PANCAKES taste like sweet parsnip soufflés. At Fleur de Lys, I used to do a similar pancake but with corn. I put a spoonful of batter in the pan, added a thin little slice of salmon folded over a tiny spoon of caviar, and then topped it with another spoonful of batter. By the time the pancake had a golden color on both sides, the fish inside was cooked as well. Then it was served with a bright-green watercress sauce. Since then Fleur de Lys's chef de cuisine, Rick Richardson, and I have made blinis with celery root, chestnuts, and parsnips. Caviar with chestnut blinis tastes really good. To ease the stress on the home cook making a holiday meal, I've garnished these little blinis more simply, but your guests will still love them. Choose smaller parsnips to avoid any with fibrous cores.

Serves 6 to 8; about 3 (2½-inch) blinis per person

Chantal's table setting featured marzipan-iced *pain d'épices* angels from Christine Ferber's Pâtisserie and Boulangerie in Niedermorschwihr on Rue Trois Epis and Villeroy & Boch holiday tableware.

1   tablespoon plus 1 tablespoon unsalted butter, plus more as needed
12 ounces parsnips, peeled and finely chopped
     Pinch of sugar
     Sea salt and freshly ground white pepper
1   large egg
3   large eggs, separated
2   tablespoons unbleached all-purpose flour
1   tablespoon whole milk
2   tablespoons crème fraîche or sour cream
1   to 2 ounces sturgeon caviar
1   tablespoon finely sliced fresh chives
     Lemon wedges for serving (optional)

Heat 1 tablespoon of the butter in a small saucepan over medium heat. Add the parsnips, sugar, and about 1 inch of water. Season with salt and pepper, bring to a boil, cover, and simmer until the parsnips are very tender, 10 to 15 minutes. If any cooking liquid remains, remove the lid and continue to cook until the pan is almost dry. Transfer the parsnips to a blender and puree until very smooth and velvety. If the puree still seems to have some fibers, push it through a fine sieve.

Add the whole egg, the 3 egg yolks, the flour, and the milk to the blender. Pulse until smooth, scraping down the sides as needed.

In a large bowl, whip the egg whites until they hold soft peaks. Scrape the puree into the whites and fold them together gently, being careful not to deflate the whites. Season with salt and pepper. The batter can be refrigerated, covered, for up to 4 hours. Stir gently, if necessary, until evenly blended before cooking.

Preheat the oven to 200°F. Heat 1 teaspoon of the remaining butter in a large nonstick skillet over medium heat. Spoon about 2 tablespoons of batter per blini into the skillet and cook over medium-low to medium heat until golden underneath, about 2 minutes. Turn and cook the second side until browned, about 2 minutes. Transfer the blinis to a warm serving platter and keep them warm in the oven. Add more butter to the skillet as needed and continue cooking blinis until all the batter is gone.

Top each blini with a small dollop of crème fraîche and another of caviar. Sprinkle with chives and serve them immediately with lemon wedges.

Oysters on the Half Shell with Citrus, Toasted Coriander, and Olive Oil

CHANTAL AND I ALWAYS BEGIN OUR CHRISTMAS DINNER with oysters and champagne. Sometimes we serve the freshly shucked oysters with a champagne mignonnette, butter, and rye bread, and sometimes we serve them this way, with toasted coriander and citrus. It's a combination I learned while working for Roger Vergé in the south of France. A platter of oysters is a smart choice for entertaining—they never fail to please your guests, and they are so festive as well as practical. You can shuck the oysters well ahead of time, prepare the garnishes, and keep them all refrigerated until serving time. Plan on a dozen oysters for every two to three people. I like Kumamoto oysters. They are small with a deep shell, a mild flavor, and a succulent texture. And I like Kusshi oysters, too—the prima donna of oysters from the Pacific Northwest that have such a clean briny flavor.

Serves 4 as a first course or about 6 as an hors d'oeuvre

Rock salt or crushed ice or both
2 dozen fresh raw oysters in their shells
1 small orange
1 small lime
1 teaspoon coriander seeds
1 teaspoon freshly cracked black pepper
About 1½ tablespoons extra-virgin olive oil

Line a sheet pan with parchment paper and then spread a layer of rock salt (it has the advantage of not melting) or crushed ice on the parchment paper. Shuck the oysters, discard the top shells (or put it in your compost!), and settle the bottom shell with the oysters into the salt so that they balance securely. Refrigerate them until ready to serve, up to several hours.

With a small sharp knife, pare away the skin and pith from the orange and lime. Working over a bowl to catch the juices, cut the segments free. Hold the fruit in one hand and cut down between each segment and the membrane. Discard any seeds. Cut the segments crosswise into tiny, thin triangles. Reserve the juice for another use.

Heat a small skillet over medium heat. Add the coriander and toast, stirring regularly to prevent scorching, until fragrant, about 2 minutes. Coarsely crush the seeds with the side of a pot pressed into the skillet (this helps prevent the seeds from hopping onto the counter and floor) or in a mortar and pestle. Set them aside.

When ready to serve, cover a serving platter or large, deep plate with fresh crushed ice. Arrange the oysters on top and then garnish each with 2 or 3 pieces of lime and 1 or 2 pieces of orange. Adjust the numbers to the size of your oysters. Very lightly dust the oysters with coriander and black pepper and drizzle with a few drops of olive oil. Serve them immediately.

Notes

♣ To save yourself time or if you are not practiced at shucking oysters, ask the fishmonger to shuck them for you. Just be sure to let the fishmonger know you plan to serve them on the half shell. He or she will then open the oysters and pack them up correctly.

♣ But you could also use crushed ice and replace it with fresh cracked ice at serving time.

"*Here's the Peruvian Prawn and Sea Scallop Ceviche that I arranged in small shooter glasses. It's fun to put these out as canapés for an elegant party.*"

Peruvian Prawn and Sea Scallop Ceviche

♣ It's nice to have something crunchy with the ceviche. Serve croutons or fried vegetable chips such as taro roots, potatoes, or a mix of root vegetables.

IN BRAZIL, WE WERE SEVERAL HOURS FROM THE WATER, so we did not do ceviche on the menu. My knowledge of ceviche—Peruvian ceviche especially—comes from sous chef Remberto Garcia at Fleur de Lys, who has been with us since 1986. He is originally from Peru. For many years, Fleur de Lys was closed on Sundays. On Saturday night, once the dinner service was over, the chefs would clear out all the fish we had not sold, and Remberto would make a staff meal of ceviche or fish stew.

Serves 4 to 6

½ pound very fresh sea scallops

½ pound very fresh prawns, peeled and deveined

Sea salt

1 medium sweet potato

1 small ear corn

1 stalk celery, cut into ⅛-inch dice

½ small red onion, cut into ⅛-inch dice

1 small habanero chile, very finely chopped

1½ tablespoons chopped fresh cilantro

2 cloves garlic, very finely chopped

1 cup freshly squeezed lime juice

12 cherry tomatoes, halved

1 head endive, separated into leaves

Cut the scallops and prawns into ¼-inch dice, place them in a large glass bowl, cover, and refrigerate while preparing the vegetables.

Bring a small saucepan of water to a boil, add a generous pinch of salt and the potato, and cook until tender, about 20 minutes. While the potato cooks, prepare an ice-water bath. When cooked, dip out the potato, plunge it into the ice water, and let it cool. Drain, peel, and cut into ¼-inch dice. Add the potato to the seafood.

Return the water to a boil and cook the corn until tender, about 6 minutes. Dip it out, plunge it into the ice water, and let it cool. Cut off the kernels and measure out ½ cup. Add to the seafood and reserve the remainder for another use.

Add the celery, onion, chile, cilantro, garlic, lime juice, and salt to taste to the seafood only a few minutes before serving. If left too long, the fish overcooks in the lime juice, releasing liquid and diluting the flavors. Toss the ceviche gently and refrigerate for 10 to 15 minutes, tossing gently every 5 minutes so that the fish cures evenly in the lime juice.

When ready to serve, gently mix in the cherry tomatoes. Present the ceviche in the bowl or scoop it into martini glasses. Garnish with the endive and serve it very cold.

My mom and dad looking through a family album.

Potato, Shallot, and Fresh Herb Potpie

CHEF HAEBERLIN'S MENTOR had been a chef at the court of Tzar Nicholas II and had brought back many recipes. The *pintade Souvaroff* we served at L'Auberge de L'Ill was a sort of potpie of truffle-stuffed guinea hen served with a rich truffle sauce. This potato pie reminds me of that Russian dish because of its puff-pastry lid and its rich filling, one you could make fancier for the holidays by mixing in sautéed mushrooms or chopped black truffle. With or without those extra ingredients, try this during the holidays. Serve it with lamb (page 71), the venison chop (page 167), or the buffalo steaks (page 165), or even on its own as a vegetarian supper with a crisp green salad.

Serves 4 to 6

2 pounds Yukon Gold potatoes, peeled
  Sea salt
1½ teaspoons extra-virgin olive oil
¾ cup very finely chopped shallots
3 large eggs
1 cup heavy cream or half-and-half
1½ cups coarsely grated Gruyère cheese (3 to 4 ounces)
1½ teaspoons finely chopped fresh thyme
2 tablespoons finely chopped fresh flat-leaf parsley
2 tablespoons finely sliced fresh chives
2 cloves garlic, finely chopped
  Freshly ground black pepper
  Unsalted butter for the baking dish
  Unbleached all-purpose flour for dusting the work surfaces
½ (11 by 15-inch) sheet puff pastry
1 large egg yolk

Preheat the oven to 375°F. Place the potatoes in a saucepan with cold water to cover. Add a tablespoon of salt and bring to a boil over high heat. Boil the potatoes until just tender; the timing depends on the size of the potatoes. Do not overcook. Drain, let cool, and slice them into ⅛-inch-thick rounds.

Heat the olive oil in a medium skillet over medium heat. Add the shallots, season with salt and pepper, and cook until very soft, about 5 minutes. Add a tablespoon of water if the pan becomes too dry. Remove from the heat and set aside.

In a large bowl, whisk the eggs until well mixed. Stir in the cream, cheese, thyme, parsley, chives, garlic, and shallots. Season well with salt and pepper.

Generously butter a 1½-quart gratin dish or pie pan. Spread half of the sliced potatoes evenly over the bottom of the dish. Ladle half of the egg mixture over the potatoes and then layer in the remaining potatoes. Fill the dish with the remaining egg mixture.

Roll out the pastry on a lightly floured work surface into a circle ⅛ inch thick with a diameter 1 inch larger than the gratin dish all around. Fit the pastry onto the top of the pie. Press the edges onto the edge of the dish and crimp the pastry all around. In a small bowl, whisk together the egg yolk and ½ teaspoon of water to make an egg wash. Brush the pastry all over with the egg wash and cut a central chimney through the pastry to allow steam to escape. If desired, use the back of a knife to make some decorative lines through the glaze onto the pastry and use leftover pastry scraps to make decorations. Brush these with the glaze.

Bake the potato pie until the pastry is browned, about 40 minutes. Let the pie rest for about 10 minutes before serving.

Braised Fennel à la Roger Vergé

IN ALSACE WE USE DRIED FIGS FREQUENTLY, especially for holiday cooking. But it was only when I worked for Roger Vergé at his three-star Moulin de Mougins in the south of France that I was introduced to the abundance of figs available there. We also often roasted whole fish on a bed of fennel fronds. This dish combines these two typical ingredients of Provençale cuisine, and then includes a twist with the addition of herbs and cinnamon. Chantal uses just about any excuse to make this; it's so easy and delicious. The flavors of the fennel, shallots, and figs, and the surprise of cinnamon make a perfect marriage.

Serves 4 (½ fennel bulb per person)

½ pound shallots, unpeeled

6 dried figs

1 cup plus ¼ cup low-salt vegetable, chicken, or beef broth

1 tablespoon extra-virgin olive oil, for oiling the baking dish

2 large fennel bulbs, halved lengthwise

¾ teaspoon finely chopped fresh thyme, or ½ teaspoon very finely chopped fresh rosemary

2 bay leaves

1 small cinnamon stick

Sea salt and freshly ground black pepper

Preheat the oven to 375°F. Soak the shallots for several minutes in a bowl of water. This prevents them from burning when you roast them. Drain and then trim off the root and stem ends. Place the shallots in a small pan and roast them in the oven until soft throughout, about 40 minutes. Leave the oven on. Let the shallots cool, then peel them and set them aside.

Place the figs and 1 cup of the broth in a small saucepan and bring to a simmer over medium heat. Simmer gently until the figs are plump and soft, about 10 minutes. Drain the figs, reserving the figs and broth separately. Quarter the figs.

Coat a baking dish with the olive oil; the dish should fit the fennel snugly in a single layer. Arrange the fennel in the dish cut side down. Scatter the roasted shallots, figs, thyme, bay leaves, and cinnamon stick over and around the fennel. Season well with salt and pepper and add the reserved broth and the remaining ¼ cup of broth. Cover the dish with a lid or a layer of parchment paper and then a layer of aluminum foil to seal the dish well. Bake until the fennel is very tender, about 1½ hours. Uncover it and serve.

Notes

♣ You could add wild mushrooms or substitute mushrooms for the figs. When fennel is out of season, try celery hearts. And any color of figs—black, white, or brown— will work. You might want to mix the colors if you have them on hand.

Above, clockwise: Chantal's tablescape. Jean Trimbach opening wine. The hors d'oeuvres buffet. Me, my brother, Francis, and my dad. Carving Yves Baltenweck's home-cured ham. Yves presenting his ham.

"The holidays are such a big deal in Alsace that Chantal and I always make a big deal of them, too."

From bottom left, clockwise: Rémy Schaal's *pain* surprise. Chantal's red, white, and green table. We had seafood including huge crabs for the first course. Rémy and his wife, Isabelle. Jean Trimbach with Dany and Michele Haas.

Beef Wellington

Notes

♣ You can cut the recipe in half and cook just half a filet to serve four. The cooking time to achieve rare to medium-rare meat is the same whether you have a larger or smaller filet: 15 minutes at 425°F followed later by 25 minutes at 375°F.

♣ You can substitute button mushrooms for the shiitakes or use a mixture of mushrooms both wild and domestic. For an even more festive dish, add truffles. Very thinly slice a truffle and, when you have spread out the mushroom filling, scatter the slices over the filling. Then follow the instructions for wrapping the filet in the duxelles. The truffle will scent the whole roast.

I HAD BEEN WORKING ON MY RECIPE for beef Wellington for the third season of my public television series *Secrets of a Chef* when Chantal and I decided to put the dish on the special Christmas Eve menu at Fleur de Lys. It's such a great old dish, and the presentation is so impressive. The flavors and textures show so well together: the earthiness of the mushrooms, the tenderness of the meat, and the crispiness of the pastry. The aroma while it's baking fills the house. Since we make up our home menu from dishes created for the restaurant, we served it at home Christmas Day. Our friends could not remember when they had had one last and raved about it.

Serves 8

1 whole beef filet (3 to 4 pounds), well trimmed
   Sea salt and freshly ground black pepper
   About ½ cup extra-virgin olive oil
   About ⅓ cup dry red wine
   Red Wine–Shallot Sauce for serving (page 211)
2 cups very finely chopped shallots (see Notes)
2½ tablespoons brown sugar (optional)
2 tablespoons finely chopped fresh thyme
2 pounds shiitake mushrooms, sliced about ¼ inch thick (about 12 cups)
1 tablespoon very finely chopped garlic
   Unbleached all-purpose flour, for dusting the work surface
3 large sheets puff pastry (11 by 15 inches)
4 egg yolks lightly beaten with 2 teaspoons water

Preheat the oven to 425°F. Tie up the roast to give it an even shape: Tie the head (thickest end) down, tuck the tail under, and tie in place. Season the fillet with salt and pepper. Heat 2 tablespoons of the oil in a large ovenproof skillet and place over medium-high heat. Add the meat and brown it on all sides, about 5 minutes. Transfer the skillet to the oven and roast for 15 minutes. The meat will register about 100°F.

Transfer the meat to a platter, let it cool to room temperature, and remove the string. Meanwhile, put the skillet back over medium heat. Add the red wine to the skillet and stir and scrape all over the bottom of the pan to loosen any browned bits. Cook until the liquid is reduced to about 1½ tablespoons. Scrape into the red wine–shallot sauce, cover, and refrigerate.

Heat 1 tablespoon of the remaining olive oil in a large skillet over medium heat. Add the shallots, a splash of water, a pinch each of salt and pepper, the brown sugar, and the thyme. Cover and cook until soft, about 3 minutes. Uncover the pan and cook over low heat until the pan is dry and the shallots have lightly caramelized, about another 8 minutes. Scrape the shallots into a bowl and set aside.

Meanwhile, cook the mushrooms in batches so as not to crowd the pan. Heat another 2 tablespoons of the olive oil in a large skillet over medium-high heat. Add the mushrooms and cook, without moving them, until browned on one side, about 1 minute. Then stir and cook over medium-low heat until well browned and very tender, about 15 minutes. For the last few minutes of cooking, add the garlic and a pinch each of salt and pepper. Scrape the mushrooms into the bowl of a food processor, let cool, and then process until evenly and finely chopped. Pulse in the shallots just to mix. Adjust the seasonings with salt and pepper. You should have about 3 cups of stuffing.

Moisten a work surface and lay out a sheet of plastic wrap large enough to

314

wrap the filet or overlap 2 sheets. Wrap a piece of string around the waist of the filet to measure its diameter and length and then use it to measure a rectangle on the plastic wrap as wide and as long as the filet. Cover the rectangle with an even layer of the stuffing. Place the filet in the middle of the stuffing and pull the wrap up and over the meat. Pat all around so the mushrooms stick to the meat and form an even layer. Roll it over and pat the bottom, too, to make sure all the mushrooms stick to the meat. Wrap the meat securely in the plastic wrap and refrigerate for at least 2 hours and up to 12 hours. Pour any juices from the meat platter into the sauce.

Preheat the oven to 375°F. Line a baking sheet with parchment paper and dust the parchment paper with flour. On a lightly floured work surface, roll one pastry sheet into a rectangle about 12 by 20 inches. It should be large enough to leave a 1- to 1½-inch border of pastry all around the filet. Put the pastry on the prepared baking sheet. Unwrap the meat from the plastic and quickly transfer it to the center of the pastry. Brush the pastry around the meat with the egg yolk glaze.

Roll the remaining sheets of pastry into a rectangle about 15 by 28 inches, roll it over the rolling pin, and then unroll it over the filet. Pat it carefully in place to remove any air pockets. Press the edge of the top crust onto the bottom crust to seal. Trim the pastry so the edges are even, leaving a border of 1 to 1½ inches, and cutting the corners on a diagonal. Make a scalloped border all the way around: Position your thumb with the tip pointing toward the meat and press down firmly. Then, with the back of a knife or spoon, pull the pastry back toward the meat, snugging it up nicely. Move your thumb to the opposite side of the scallop and repeat all the way around to form a deeply wavy, decorative edge.

Brush the pastry generously with the egg glaze. Make decorative lines on the pastry by running the back of a knife through the egg glaze. Cut 3 or 4 slits in the pastry to let steam escape and cut decorative shapes out of the pastry trimmings. Arrange them on the pastry and then brush them with more egg glaze. Place the beef in the 375°F oven and bake for 25 minutes for medium-rare meat. The temperature of the meat will register about 120°F. Warm the sauce over low heat while the beef cooks. Let the meat rest for 5 to 10 minutes before carefully cutting it into thick slices to serve. Pass the sauce at the table.

Wild Salmon Variation

Choose a single thick, skinless fillet of salmon and pull out any pinbones. Estimate about 5 ounces of fish per person. Make the duxelles (the mushroom stuffing in the main recipe) and spread a layer on the pastry. Place the fish on top, season, and spread with a second layer of duxelles. You can add a layer of finely chopped scallions, herbs, and capers if desired before adding the top layer of mushrooms. Enclose with the pastry and bake as directed until the pastry is very brown. Serve with a béarnaise sauce (page 80).

♣ Chop the shallots by hand; in a machine, they may turn into a puree. And although it is an extra step to cook the shallots separately from the mushrooms, only in this way can you be sure they are well cooked and really dry before mixing them with the mushrooms.

♣ You will be wrapping the whole filet in plastic wrap and refrigerating it for several hours. In order to wrap such a large piece, you will need to overlap 2 sheets of plastic wrap or use restaurant-sized wrap. This size is available at restaurant supply stores and warehouse stores.

Galette des Rois / Three Kings Cake

MY BROTHER AND I COULD HARDLY WAIT for holiday desserts such as *galette des rois*, served in French homes on Epiphany, the twelfth day after Christmas. It's a handsome, buttery puff-pastry sandwich stuffed with almond cream. Traditionally it's decorated with a paper crown and has a fava bean, a peeled baby carrot, or a whole almond baked inside. Whoever gets the piece with the bean becomes the king or queen of the feast. Parents cut the cake into slices, and each child chooses one. They try to peek and guess before taking one. After the French Revolution in 1789, the cake became associated with the royalist cause and baking it was strictly forbidden. Only after the Restoration of King Louis XVIII could bakers once again make the cake and families celebrate the holiday in the usual way.

Serves about 8

8	tablespoons (1 stick or 4 ounces) unsalted butter
½	cup (3½ ounces) sugar
1	large egg
3	large egg yolks, divided
1	cup (3¼ ounces) finely ground almonds
2	tablespoons unbleached all-purpose flour, plus more for dusting the work surface
2	tablespoons dark rum
1½	pounds puff pastry, divided
1	dried bean or 1 peeled baby carrot
1	tablespoon powdered sugar

In a mixing bowl, beat the butter and sugar together until very light and fluffy. Beat in the whole egg and 1 of the egg yolks until smooth. Stir in the almonds, 2 tablespoons flour, and rum until evenly combined. Cover and refrigerate.

Brush an ungreased baking sheet very lightly with water. Dust a work surface lightly with flour and roll 10 ounces of the pastry until 1/16 inch thick and trim into an 11-inch circle. Transfer it to the prepared baking sheet. Mound the almond filling on the dough, leaving a 1-inch border all around. Press the dried bean into the filling. In a small bowl, whisk the remaining 2 egg yolks with 1 teaspoon water. Brush the border with a little of the egg wash.

On a lightly floured work surface, roll the remaining dough until 1/8 inch thick and trim into an 11-inch circle. Lay it over the filling and press the top and

bottom pastry layers together to seal. Trim the pastry so the edges are even. If you like, make a scalloped border all the way around: With your thumbnail facing toward the cake, press your thumb down onto the pastry border. Position a teaspoon on one side of your thumb and pull the pastry back toward the cake with the spoon, snugging it up nicely. Move your thumb to the opposite side of the scallop and repeat all the way around to form a deeply wavy, decorative edge. If the dough warms too much and becomes soft and sticky, refrigerate the cake to allow it to firm up.

Brush the egg wash over the entire top of the cake. With the back of a paring knife, without cutting into the pastry, draw a decorative pattern of cross-hatched lines or petals by marking sets of curved lines like open and closed parentheses.

Chill the cake while the oven preheats to 425°F. Pierce a few holes through the pastry to allow steam to escape and dust the top with the powdered sugar. Bake until puffed and golden brown, 20 to 25 minutes. Lower the heat to 400°F and continue to bake until the cake is firm, shiny on top, and toasty brown, about 5 minutes. If the sugar has not melted, run the cake quickly under a very hot broiler to finish glazing. Serve it warm or at room temperature. The cake is best served the same day it is baked. Any leftovers can be rewarmed gently before serving.

I went into La Boulange in San Francisco for bread and could not resist the puff pastry palmiers *(top)* and the handsome, generous *galette des rois (opposite).*

Black Forest Cake

UNDER ALL THE WHIPPED CREAM ICING of the Black Forest cake are three layers of chocolate génoise soaked in kirsch. My father finished his génoise by hand, using a huge whisk with widely spaced wires to fold the flour and then the butter into the batter with big, efficient strokes so it would not deflate. On a daily basis, he would grab one of us kids to help. He sifted the flour, cocoa, and salt onto a sheet of parchment paper. When he was ready, my brother or I would hold the parchment paper folded above the bowl and tap the flour over the batter while Dad folded it in, telling us to tap faster or slower. As with many fancy cakes, the assembly is easy; it just takes lots of words to describe.

Once you have baked the cake, you have completed the part that needs the greatest attention. The cake's flavor develops as the kirsch soaks into the layers. Give the finished cake a minimum of four hours in the refrigerator before serving, but it's even better made a whole day in advance. My recipe uses home-preserved sour cherries. But if you want to make this cake and did not start in June during cherry season, you still have plenty of options. You can use fresh or frozen fruit or shop for jars of preserved sour cherries such as morello and amarena cherries. Depending on what you find, the syrup will contain more or less sugar, so be sure to taste first and adjust your ingredients accordingly. (See the Note on the next page for details on substitutions.) A good Black Forest cake should be very moist and have a distinct kirsch flavor. So be sure to use good-quality kirsch.

Serves 8

Notes

♣ In French pastry, the difference between a plain sponge cake and a génoise is the addition of butter to the batter. Unfortunately, folding in the butter can cause the batter to deflate and your cake to be heavy. If you feel confident making génoise, go ahead and add the 3 tablespoons of unsalted butter. Otherwise, leave it out. The cake will still be delicious.

Cake

- 3 tablespoons unsalted butter, melted and cooled, plus more for buttering cake pan
- ½ cup (2½ ounces) unbleached all-purpose flour plus more for dusting cake pan
- ¼ cup Dutch-process cocoa
  Pinch of salt
- 6 large eggs, at room temperature
- ¾ cup (4¾ ounces) superfine sugar
- 1 teaspoon vanilla extract

Syrup

- ½ cup sugar
- 1 ounce (2 tablespoons) kirsch

Assembly

- 4 cups heavy cream
- 1 cup (4 ounces) powdered sugar
- 2 teaspoons vanilla extract
- 2 cups Spirited Sour Cherries, drained (page 46), or a 24-ounce jar sour cherries such as morello or amarena
- 8 fresh cherries with stems (optional)

About 2½ ounces dark chocolate (at least 60% cacao) in a single block

About ½ cup ground dark chocolate (at least 60% cacao) or chocolate cookie crumbs

Powdered sugar for dusting

To make the cake: Preheat the oven to 350°F. Place the rack in the center of the oven. Butter and flour a 10-inch cake pan that is 3 inches deep such as a springform mold.

Sift the ½ cup flour, the cocoa, and the salt together onto a sheet of parchment paper and set aside. In the bowl of a stand mixer fitted with the whisk attachment, beat the eggs, sugar, and vanilla at high speed until the mixture has tripled in volume and is very thick, about 8 minutes. When the whisk is lifted, the batter will form a thick ribbon as it falls back into the bowl.

Lower the speed to stir and carefully tap the dry ingredients into the egg mixture. As soon as all the flour has

Notes

♣ If using jarred cherries, drain them, reserving both the syrup and the cherries. Measure the amount of syrup and set aside. Macerate the cherries in a glass bowl in ½ cup of kirsch for 1 hour, tossing them occasionally. Drain the cherries, reserving them and the kirsch separately. Pour the syrup into a small saucepan with the kirsch and add sugar, if needed, to make a slightly sweet, cherry-flavored syrup. Bring to a boil over high heat, stirring until the sugar dissolves. Remove from the heat and set aside until needed. You need about 1 cup of syrup for the cake. Use the rest as a sauce for ice cream.

been added to the eggs, stop the machine. Pour in the melted butter, making sure to leave the white, milky solids behind. With a large rubber spatula, using as few strokes as possible, finish folding the flour mixture and butter into the batter until evenly mixed.

Immediately scrape the batter into the prepared pan, place the pan on a baking sheet, and bake until the cake feels just firm to the touch, about 40 minutes. Transfer the cake to a rack and let it cool for about 5 minutes. Then turn the cake upside down onto a rack to cool. This will flatten the slightly domed top.

To make the syrup: Place the sugar and ½ cup water in a small saucepan over medium-high heat. Bring the mixture to a boil while stirring to dissolve the sugar. Add the kirsch and remove from the heat. Pour the syrup into a small cup or bowl and set it aside.

To assemble the cake: In a large bowl, whip the cream with the sugar and vanilla on medium-high speed until it holds firm peaks. Do not overbeat; the whipped cream should be smooth and firm. Divide the cream into 4 equal portions and set them aside. (This helps prevent getting to the last bit of decorating and discovering you have run out of cream.) Drain the cherries and divide them into 2 equal piles. Reserve 8 to 12 cherries to garnish the top of the cake if you do not have fresh cherries.

Place the cake on a work surface with its original top up. Trim off any hard crusts. With a long serrated knife, cut the cake horizontally into 3 even layers. Transfer the top layer to a serving plate, arranging it top side down. Brush it liberally with the syrup. With an offset spatula or rubber spatula, smooth on a ½-inch layer of whipped cream. Push the cream a little beyond

the edge of the cake. (This prevents gaps when you settle the next layer on top.) Nestle half of the cherries into the whipped cream, scattering them evenly over the top.

Place the middle cake layer on top of the cherries, pressing it lightly into the whipped-cream layer. Brush with syrup, spread with whipped cream, and scatter the remaining half of the cherries over the cream.

Finally, add the last cake layer, cut side up, on top of the cherries, again settling it into the whipped-cream layer. Brush with syrup. With an icing spatula or a large rubber spatula, spread a thin layer of whipped cream over the top of the cake. Spread a thicker layer onto the sides.

Pastry shops add a decorative scalloped edge of ground dark chocolate around the base of the cake. Fill your cupped palm with some of the ground chocolate and lift and tilt it onto the base of the cake all around the bottom edge. Rotate the cake between handfulls. It's the heel of your hand that forms the scalloped edge.

Rotate the edge of a sharp knife against the block of chocolate to make curls or cut shavings with a vegetable peeler. Pile them on top of the cake.

Scoop the remaining whipped cream into a pastry bag fitted with a medium star tip. Pipe fat rosettes all around the top edge of the cake. Press a fresh or spirited cherry into the center of each rosette. Refrigerate the cake for at least 4 hours to let the flavors meld. Just before serving, dust the top with powdered sugar.

Alcohol-Free Variation

Use about 24 ounces of preserved sour cherries in syrup. Drain the cherries, reserving the syrup and cherries separately. In a small saucepan, bring to a boil ⅓ cup espresso or strong coffee, the reserved syrup, and ¾ cup sugar (or to taste), stirring until the sugar dissolves. Remove from the heat and reserve until needed.

Bûche de Noël de Henri Variation

For our Christmas menu in 2010, we used Black Forest flavors for our bûche de Noël. We baked the génoise as a sheet cake, soaked it with the kirsch syrup, spread it thickly with the whipped cream, and then scattered the cherries over the cream before rolling up the cake. We iced it with the traditional chocolate buttercream. This makes a lighter-than-usual bûche, and our guests cleaned their plates.

ACKNOWLEDGMENTS

I NEVER THOUGHT I'D WRITE A MEMOIR, but as I worked with my coauthor, Penni Wisner, downloading favorite stories and memories into her recorder, I realized I had an opportunity to look back at my journey. So many people have helped me on my way, beginning with my parents, Yvonne and Henri; my first mentor, chef Paul Haeberlin and all the Haeberlin family; my best friend and wife, Chantal; my partner in Fleur de Lys, Maurice Rouas, who supported me even when his longtime customers expressed dissatisfaction; Marjorie Poore, who produces my *Secrets of a Chef* television series for PBS, and Mary Rogers of Cuisinart, our sponsor; and Penni, who dug into the material I gave her and then wrote and cooked and wrote and cooked until she was satisfied. To all of you who support and challenge me on a daily basis to do my best, especially the chefs and staffs of all my restaurants and our customers, thank you for your understanding and friendship.

A big thank-you to our agent, Carole Bidnick, for her firm belief and support, and to the team at Andrews McMeel Publishing, especially Jean Lucas, our editor, and Kirsty Melville, our publisher, for their insights, enthusiasm, and patience.

Thank you to Don Morris, our book designer, and Eric Wolfinger, our photographer, for taking a strong personal interest and going the extra mile to make the design and photography great.

To our recipe testers—Alison Thoreau, Anita Chu and husband Mike Dimmel, Brian Banuelos, Chad Schmidt, Francesca Bannerman, Robin Wirthlin, Elspeth Martin, Laura Martinez, and Nikki Blum—Penni and I thank you so much for your care and insights. What a lot of great work.   —*Hubert Keller*

Once or twice a week for months in 2011, Kyle Anderson, then the Burger Bar sous chef, and I test cooked at Fleur de Lys in San Francisco in the morning while the kitchen was quiet. Kyle cheerfully gave up days off or worked a double shift in order to help me make sure the recipes were right. Hermenegildo "Gilberto" Banuelos Villarreal, the pastry chef, worked alongside us, and often with us, mentoring us and giving us the benefit of his more than twenty years' experience at Fleur de Lys. When our work extended later into the day, everyone flowed around us, accommodating us into the rhythm of the kitchen. Often the chefs taught me techniques and prevented my errors. The waitstaff and Marcus Garcia, dining room manager, demonstrated the authentic sense of hospitality and the graceful dance that characterize great service. To all of them, I am so grateful for their generous welcome. I also want to thank Robin Wirthlin and Francesca Bannerman on whose energy, advice, and cooking prowess I relied. And to my family and friends for their compassion and understanding as I took them on the roller-coaster ride that is writing such a big, complex, and exciting book. With my whole heart, I especially thank Chantal and Hubert for entrusting me with their stories and food.   —*Penni Wisner*

METRIC CONVERSIONS & EQUIVALENTS

APPROXIMATE METRIC EQUIVALENTS

Volume	Metric
¼ teaspoon	1 milliliter
½ teaspoon	2.5 milliliters
¾ teaspoon	4 milliliters
1 teaspoon	5 milliliters
1¼ teaspoons	6 milliliters
1½ teaspoons	7.5 milliliters
1¾ teaspoons	8.5 milliliters
2 teaspoons	10 milliliters
1 tablespoon (½ fluid ounce)	15 milliliters
2 tablespoons (1 fluid ounce)	30 milliliters
¼ cup	60 milliliters
⅓ cup	80 milliliters
½ cup (4 fluid ounces)	120 milliliters
⅔ cup	160 milliliters
¾ cup	180 milliliters
1 cup (8 fluid ounces)	240 milliliters
1¼ cups	300 milliliters
1½ cups (12 fluid ounces)	360 milliliters
1⅔ cups	400 milliliters
2 cups (1 pint)	460 milliliters
3 cups	700 milliliters
4 cups (1 quart)	0.95 liter
1 quart plus ¼ cup	1 liter
4 quarts (1 gallon)	3.8 liters

Weight	Metric
¼ ounce	7 grams
½ ounce	14 grams
¾ ounce	21 grams
1 ounce	28 grams
1¼ ounces	35 grams
1½ ounces	42.5 grams
1⅔ ounces	45 grams
2 ounces	57 grams
3 ounces	85 grams
4 ounces (¼ pound)	113 grams
5 ounces	142 grams
6 ounces	170 grams
7 ounces	198 grams
8 ounces (½ pound)	227 grams
16 ounces (1 pound)	454 grams
35.25 ounces (2.2 pounds)	1 kilogram

Length	Metric
⅛ inch	3 millimeters
¼ inch	6 millimeters
½ inch	1¼ centimeters
1 inch	2½ centimeters
2 inches	5 centimeters
2½ inches	6 centimeters
4 inches	10 centimeters
5 inches	13 centimeters
6 inches	15¼ centimeters
12 inches (1 foot)	30 centimeters

METRIC CONVERSION FORMULAS

To Convert	Multiply
Ounces to grams	Ounces by 28.35
Pounds to kilograms	Pounds by .454
Teaspoons to milliliters	Teaspoons by 4.93
Tablespoons to milliliters	Tablespoons by 14.79
Fluid ounces to milliliters	Fluid ounces by 29.57
Cups to milliliters	Cups by 236.59
Cups to liters	Cups by .236
Pints to liters	Pints by .473
Quarts to liters	Quarts by .946
Gallons to liters	Gallons by 3.785
Inches to centimeters	Inches by 2.54

OVEN TEMPERATURES

To convert Fahrenheit to Celsius, subtract 32 from Fahrenheit, multiply the result by 5, then divide by 9.

Description	Fahrenheit	Celsius	British Gas Mark
Very cool	200°	95°	0
Very cool	225°	110°	¼
Very cool	250°	120°	½
Cool	275°	135°	1
Cool	300°	150°	2
Warm	325°	165°	3
Moderate	350°	175°	4
Moderately hot	375°	190°	5
Fairly hot	400°	200°	6
Hot	425°	220°	7
Very hot	450°	230°	8
Very hot	475°	245°	9

COMMON INGREDIENTS & THEIR APPROXIMATE EQUIVALENTS

1 cup uncooked white rice = 185 grams

1 cup all-purpose flour = 140 grams

1 stick butter (4 ounces • ½ cup • 8 tablespoons) = 113 grams

1 cup butter (8 ounces • 2 sticks • 16 tablespoons) = 227 grams

1 cup brown sugar, firmly packed = 200 grams

1 cup granulated sugar = 200 grams

Information compiled from a variety of sources, including *Recipes into Type* by Joan Whitman and Dolores Simon (Newton, MA: Biscuit Books, 2000); *The New Food Lover's Companion* by Sharon Tyler Herbst (Hauppauge, NY: Barron's, 1995); and *Rosemary Brown's Big Kitchen Instruction Book* (Kansas City, MO: Andrews McMeel, 1998).

INDEX

A